RECESS

Its Role in Education
and Development

The Developing Mind Series

Series Editor
Philip David Zelazo
University of Toronto

Co-Editors
Dare Baldwin, *University of Oregon*
David F. Bjorklund, *Florida Atlantic University*
Judy DeLoache, *University of Virginia*
Lynn Liben, *Pennsylvania State University*
Yuko Munakata, *University of Colorado, Boulder*

The Developing Mind Series brings you readable, integrative essays on fundamental topics in cognitive development—topics with broad implications for psychology and beyond. Written by leading researchers, these essays are intended to be both indispensable to experts and relevant to a wide range of students and scholars.

RECESS

Its Role in Education and Development

Anthony D Pellegrini
University of Minnesota

LEA   LAWRENCE ERLBAUM ASSOCIATES, PUBLISHERS
2005   Mahwah, New Jersey   London

Lawrence Erlbaum Associates, Inc., Publishers
10 Industrial Avenue
Mahwah, New Jersey 07430
www.erlbaum.com

Cover design by Kathryn Houghtaling Lacey

LIBRARY OF CONGRESS CATALOGING-IN-PUBLICATION DATA

Pellegrini, Anthony D
    Recess: its role in education and development / Anthony D. Pellegrini.
       p.   cm.
    Includes bibliographical references and index.
    ISBN 0–8058–5324–3 (cloth) — ISBN 0–8058–5544–0 (pbk.)
    1. Recesses. I. Title.
LB3033.P44 2005
371.2'424—dc22   2004061926

Books published by Lawrence Erlbaum Associates are printed on acid-free
paper, and their bindings are chosen for strength and durability.

Printed in the United States of America
10 9 8 7 6 5 4 3 2 1

To the memory of Greta,
who enriched our understanding
of children and their play

Contents

Preface

Writing a book about recess could be a very questionable endeavor for a serious academic psychologist. At first blush it seems to be a pretty trivial topic. It's the time during the school day when there's a break from what's typically considered the most serious work of the day—reading, writing, and arithmetic. Reflecting this trivial sort of tenor, it's also that time that kids will, perhaps only half-jokingly, say is their favorite part of the school day. There's even a cartoon TV show for kids called *Recess!* All of this reinforces the popular notion that recess is indeed trivial and certainly not worthy of serious academic and scientific attention. This perception has, I think, led to many schools questioning the role of recess in the school day. This orientation, I think, has done much more harm than good.

If studying the role of recess during the school day seems questionable, so too, some people think, is the idea of taking recess away from kids in primary school. When people first hear of this state of affairs, a frequent initial reaction is disbelief—"You've got to be kidding!"

This book attempts to broach these two views of recess—the perceived value of recess and the movement to eliminate or reduce the school recess period from the primary school day. Over the past 10 years, I have been contacted by a number of folk concerned with this trend. They know, in their hearts, that something is wrong here. When they speak with me, they ask for advice on how to counter the trend. I hope that this book helps them in this important job.

Acknowledgments

In writing this book, I must acknowledge a whole array of folk. Over the past 10 to 15 years I have received numerous telephone calls, letters, and e-mails from parents concerned about the loss of recess in their kids' schools. This constant reminder made it clear to me that there was a need for this type of book. So to all parents, kids, teachers, and others who have voiced concerned over the place of recess in schools: Thanks.

My research on kids' behavior on the playground has been funded, across the past 20 years or so, by the following agencies: The WT Grant Foundation, The National Institutes of Health, The Sara H. Moss Foundation, and The Spencer Foundation. Without this support, the research reported here would not have been possible. Thanks. Related to financial support, I also acknowledge the College of Education and Human Development and the Department of Educational Psychology at the University of Minnesota for providing me with a semester leave to write this book. As worn as the expression is, it is true and worth re-stating: Having time to think and write is important.

I also must thank the people closely connected to the publication of this project at Lawrence Erlbaum Associates. Bill Webber has supported and encouraged this project from the start. Also the editors of this series— Dave Bjorklund and Phil Zelazo—have provided great feed back on the drafts of each chapter. Thanks for saving me from the embarrassment of having earlier drafts appear in public!

I also acknowledge, Dom Cavallo, Barbara Finkelstein, Barney Mergan, and Brian Sutton-Smith for providing me with information on the history of play and recess, and Ithel Jones for statistics on current recess practices in the United States.

Chapter 1

The Debate Over Recess: A Sad Tale of the Disjuncture Between Educational Policy and Scientific Research

In this chapter, I begin with an outline of the "recess debate." I present cases from both the United States and the United Kingdom (UK) because the debate in both places began around the same time (the early 1980s) and revolves around very similar issues. First, I spell out the arguments presented by the "antis"—those individuals who want to minimize the place of recess in the school day. Next, I present data on the frequency and duration of recess periods in schools across the USA and the UK. I also present parallel discussion of the USA and UK cases because I've spent a great deal of time in the UK studying kids' play and recess behavior. In the third section, I present a personal history, of sorts, of my interest in the topics of children's play and recess in schools.

I then present a brief overview of theories used to generate hypotheses about the role of recess and play in children's learning and development. Theories are needed to guide us in understanding the phenomena. Theories also provide road maps to the questions we ask within the scientific enterprise. That is, theories offer us a frame around which to understand the data generated in empirical research. The quip, "there is nothing as practical as a good theory," is very true. Without theory, we cannot ask good scientific questions, make sense of our data, or progress toward a deep understanding of our areas of study.

Finally, this chapter and each one to follow ends up with a series of questions and issues to "Think About." The intent of this section is to stimulate discussion among people who've read the book (kind of like the discussion questions presented in book clubs). Ultimately, I hope these issues will stimulate action to keep recess in schools.

THE DEBATE OF THE ROLE OF RECESS IN SCHOOLS

It has been a "given" for as long as most of us can remember that recess is part of the primary school day. Walk around 19th-century primary school buildings in the UK and early 20th-century American schools, especially in cities, and you might notice the quaint labels over the school house doors on different sides of the schools. The labels tell us that "Boys" and "Girls" had separate entrances to the schools. In fact this was because boys and girls had different play areas for their play breaks during the school day.

Breaks during the school day, like breaks from work on the factory assembly lines, have been with us for at least for as long as each of those institutions has existed. Indeed, the rationale for breaks in each of these work places is similar: After a reasonable amount of work, you need a break. You need a break, if for no other reason than because breaks may help you be more productive. If you've never worked on an assembly line or do not remember your primary school days, perhaps you can remember driving on a long trip. You probably remember that the longer you drove the less attentive (and less safe) you became. You pull over for a rest, or break, and start over again, being more attentive (and safer). This is related to the laws in many states governing the length of time truckers (and airline pilots) can drive without a break.

The "Anti's"

This rather simple but powerful message has not deterred the movement to eliminate or minimize the recess period from the school day. The reasons given, most often by "no nonsense" superintendents of schools and politicians (not often by teachers, parents, or kids) are as follows: Recess is a waste of valuable time—time that could be more profitably used for instruction; and moreover, the playground at recess is the place where kids get bullied and aggression is learned.

The first argument, that recess is a waste of instructional time, is the one that politicians and superintendents use to demonstrate that they mean business in making schools more effective. I remember vividly a number of years ago when then superintendent of the Atlanta Public Schools, Benjamin Canada, and I encountered each other on the *Good Morning America* TV show. The section of the show was to address the role of recess in schools. I was touted as the expert on recess, whereas Mr. Canada had made national news for his policy of eliminating recess in Atlanta schools and replacing it with physical education. His claim was that by eliminating recess from the whole school system, he had raised kids' achievement scores. Recess, he said, was a waste of time, and kids did not learn by "hanging on monkey bars." They could "blow off steam" in physical education, and as part of this package, they could also learn some skills. When pressed by both me and the TV host, who I inferred was sympathetic to the recess cause, about exactly what he meant by achievement going up as a result of eliminating recess, he began equivocating. He equivocated because he had no data. Indeed, there is no evidence to support his claim! The Atlanta school system did not carry out a systematic study tying the elimination of recess to increased achievement, at least that I'm aware of.

As we will see later in this book, the evidence is exactly the *opposite* of Mr. Canada's claims. That is, in numerous controlled experiments, children's attention to school tasks decreased the longer they were deprived of a break, and they were significantly more attentive after a recess than before! Kind of like driving on a long highway trip, isn't it?

Furthermore, the idea of replacing recess with physical education has been denounced by a national organization of physical education teachers—certainly a group that would have a vested interested in promoting physical education (Council on Physical Education for Children, 2001). As I discuss in more detail later, one of the values of recess is that it provides a break from stringent instructional regimens. Physical education, like other instructional disciplines, rightfully, imposes rigorous demands on children and adolescents so as to stretch their skills. After such demands, a break is necessary. Remember the example of driving on the long car journey.

Also, the idea that children, or any other animals for that matter, need to "blow off steam" is without scientific merit. Such hydraulic models of learning and growth have no current scientific credibility (Evans & Pellegrini, 1997). I discuss this in greater detail later in this chapter.

In short, there is, to my knowledge, not one bit of scientific data to support the sort of claims Mr. Canada made. Why do people make claims that are totally lacking in empirical support? I can only speculate, but it probably makes good grist for the political mills and media sound bites. It sends a "tough love" sort of message, if there are data to support the tough love—I'd advise to hold your nose and swallow—but there simply is no evidence. The specifics of the empirical research addressing the role of recess in learning are addressed in chapters 7 and 8.

And perhaps more cynically, children are a vulnerable population. They have little power in relation to superintendents and little recourse to challenge such dicta. It rests with parents, guardians, and other concerned adults to exert pressure. As I argue, this group of adults should demand accountability from their school leaders on policy that they advocate. They should demand that all educational policy be "evidence-based," to use a current buzz word. The assumption here, I assume, is that earlier policies were something other than evidence-based (which was and is true with recess policy). Tax and tuition dollars, as well as student and teacher time, should not be expended on practices with little or no evidence supporting their implementation, especially when the policies that they are trying to replace *do* have evidence to support them. We would not advocate building a road or a bridge or instituting a surgical procedure without such support. Are kids in school any less important?

The next popular claim in the "anti's" argument against recess is that recess, especially playground recess, is the place where kids get bullied. Though kids do get bullied on the playgrounds, they also get bullied in cafeterias, hallways, toilets, locker rooms, and other places where there is little adult supervision (Pellegrini, 2002). Even in these cases, the base *rate* of aggression on playgrounds is incredibly low. Specifically, of all the behaviors observed on preschool and primary school playgrounds in many countries, such as Canada, the USA, and the UK, physical and verbal aggression accounts for less the 2% of all behavior (Pellegrini, 1995; Smith & Connolly, 1980). These are very good odds! Indeed, if you could bet on aggression *not* occurring on the playground, I'd recommended placing many bets, as you'd be very rich: 98 of every 100 behaviors would not be aggression!

Some adults may confuse children's rough-and-tumble play on the playground as aggression. Rough-and-tumble play is a form of play fighting, and as I discuss in a separate chapter, is not aggressive for the majority of children nor does it tend to "escalate" into aggression.

That rates of aggression are low at recess does not mean that there are not cases of aggression that damage kids; we can have high intensity levels even when rates are low. Like other forms of school violence, such as the all too frequently observed school shootings, they do not happen often, but when they do, people get hurt. Adult supervision of recess periods, like adult supervision of the cafeteria and the hallways between classes, has a potent effect on dampening aggression.

The flip side of the negative behavior argument is that recess is one of the only times during the school days when children have the time and opportunities to interact with their peers on their own terms. Children learn social skills, such as how to cooperate and compromise and how to inhibit aggression, by interacting with other kids. They do not learn them by getting lectures on the topic or by having a course of "values education"! In chapter 3, I discuss the value of recess for children's social skills learning and development.

A PERSONAL HISTORY OF MY RESEARCH ON RECESS

As a "serious" academic psychologist (most of the time, at least) concerned with children's education, learning, and development, some popular pictures of recess may present some problems. At one level, I should be studying the ways in which children learn and develop in school. Studying the ways in which children learn to read and write seems a more legitimate venue for an educational psychologist.

Because I have studied the role of children's play in their social and cognitive development for many years, it was an easy extension to recess, especially as I spent time studying the play fighting (Pellegrini, 2003; Pellegrini & Smith, 1998) and games of boys and girls on their school playgrounds (Pellegrini, Kato, Blatchford, & Baines, 2002).

What really piqued my interest in the topic of school recess was the "debate" over the role of recess that emerged in the early 1990s in the State of Georgia (well before Benjamin Canada's claims on *Good Morning America*) and the simultaneous use of standardized tests as the sole criterion for promotion from kindergarten to first grade. As part of this very questionable (in my view, at least) venture, there was talk of eliminating recess so kids could spend more time on the "important skills" necessary to pass the test. Their logic was as follows: Kids' test scores are declining, and given the limited number of hours in the school day, it made clear sense to eliminate (or minimize) a practice that was viewed as trivial (at best) or antithetical to the more serious educational enterprise.

My first reaction to the testing question was disbelief. I could not believe that such an ill-informed policy (to put it mildly and politely) could be implemented. We've known for decades, for example, that kindergartners are unreliable test takers (Messick, 1983). By this I mean that kids tend not to perform consistently across time. They could score in the 99th percentile on Tuesday and in the 65th percentile on Wednesday. (This actually happened to my daughter.) Young kids are simply susceptible to too many distractions to be reliable test takers.

For example, Anna, a kindergarten student, may be having a very bad day because her mother made her wear her green socks to school; she wanted to wear her red socks, not her green ones, so she left home very upset. When Anna gets to school, she is still feeling bad and chooses not to put her "all" into the test. The test is simply not motivating enough for Anna to change her state of mind. The morning incident of the socks could cause such a swing in test scores from Day 1 to Day 2. Being susceptible to such swings in motivation means that young children are often unreliable test takers. Without reliability we cannot have validity, or truthfulness, in our assessment. That is, if test scores change from day to day, they tell us nothing about the truthfulness of the scores.

That children are unreliable test takers is an important reason for educators to use a number of different assessment strategies. That is, tests can and should be used but in conjunction with other measures, such as attendance, grades, teacher assessments, and behavioral observations of competence. When all of these things are aggregated, we get a more valid picture.

At the time of this kindergarten testing debate (or debacle), I had been studying kids' (beginning in kindergarten) rough-and-tumble play on the school playground during recess for a few years. As part of this research, I also had access to kids' test scores from kindergarten through at least first grade. I also knew that what kids did on the playground requires pretty high levels of social cognitive competence. So, I wondered if what kindergarten children did on the playground could be a valid predictor of their first-grade achievement as measured by a standardized tests. That is, does kindergarten kids' playground behavior predict their first-grade test scores, even after we control statistically for children's academic achievement in kindergarten? In essence, I was asking if there was predictive academic value in what kindergarten kids did at recess, beyond that information provided in their kindergarten academic achievement as measured by a standardized test score. How much did it tell us, beyond their kindergarten test scores, about how well they'd do in first grade?

My hunch, or hypothesis, was that the recess behavior would tell us a great deal. After all, when kids are on the playground they are typically interacting with their peers and to do so takes some pretty sophisticated skills. For example, to play cooperatively with their peers, children have to be able and willing to see things from their peers' perspective, use compromise to resolve conflicts, follow rules of play and games, and use language to negotiate all of this. Indeed, we know that the types of language that kids use to negotiate conflicts and compromise are very similar to the language of school instruction (Heath, 1983) and the language of literacy (Pellegrini & Galda, 1982).

Further, during play and games with their peers, kids are motivated to marshal their social cognitive resources to meet these demands. Kids, generally, like to interact with their peers at recess so they try their best to initiate and sustain play. For example, they may have to compromise (share a toy or a turn) to continue to play with their best friend. They typically do this because they are motivated to do so, perhaps more so than to perform on an achievement test. Tests, at least for most young kids, are not that motivating! My guess is that they are not aware that performance on these tests in kindergarten may jeopardize their chance for admission to Princeton in 15 years!

As I will discuss later, these kindergarten behavioral measures did predict first-grade achievement, beyond their kindergarten test scores. That both the behaviors and the test scores did so reinforces the notion that multiple measures should be used in "high stakes" assessments.

In an effort to change policy in the State of Georgia, my friend and colleague, Carl Glickman, and I wrote an editorial in the *Atlanta Journal Constitution* and articles for *Young Children* (1992) and *Principal* (Pellegrini, 1991) to publicize our finding to the general public and the community of teachers of young children and primary school principals. Testing policies did change in Georgia, but the press to minimize or eliminate recess gained steam, and actually continued to grow!

As a result of these actions, policy makers, teachers, parents, newspaper reporters, and radio and TV stations around the country and in the UK, where I was also working, began contacting me about recess. One of my earliest memories of this was in the autumn of 1991 when I was in a hotel room in Leiden, the Netherlands. I got a call from a newspaper reporter in

Pittsburgh! I was, to say the least, surprised. Why, I asked would he spend the time and money to track me down in the Netherlands. He (Bill Zlatos) said that Pittsburgh was in the midst of a controversy gripping the public and parochial schools over the role of recess: Should it be kept or eliminated (see the *Pittsburgh Press*, 27 October 1991)? I was amazed that there was another place considering the elimination of recess and that there was such a felt sense of urgency. I was, at the same time, on leave in Sheffield, England, and the anti-recess debate was gaining steam there as well.

THE STATE OF RECESS IN THE USA AND THE UK

Perhaps the most important indicator of the recess debate is the way in which recess time has eroded across the last 15 years. One of the first surveys of recess in the United States, to my knowledge, was conducted by the National Association of Elementary School Principals (NAESP, 1989). The survey was sent to school superintendents in all 50 states plus Washington, DC. Responses were received from 47 states and the results showed that recess existed, in some form, in 90% of all school districts. Generally, it was found that individual schools (in 87% of the reporting schools with recess) determined recess policy. Consequently, there seems to be quite a bit of variation both within school districts and within states. In 96% of these cases, recess occurred once or twice per day. In 75% of the cases, the recess period lasted 15 to 20 minutes. Of course we do not know, from these data, the form that the recess period took; for example, we do not know if organized physical education was counted as recess. Indeed, about one half of those districts having recess had "structured" recess times.

In terms of the ways recess is supervised, this survey indicated that teachers assumed responsibility in 50% of the cases, and in 36% of the cases, teachers' aides supervised. Of these aides, 86% had no formal training for supervision. I do not know about the supervision policies of the other 14% of cases. As I discuss in the final chapter, training for supervisors is not a trivial issue. A well-trained supervisor can both support children's positive social interactions and guard against aggression and bullying.

Ten years later another survey was conducted, this time by the U.S. Department of Education, but it surveyed only recess in kindergarten. (I acknowledge Ithel Jones for providing me with these data.) Seventy-one percent of all American kindergartens surveyed reported having a daily recess period; 14.6% and 6.7% had recess three to four and one to two times per week; 7.7% did not have any recess. In terms of the duration of the recess period, 27% had 30 minutes of recess, 67.4% had 16 to 30 minutes, and 6% had less than 15 minutes. Children attending private kindergartens were twice as likely to have recess as children attending public schools (48.3% vs. 22.2%).

Though a direct comparison with the 1989 survey is not possible, there are some interesting points to consider. Most interesting, I think, is the fact that in kindergarten only 70% of the children had daily recess. If there is one grade where we would assume that *all* children would have recess daily, it would be kindergarten. This is clearly not the case.

The public/private contrast, too, is interesting. It is also consistent with my own experience. Many years ago when I was studying the playground behavior of middle school students in Athens, Georgia, no public middle schools in that city had recess. A private school did! Why is this the case? It could be because parents, generally, favor recess, and they make their wishes known to the schools to which they are sending their children and their money. That these schools depend on tuition may also mean that they are more responsive to parents. When I asked the headmaster of this particular school in Athens why they had recess, she told me that they considered it an important way for children to develop their social skills! Not that different from the Rugby School model I present later.

Speaking of England, Peter Blatchford and his colleagues (Blatchfrod & Sumpner, 1998) conducted a national survey of recess (called "break-time" in the UK). They chose a random sample of primary and secondary schools (1:10 schools) from across England, with a 60% return rate. This resulted in a sample of 6% of all English schools (1,500 in all). Importantly, recess in the UK is uniform compared with the USA. Schools have a morning, a lunch time, and an afternoon break. Though students across all grades had breaks, the duration of the break periods decreased with age: 93 minutes for children in infant school (5 to 7 years of age), 83 minutes for junior school (7–11 years of age), and 77 minutes for secondary school students (11–16 years of age). Clearly, English children have much more recess than their American counterparts and the duration of the periods seems more sensitive to the developmental levels of the students.

There is, however, an "anti" movement in the UK as well. The issues propelling this movement are very similar to those in the United States and they have been very visible—being featured in newspaper stories and on radio and TV. This pressure has resulted in a reduction in break time. Blatchford and Sumpner specifically asked in their survey about changes across the 5-year period from 1990/1991 to 1995/1996 and they found that 38% and 35% of junior and secondary schools, respectively, had reduced the duration of the lunch break. For infant schools, 26% had reduced lunch breaks. Regarding the afternoon break, it was eliminated in 12% of infant schools, 27% of the junior schools, and it was also eliminated in 14% of the secondary schools! One would think that such drastic change should be directed by good theory and empirical support; but as we see next, most of the theory supports keeping recess in schools.

THE ROLE OF SCIENTIFIC THEORY AND EVIDENCE IN THE RECESS DEBATE

The urgency has not abated. Indeed, it has actually increased. From the beginning of the recess debate, I have been contacted literally hundreds of times by journalists, parents, and educators about recess, and the issue is always the same. Recess is being eliminated or minimized, and what can be done to save it?

I see my role here as a public advocate for kids and good sense. As I outline in the course of this book, overwhelming evidence shows that the benefits of recess clearly out weigh its costs. To ignore this evidence, as is all too frequently done, is a tremendous waste of resources (kids' and teachers' time and effort and of taxpayers' money). All these stakeholders in the educational enterprise should demand accountability from their school boards, principals, and teachers.

In this book, I present the theory and empirical evidence to support these claims. Though the style of the book is user friendly, that is, understandable to the educated lay person, I think it is also important for credibility purposes to present the scientific side of the argument. Specifically, I present (usually in appendices of each chapter) the formal research methods by which this research was conducted as well as the statistical analyses. I present the scientific side of the argument because this sort of information is (rightfully) needed to argue a case to change school policy. Better to be too thorough in these matters than not thorough enough. The reader not interested in these details can simply skip these parts, as the results are summarized and discussed in each chapter.

Some Theoretical Debate

Work Is Good, Play Is Bad. Questioning the role of recess in the primary school educational process is similar, I think, to the ways in which children's play has been questioned by some early childhood educators (though not many contemporary early childhood educators do question play; National Association for the Education of Young Children, 1992). Play, like what goes on at recess, is often seen as a force opposing work. Work is viewed as good and play is not. Some trace this dichotomy to the Puritan/Calvinistic ethic in America and much of the Anglo Saxon world (e.g., Sutton-Smith, 1995; Tawney, 1969). Sloth, remember, is one of the seven deadly sins, portrayed in many Renaissance paintings.

We cannot just blame Calvinism or the Protestant work ethic for devaluing play and leisure in relation to work. The positive role of labor and work was certainly stressed by explicitly anti-Christian theorists such as Karl Marx (1906). Marx believed that one's labor, realized in one's place in the means of production, defined and formed one's consciousness. Further, the idea that one could accrue benefits without engaging in labor was frowned upon in Marx's notion of the unearned increment.

By extension, the benefits of manual labor were stressed by Mao Tse-tung, especially during the Cultural Revolution. The virtues of manual labor were stressed over the enterprise of intellectual activity. Those individuals in Mao's China who engaged in activities of the mind were re-educated (to put it very mildly). In short, the value of work over less visibly productive activities has a long history and has had appeal to a very wide audience. Bertrand Russell (1932/1972) referred to this bias as the cult of efficiency.

Is There "Educational Value" in Leisure and Play?   In direct opposition to this view of efficiency is the idea that there is real value in leisure and play. One of my favorite discussions on this topic comes from Bertrand Russell, arguably one of the more productive and original scholars of the 20th century. Important to our evidence-based perspective, Russell was no soft touch. He was an adamant empiricist (literally) who insisted on rigorous scientific and logical methods to generate and test hypotheses (Russell, 1931/1959).

I quote from Russell's (1932/1972, pp. 9–10) essay, *In Praise of Idleness,* at length:

> I think there is far too much work done in the world, that immense harm is caused by the belief that work is virtuous, and that what needs to be preached in modern industrial countries is quite different from what has been preached. . . . I hope that after reading the following pages, the leaders of the YMCA will start a campaign to induce young men to do nothing. If so, I shall not have lived in vain.

Russell's argument is not aimed at children and schools per se but at the role of work and leisure for adults and modern society at large. His notion of idleness, however, is close to our definition of play—a capacity for light-heartedness and play (p. 24). His larger point is that leisure does have benefits and, in this case, to the economic well-being of society. Specifically, he suggested that the workday be reduced to four hours (remember this was written in 1932) so that people would have more time to spend in leisure activities, such as playing games, dancing, listening to music, and going to the cinema.

The benefit associated with this extension of leisure, for Russell, was that people, in their leisure time, might choose to learn more about their professions, such as teachers or physicians, learning more about allied fields, or volunteer in public causes. All of this would, he argued, make the world a better and more productive place. Historians, such as Johan Huizinga (1939/1995), also make the connection between play and leisure and the flourishing of arts and civilization.

Russell was not the first Englishman to exhort the possible benefits of play and games. Perhaps most famous was Thomas Hughes' (1895) praise for the moral instruction afforded by game playing in childhood. In his book, *Tom Brown's School Days*, Hughes talked about the moral and social lessons learned when youngsters engaged in games played on the fields of Rugby School. The timeliness of his opinion is expressed in this frequently cited quote:

> You say you don't see much in it all; nothing but a struggling mass of boys, and a leather ball, which seems to excite them to a great fury, as a red rag does a bull. My dear sir, a battle would look much the same to see, except that the boys would be men, and the balls iron; but a battle would be worth your looking at for all that, and so is a football match. You can't be expected to appreciate the delicate strokes of play, the turns by which the game is lost and won,—it takes an old player to do that, but the broad philosophy of football, you can understand if you will. (p. 99)

From Hughes' view, the social skills learned when playing rugby are similar to those of leading men in battle. The lessons learned on the playing fields at Rugby were generalized to Waterloo. Interestingly, Hughes' view of games and play is much more behavioral than that of Russell. For Hughes, specific skills and attitudes are associated with games. This view is very similar to the view of play espoused by ethologists who study the play of nonhuman animals and make inferences about the value of play fighting, for example, in males' later fighting and hunting ability.

This position is contrasted with Russell's model in which, after a certain amount of work, individuals needed to re-charge to be productive. As I discuss in a later chapter, there is scientific merit in some dimensions of each of these theories. Relatedly, it is probably no accident that games and sports are *required* for all students in so many "public schools" in England and private schools in the USA. For these places, instruction is not limited to the classroom; instruction in morals and social skills takes place in the classroom *and* on the playing fields. This ethos may be responsible for the early place of sport in many colleges. Currently, in big-time college sports in the USA, a different moral lesson is being taught!

Let's Get Real. At one level, children certainly benefit from receiving quality instruction, and increasing the number of hours of instruction per year that a child receives may indeed increase learning, at least under many circumstances. This is not the same thing as stating, however, that more intense, break-free hours of instruction will enhance learning. In fact, I argue just the opposite. As early childhood educators and child developmentalists, we decry the claims for a "cult of efficiency" (p. 24), to quote from Russell again. I base my protests on our unbridled belief in the value of play and practices such as break times and recess periods that support play and leisure activities for children in schools.

The second valuable point about Russell's quote is that it forces us to reconcile an important educational conundrum. On the one hand, we have calls for more play and leisure time in school. On the other hand, we have the very real problem of declining levels of achievement. This apparent contradiction begs serious attention, given the stature of the person advocating more leisure time.

Russell's solution to the problem as it might relate to schools and recess (his solutions dealt mostly with the economics of the duration of the workday) proposed that leisure time results in happy lives instead of frayed nerves associated with overwork. Happy people live better, and more productive, lives.

I argue that there is not enough leisure time in school in the form of recess. Play and recess time can actually help students learn; they do not detract from learning. On the other hand, the relation between work (both in terms of duration and intensity) and efficiency are certainly reflected in our schools. The time-on-task literature in American educational research is one of the clearest examples of this point (see Brophy & Good, 1974, for a summary). The basic idea behind this influential practice was that educational attainment was directly and positively related to the amount of time spent working on tasks. Calls for longer school days and school years and the elimination of recess periods from the school days are logical extensions of this practice. One solution might be a longer school day with frequent breaks and an extended school year. Such as practice would probably improve achievement and provide working parents with a safe and enriching place for their children while they are at work. I address this issue in greater depth in the concluding chapter of this book.

The realist might say (and rightly so) that discussions of play and school recess must be conducted in light of the world of real school policy. That is, parents, educators, and politicians are concerned about children's academic achievement as well as their safety in schools. Where they raise concerns that recess may interfere with safety and learning, those concerns must be addressed. We, as researchers, typically address the concerns by noting how play is beneficial to immediate and later social and academic competence. I argue that play and recess do have beneficial consequences. I present some psychological theory that has guided, and will continue to guide, research in the field.

Classical Psychological Theory: The Role of Recess, Play, and Games in Children's Competence

Probably the most famous play theorists are Jean Piaget (1962), the Swiss psychologist, and Lev S. Vygotsky (1967), the Russian psychologist. Both men stressed the role of children's pretend, or make-believe, play in cognitive development. Make-believe play is observed most frequently during the preschool years, peaking around 5 years of age (Fein, 1981). Furthermore, though it is commonly observed in classrooms, it is not frequently observed on the playground at recess. For both of these reasons, I will discuss Piaget's and Vygotsky's theories only briefly, spending more time on what I view are more relevant theories.

Jean Piaget's Theory. For Piaget the development of children, and indeed adults, was motivated by a never-ending battle to maintain mental balance (what he termed *equilibration*) and to minimize mental conflict between already established concepts and new information. Let's take an example of a 3-year-old child, Anna, having a concept of *dog* as being comprised of the following: four legs; black-and-white in color, furry, friendly, about 8 inches in height, and about 2 feet long. One day Anna and her parents are driving down a country lane and in a field next to the road is a Holstein cow. Anna points at the cow and says DOG! After all, this thing has four legs, is black-and-white, furry, and (seemingly) friendly. It is, however, much bigger. By calling the cow a dog Anna is *assimilating* this new information into an extant concept. That is, she is treating something new in terms of what she already knows. But her new, expanded concept is short-lived. Her parents tell her this novel animal is not a dog but a cow. Anna modifies, or *accommodates*, her concept of dog so that it does not include such large, bovine-like creatures. And in the process, she develops a new concept.

For Piaget, children's play was the paradigm example of assimilation. When children play, they take the outside world and define it in terms of what they already know. So, in pretend play a child calls a doll "My baby"—subordinating the meaning of the outside world to her inner world. The polar opposite for Piaget was accommodation, where children imitate what someone else says or does, with little if any extant knowledge. For example, an adult points to an animal that a child has never seen and says "cow." The child imitates and says "cow," with little or no knowledge in the concept.

In actuality, most encounters involve both assimilation and accommodation, but one is usually more pronounced than the other. So if a child is engaged in pretend play about her "baby," she may be subordinating the world (the doll) to her view, but her concept of baby in the process is also being enriched. For example, in the course of play, especially if it is social play where children are exposed to different views, the child probably discovers something new about babies. From this view, pretend play is primarily assimilation, but it also has some components of accommodation.

Lev S. Vygotsky's Theory.   Pretend play was important for Vygotsky, too. For Vygotsky, children's play involves a tension between their desire to attain the unattainable and the realization that their behavior should conform to societal expectations. Let's take the example of the 3-year-old Adam having the desire to ride a horse. This goal is unattainable because he does not have a horse! This desire to attain the unattainable is also an important motivator for children—they want to do something because it should bring pleasure. So, they'll expend social and cognitive resources to attain this goal. Wanting to ride the unattainable horse, for Adam, is moderated by his knowledge that he does not have a horse so he knows he can pretend to have one; he takes a broom and straddles it. His pretend play with the horse, further, follows roughly societal rules governing horse riding. So he gallops in ways that he has seen on TV and makes appropriate horse noises. The importance of pretend play for Vygotsky was that he viewed children as learning to use socially defined symbols (such as a broomstick to represent a horse) to represent concepts. This is important in their development of both oral and written language, where arbitrary but socially agreed upon signs, such as the word *horse,* represent a real animal.

Recess Specific Theory: The Role of Recess and Free Time in Children's Schooling

It is uncontroversial that young children think differently than older children, who in turn think differently than adults. Regardless of the much debated underlying reasons for these differences (see Bjorklund, 2004; Flavell, Miller, & Miller, 1993; and Siegler, 1996, for in-depth discussions), the result is that younger children learn most things at a slower rate than older children. Despite young children's limitations, research over the past several decades has demonstrated that preschool and early school-age children can be taught skills that are spontaneously acquired only by older children, providing the impression that more rigorous instruction during the early grades will result in enhanced cognition, both immediately and later in development. It is from this perspective that recess is seen as a superfluous activity, perhaps necessary to some degree to combat boredom but an essentially nonproductive part of the school day.

An alternative, and developmental, perspective holds that children's immature cognitions are often well suited to the peculiar demands of childhood—that immaturity is not just something to overcome but that children's immature nervous systems may be adapted to deal effectively with the cognitive demands they face in their daily lives at those particular developmental periods (Bjorklund, 1997; Bjorklund & Green, 1992; Bjorklund & Schwartz, 1996). This position is consistent with the view that behaviors and cognitions within the early childhood period have value or function inherent to that period and should not be considered "imperfect" variants of adult behavior (Bateson, 1981; Bjorklund & Pellegrini, 2002).

IMMEDIATE BENEFITS OF RECESS FOR SCHOOL PERFORMANCE

In this section, I sketch two arguments for the continued presence of recess in primary schools. I first present evidence of the benefits on learning of distributed practice (like the "taking a break during highway driving" example given earlier in this chapter), which recess affords, followed by a brief discussion of the development of cognitive efficiency and how recess may especially facilitate learning in younger and cognitively immature children. Both arguments propose that benefits associated with recess are immediate (that is, they occur almost simultaneously with the recess behaviors themselves). I assume that much of what goes on during preschool and primary school recess periods can be considered play, thus the view that play has immediate benefits (Bateson, 1976). In this view, play is not considered an imperfect or incomplete version of some adult behavior. Play has benefits for the unique niche of childhood. I conclude this section with a summary of research from our lab that provides evidence for the beneficial effects of recess on children's school performance.

Massed Versus Distributed Practice

Recess may be beneficial for children in schools because it provides a break from sustained periods of work. We have known for many years (e.g., Ebinghaus, 1885/1965; James, 1901) that children learn better and more quickly when their efforts on a task are distributed, or when they are given breaks during tasks, rather than concentrated, or when effort is grouped into longer periods (Hunter, 1929). The positive effects of distributed effort have specifically addressed the ways in which children learn numerous school-like tasks, such as native and foreign language vocabulary, recall from text, and math facts (see Dempster, 1988, for a review). These laboratory studies yielded reliable and robust effects, documenting the efficacy of task spacing on learning. Indeed, the theory has been supported with humans across the life span and with a variety of other animals.

Classroom studies have been less frequently undertaken, and when they have, have generally produced less impressive results. Factors associated with the nature of the task (e.g., simple vs. complex) seemed also to influence the effects of distributed practice on classroom learning (Dempster, 1988). When the nature of the criterion variable is changed from material learned to attention to the task at hand, however, the results of the classroom research match those of the laboratory. Spacing of tasks may make them less boring and correspondingly facilitate attention. Attention to task, in turn, may be important to subsequent learning (Dempster, 1988; Eder & Felmlee, 1984).

Given the positive effects of distributed practice on children's attention to school tasks, it is quite puzzling why it has not been more readily used in classrooms. One possibility, as suggested by Frank Dempster (1988), is that the complicated contingencies of running a school may not readily accommodate the added complexities of a distributed practice regimen. There is a simple solution to this conundrum, using a well-established school institution: recess. Recess provides a break between school tasks, thus distributing practice. The same principle also applies to highway driving!

Deferred Benefits of Behavior Observed at Recess

Researchers and theorists have nominated one aspect of children's recess behavior, play, as serving deferred, not immediate benefits. *Scaffolding* has been proposed as a metaphor for deferred benefits of play (Bateson, 1976). In play, children assemble a skill; play is disassembled when the skill is completed.

Traditionally, the deferred benefits of play are gauged in terms of a cost/benefit ratio. Play is beneficial if the deferred benefits outweigh the immediate costs. Most theories of child development posit that play is beneficial in terms of preparation for adulthood. Play is often viewed as the way in which the juvenile, through his/her extended childhood, learns the skills necessary in adulthood. For example, a girl's play with dolls may help prepare her for the role of mother. By implication, it is also assumed that play is costly for children. Cost is often measured by the amount of time spent in play (Smith & Dodsworth, 1978), energy expended in play (Pellegrini, Horvat, & Huberty, 1998), or in the dangers inherent in play, such as injury (Fagen, 1993). Though there have been very few studies of the costs of play for children, what work has been done suggests that it is moderately costly. For example, children spend a substantial portion of their free time in play (Smith & Dodsworth, 1978). Further, when they do play they expend substantial amounts of stored energy; energy expenditure during outdoor recess exceeds basal levels of expenditure by a factor of 7.5 (Pellegrini & Smith, 1998; Pellegrini et al., 1998), and many childhood injuries are incurred during play (Fagen, 1993).

Now that we have established that play is costly, we must link play to some beneficial outcome. If play did not provide some advantage to children, given its costs, it would not have been naturally selected for in human evolution (Fagen, 1981). In short, there must be some sort of beneficial payback for the costs incurred in play. We assume that the benefits that result from those behaviors exhibited during the school recess period are related to the physically vigorous social play that children exhibit. Consequently, we would expect children's recess behavior to relate to subsequent cardiovascular fitness and social competence. Unfortunately, the empirical record has not addressed systematically the long-term effects of vigorous social play. This limitation is probably because of the logistical and financial problems of conducting such sustained longitudinal research from childhood into adolescence and adulthood.

Consequently, most of the studies have not been longitudinal and those that have been, did not extend across the theoretically relevant period, from childhood to adolescence or adulthood. Briefly, experimental studies have shown a positive and *immediate* effect of vigorous physical activity on cardiopulmonary functioning (e.g., Simon-Morton et al., 1987). Regarding the social dimensions of recess behavior, short-term longitudinal research has shown that forms of primary school children's reciprocal social play, such as rough-and-tumble play, predict social competence one year later (see Pellegrini & Smith, 1998, for a summary). Specifically, the variety of roles that children enact during social play predicts their perspective-taking status and ability to solve hypothetical social problems.

DEVELOPMENTAL DIFFERENCES IN COGNITIVE EFFICIENCY AND ITS RELATION TO RECESS

David Bjorklund and I have suggested previously (Pellegrini & Bjorklund, 1996, 1997), and based on Bjorklund's theory of "cognitive immaturity" (Bjorklund & Green, 1992), that the facilitative effects of distributed practice should be greater for younger than for older children. Young children do not process most information as effectively as older children. The immaturity of their nervous systems and their lack of experiences render them unable to perform higher level cognitive tasks with the same efficiency as older children and adults and directly influences their educability. As a result, young children are especially susceptible to the effects of interference (see Dempster, 1992, 1993) and should experience the greatest gains from breaks between focused intellectual activities, which recess provides.

Evidence in support of this hypothesis is drawn from the literature on memory and cognitive inhibition. Research using a wide range of tasks has shown that children are increasingly able to inhibit task-irrelevant thoughts and to resist interference from task-irrelevant stimuli and that such skills contribute significantly to overall cognitive functioning (e.g., Bjorklund & Harnishfeger, 1990; Brained & Reyna, 1990, 1993; Dempster, 1992, 1993; Harnishfeger & Bjorklund, 1993, 1994). Inhibition abilities have been proposed to play a significant role in attention, permitting children to focus on task-relevant information and not to be distracted by task-irrelevant, peripheral information, and have also been proposed to be of central importance to functional working-memory capacity. Young children have a difficult time keeping extraneous information from entering short-term store. As a result, their working memories are often cluttered with irrelevant information, leaving less mental space (cf. Case, 1985) for task-relevant information or for the execution of cognitive strategies (Bjorklund & Harnishfeger, 1990; Harnishfeger & Bjorklund, 1993).

From this perspective, there may be a general increase in interference when children perform a series of highly focused tasks, regardless of the nature of those tasks. Although one would predict that changing from one type of focused activity to another would yield some cognitive benefit, children (especially young children) may experience a continued build-up of interference with repeated performance of even different highly focused tasks, and thus experience greater benefit from a drastic change in activity, such as is afforded by recess. This is consistent with the evidence that younger children may require a greater change in activity or stimulus materials before they experience a release from interference (e.g., Bjorklund, 1978; Douglas & Corsale, 1977; see discussion in Pellegrini & Bjorklund, 1996, 1997). This should make school learning particularly difficult for young elementary school children, and opportunities to engage in non-focused, nonintellectual activities should afford them the needed respite to "re-energize" their nervous systems (perhaps literally) so that they can continue to learn in school. Consistent with this reasoning, recess periods across the school day should minimize cognitive interference. Importantly, instructional regimens, such as physical education, would not serve the same purpose.

CONCLUSION

In this chapter, I "mapped" the basic territory in the recess debate. Basically, recess, like play in young children, is debased because it is assumed to be a waste of time—time that could be otherwise more "efficiently" spent. The counterargument (why recess is good) is backed by a large body of theory and empirical research. I recommended that those advocating the elimination of recess present sound theoretical and empirical support for their arguments. As I demonstrate later in this book, there is clear evidence that recess has beneficial effects on children's social competence and academic performance.

SOME THINGS TO THINK ABOUT AND DO

1. Poll different groups of educators in your area on recess practices.

	Kindergarten	Primary Grades (1–3)	Middle Schools (4–6)
How many/day?			
Length of each			
Structured/Unstructured			
Teacher/Aide Supervised			

2. Ask different people what they think about recess.

	What's good	What's bad	How improve it
Children			
Teachers			
Administrators			
Parents			
Nonparents			

Chapter 2

A Brief History
of the Place of Play and Recess
in American Schools

As you will see throughout this book, as we discuss recess, I state that some aspect or another about the school recess period has not been studied systematically. This dearth of research interest probably reflects the perceived importance of recess to the academic community, educators, and to the general public. So, at some level, the degree to which a topic is subjected to scholarly scrutiny may reflect its perceived importance in that community. In contrast, the amount of research attention paid to reading and mathematical learning in schools is substantial and corresponds to the perceived importance of literacy and numeracy in both schools and in society at large.

As I illustrate later in this book, the relatively low status of the study of children's play, games, and recess in child psychology and education is reflected in the lack of scholarly attention paid to these topic. For example, in one of the archival collections of child psychology, the *Manuals of Child Psychology* (Carmichael, 1946, 1954; Eisenberg, 1998; Mussen, 1970, 1983), there has been only one chapter (in the 1983 volume) dedicated to the study of play. Further, there is no chapter on games and a very few total cited references to games at all.

With all of this said, I was still amazed to find virtually nothing written about the historical origins of recess in American schools. In keeping with the idea that scholarly activity in a subject is related to its perceived importance, much research has been conducted on the history of literacy in American schools. A few historical accounts of the role of play in American schools have been written (e.g., Cavallo, 1981; Mergen, 1995), and even some histories of playgrounds in American cities and schools have been written (Cavallo, 1981). But nothing has been published, to my knowledge anyway, on the historical origins of recess in primary schools.

As part of my quest into this topic, I contacted a number of people to see if I was missing the obvious. The first person I contacted was Brian Sutton-Smith. Brian knows more about play (and indeed most things) than most people I know. To his knowledge, there is no work done on the topic. His book on play in his native New Zealand (Sutton-Smith, 1981) provides a history of recess in that country—but not the United States.

I then contacted a number of historians. Barney Mergan, Dom Cavallo, and Barbara Finkelstein were generous enough to respond. They each have authored several books and papers on the history of play and playgrounds in the USA. They, too, said, that no one had studied this. Amazing! Or maybe not really.

Typically, and as noted in the last chapter, scholars suggest that a reason for play and games being given limited scope in American research is due to the influence of our Puritan/Calvinist past. That is, the work ethic associated with Calvinism has permeated American (and indeed Anglo-Saxon) culture (see Tawney, 1926/1969). Consequently, this ethos tends to devalue all enterprises associated with pleasure and leisure. The result of this orientation has been that play and recess are devalued by most schools in the industrialized world. As I discuss below, this orientation is not limited to countries with a Puritan/Calvinistic history.

In this chapter, I discuss the history of recess in schools in the larger context of the place of play in schools. As I will illustrate in subsequent chapters, what goes on in the playground at recess is play-like. That is, children interact with peers and materials on their own terms, relatively unfettered by adults. For these reasons, adults typically consider these activities to be counter forces to quality education. As I illustrate, societies of very different political orientations typically have little value for play and recess in schools.

AN EQUAL OPPORTUNITY TARGET: VIEWS ON PLAY FROM THE PEOPLES' REPUBLIC OF CHINA AND THE SOVIET UNION

This, I think, is too simple. As I noted in the first chapter, stressing the importance of work and correspondingly diminishing the role of play and leisure is not the sole purview of Calvinists! Marxist theory certainly followed this line as well, with value being placed on labor and corresponding disdain for pursuits associated with frivolous leisure. This orientation reached a high point (or low point) during the Cultural Revolution in China when intellectuals (viewed as a nonlaboring class) were "re-educated."

The Chinese Case

A team of American observers to Chinese schools in the mid-1970s found that schools continued to discourage intellectual elitism (Kessen, 1975). Correspondingly, Chinese kindergartens' love of labor is considered a virtue, and an objective of primary school education is participation and love for productive labor (Kessen, 1975, p. 119). The American team observed cases where primary schools were paired with a neighboring factory and children were given jobs to complete that in some way were connected to the neighboring factory. For example, children helped to assemble badminton birds and shaped chess pieces.

Chinese nurseries and kindergartens did make provision for children's play. In the nurseries (that is, prekindergartens) the team of Americans observed, they found that indoor play was minimal, and where it was observed, was initiated by an adult with a child (Kessen, 1975). Further, there was a paucity of play materials in the nurseries as well. Indeed the observer noted a uniform absence of toys in many nurseries (p. 69). They concluded, however, the children did not seem the worse for it.

In kindergarten, however, there was a great variety of play materials, such as toy trucks and plastic animals and art materials available, and most kindergartens had an attached play yard with "substantial" play equipment (Kessen, 1975). Additionally, play periods were scheduled before classes and for 10 minutes in between each class (about every hour). This, it seems, it similar to a periodic recess, or play break.

Children's behavior, both indoors and outdoors, was, however, adult directed, not spontaneous or play-like. For example, in outdoor play, children moved as a group from one activity to another—more like physical education than play, as we've described it. Similarly, the indoor play was also highly organized. The American observers concluded that children did not seem free to pursue their own interests. So, for example, children would be seated at a table with drawing materials, and though they were not free to choose the activity, they could choose what to draw. Further, and perhaps most telling, the Americans did not observe instances of kindergarten-age children engaging in dramatic play! Contrast this with the high frequency of dramatic play observed during the free play periods even in the most traditional American preschool classrooms.

When we move into Chinese primary school and examine the frequency of breaks during the school day, we find that a 30-minute break is given after the first and the third class periods (where each period is about 40 minutes). As with the breaks in kindergarten, they are structured and more like a physical education class than a recess period as we know it. Children were observed being guided through eye exercises (to prevent near-sightedness) and then doing calisthenics to recorded music.

The Soviet Russia Case

The extent to which play has been pursued as an area of scholarly activity or stressed in schools in Soviet Russia is both similar and different from the Peoples' Republic of China. It is different to the extent that there was a history of Western-oriented developmental psychology at the very beginning of the Soviet experiment. Specifically, research on play in the Soviet Union in the 1920s was guided by Vygotsky. Vygotsky was a developmentalist and influenced by the American psychologist G. Stanley Hall's notion of stage theory and of "ontogeny recapitulating phylogeny" (see next section for a fuller discussion of Hall; Rahmani, 1973), and by that of his contemporary, Piaget (1932/1965). This work, and the subsequent work of Zaporozhets and Elkonin (1971) and Repina (1971), stressed the role of play in children's development. Specifically, and following the contemporary *zeitgeist* of Western psychology, play was conceptualized as practice for practical ends—learning and development. Play in childhood was practice at learning the skills necessary to become an adult. This view is consistent with that Piaget advanced. For Vygotsky, play was motivated by the tension within the child to fulfill desires and wants that are unattainable within socially acceptable norms. Take, for instance, the example I discussed in chapter 1: A child has a desire to own a horse. Because, in reality, he cannot attain that goal he pretends a broom is a horse. From this view children develop the ability to both control emotions and desires as well as gain practice at symbolic representation—or having one thing (a broom) represent something else (a horse).

These Western and non-Pavlovian principles, however, were suppressed with the succession of Stalin (Rahmani, 1973). At this time, psychology became much less developmental and much more oriented towards pedagogy, "shaping" the new Soviet man. Indeed, Western influences in psychology were suppressed and only Pavlovian theory was given currency (Rahmani, 1973).

In terms of Soviet pedagogy, schools stress the role of "work" in the form of class projects and learning specific skills, such as carpentry and dress making (Bronfenbrenner, 1973, p. 52). Schools did, however, have recess periods and the goal of recess, like education more generally, was to educate Soviet citizens (Bronfenbrenner, 1973). This entailed learning to cooperate with peers and internalizing socially minded, collectivist values. On the playground, this was accomplished by peer-guided games. So, not unlike Western views, play was seen by Soviet psychologists and educators as training for adulthood. Consistent with Vygotsky's theory (1978), this was accomplished through social interaction.

So, the West and the East have treated recess and play in similar ways: an equal opportunity target. This shunning of recess and play would not be so interesting if recess were not such a ubiquitous part of the school day. It is this entity that is part of the school day for primary school children across most of the industrial world, but we know virtually nothing about it! So for those of you looking for a research topic that has not been studied—go no further.

HISTORICAL ORIGINS OF RECESS AND PLAY IN THE UNITED STATES

With that said, it would be very interesting and important if we had some archival evidence for when the recess period first was instituted in schools across the United States. Correspondingly, if we also had some policy documents about the roles of supervising teachers on the playground, we might get some insight into what contemporaries saw as the role of recess. I wonder if these sorts of documents are archived in state historical societies that index local school policies, curriculum guides, and teacher guidelines. Someone should look!

As it stands, we can only make very indirect inferences. In terms of when recess was instituted, I simply do not have a clear answer. The more complex question of motive is even more obscure. Even if we had historical documents in hand specifying policy, what is stated in official documents may not correspond to the real intent of the practice. Instead, what we seem to have (and I say this cautiously because I am not an historian) is two general lines of inquiry that approach convergence on recess. First, we have historical studies of the role of play in schools associated with the child study movement of the late 19th and early 20th centuries. Second, there is a substantial literature of the history of playgrounds in the USA and to a lesser degree in schools.

I say these two research streams *approach converging* on recess because no one, to my knowledge, has explicitly linked the two. Instead, we tend to have groups of scholars who study play and playgrounds and make inferences about the role of each in schools. Further, these scholars are divided into two groups that seem diametrically opposed to each other. One group sees play in school as a liberating force and the other sees play in schools being used to control children.

As can be seen in Figures 2.1–2.3, schools in the early 20th century uniformly did not have playgrounds attached to the school grounds. From

FIG. 2.1.   School house without playground.

FIG. 2.2.   School without a playground (1938).

FIG. 2.3.   School house with added playground equipment
(1918).

this, albeit very indirect, evidence, we assume that recess was not an
important part of the school day early in the 20th century.

The Child Study Movement and the Importance of Play

The Child Study Movement in the United States began in the early 20th
century. Its origins can be traced to the influences of Darwinian theory as
applied to child psychology. This influence was due, perhaps most directly,
to the theories and influence of G. Stanley Hall (1904, 1916). Hall was
called by many (e.g., Cairns, 1983) the father of American psychology,
generally, and a founder of child and developmental psychology in the
United States, more specifically. Hall was the first American to receive a
PhD in psychology (from Harvard in 1878, under the supervision of Wil-
liam James) and the first American to be awarded a chair in psychology (at
Johns Hopkins in 1884; Cairns, 1983).

He was much more, however. He was a minister, an educational psychologist, a university professor and president, the first president of the
American Psychological Association, and the founder and editor of a
number of psychological journals. It may have been this great willingness
and ability to cross intellectual boundaries and integrate a variety of dis-

ciplines that led to his having such a great influence on our field. He took this knowledge of biology, psychology, and philosophy to guide the Child Study Movement across the United States

As a child/developmental psychologist, Hall may be most remembered for his stress of the stage-like progression of human development. For Hall, these stages were thought to re-enact the history of the species (phylogeny). In this vein, Hall is perhaps best remembered for the phrase "ontogeny recapitulates phylogeny" (borrowed from the German biologist Ernst Haeckel). For Hall, this meant that development within an individual (ontogeny) recapitulates, or repeats, the evolutionary history of the species (phylogeny). Some of Hall's famous examples include the following. Boys' tree climbing is a recapitulation of our primate past. Similarly, boys' play fighting (then it took the form of cowboys and Indians) was a re-enactment of our hunter-gatherer past.

It must be noted that the accuracy of the notion that ontogeny repeats phylogeny is not credible (see Bjorklund & Pellegrini, 2002; Hinde, 1983). Specifically and without going into detail (though see Bjorklund & Pellegrini, 2002, chapter 3, for an extended discussion), it is probably more likely that ontogenetic development influences phylogeny. In the course of individual development, for example, the age of sexual maturity influences the development of the species.

A Cautionary Note.   We should not be too hasty and laugh too visibly at the apparent foolishness of Hall's claim: Take pause. The history of science is too full of examples that seemed like certainties, only to later be discredited. That Newton's theory was displaced by Einstein's (Clark, 1971) should not discredit the historical importance of Newton for the physics of his day. In short, we should minimize the extent to which we view historical events from our eyes and try to view those events through the eyes of the actors of that day (Butterfield, 1931/1965). From that view, Hall was very innovative.

Probably the most enduring aspect of Hall's theory was the stress on stages of human development and the corresponding importance he placed on the role of play during childhood. Hall saw play as integral to childhood. Hall viewed childhood as a period during which children should be allowed unfettered time to explore and play. He warned against unnatural and artificial educational and pedagogical regimens in that they interfered with the natural unfolding of children's developmental processes (Cairns, 1983, p. 52). Play, for Hall, had children choosing activities and enacting them on their own terms. In this regard, play during childhood was stressed as a way in which children expressed their phylogenetic history. So children's play hunting or fishing expressed their foraging past!

Perhaps more interesting was Hall's view that play was not something that prepared individuals for adulthood. Unlike most of his contemporaries, such as Karl Groos (1898, 1901) and later Piaget (1932) and Vygotsky (1967), Hall considered play important to childhood—not as practice for adulthood. Indeed, this view is current among many developmental psychologists today (Bjorklund & Pellegrini, 2002; Pellegrini & Smith, 1998)!

This work, along with that of other Darwinians such as Groos (1898, 1901), stressed the notion of childhood as a distinct stage of human development. Correspondingly, play was seen as the way in which youngsters of this age came to know their world. Through play, children interacted with their physical and social world and "constructed" the mental worlds. If this view sounds reminiscent of Piaget—it is. After all, Piaget was trained as a biologist, and his general systems theory was a biological theory and his more specific notions of assimilation and accommodation are biological constructs.

The general Darwinian world view and Hall's theories, specifically, had an enormous impact on the new fields of developmental and child psychology, as well as nursery and primary school education in America (Cairns, 1983; Kessen, 1965). Specifically, Hall was the first president of Clark University, in Worcester, Massachusetts. Clark, traditionally, has been a bastion for the training of some of America's leading developmental psychologists. Clark's Child Study Institute was a laboratory where children were studied and this knowledge was used to develop school curriculum. John Dewey, another advocate of play, was among Hall's students (Cairns, 1983). Members of its faculty are a who's who in American developmental psychology, for example, Heinz Werner (e.g., Werner & Kaplan, 1952), Jack Wohwill (1973, 1984), as are some of its graduates, such as John Flavell. When Piaget first visited the United States he gave a series of lectures at Clark, as did Sigmund Freud.

At the same time Hall was instrumental in founding the *Pedagogical Seminary* in 1891, renamed in 1927 to the *Journal of Genetic Psychology* (Smith & Connolly, 1980). This scientific journal was the archival outlet for studies in child and developmental psychology. This journal provided an intellectual forum for the nascent science of child development. Indeed, the use of the term *genetic* in this context was synonymous with ontogeny—not with the influence of genes on behavior, as it is currently used. The result was that American psychology was shaped by Darwinian and

Hallian developmental theory. Childhood was seen as a unique stage and children of this age should "play in order to develop properly."

The intellectual ethos of the child study movement was directly translated into educational programs and interventions for young children. The "nursery school" movement was being formulated at academic institutions in the United States (Teachers College/Columbia under the influence of John Dewey) and at the child welfare stations at the Universities of Iowa and Minnesota.

Laboratory nursery schools were formed at both Iowa (see Thompson, 1944) and Minnesota (see Parten, 1932). Both being land-grant institutions, they were based on the agricultural extension model (Cairns, 1983). Apparently, an Iowa housewife and mother, Cora Bussey Hill, queried that if universities could help farmers grow bigger cattle and better corn—they could help grow healthier children (Cairns, 1983)! From this view, a "child welfare station" was set up at Iowa (1917) and a laboratory nursery school was established in 1921 (Cairns, 1983). Similar institutes and nurseries were established during the 1920s and 1930s at Minnesota, Toronto, Berkeley, Yale, and the Merrill-Palmer Institute, not only as child advocates but also as centers where research knowledge and excellent pedagogy was designed and tested. The labs were used both to test developmental theories and to design curricula based on these theories. The Shirley G. Moore Laboratory Nursery at the University of Minnesota is still carrying out this work today! It is the center of a number of very active research programs and a place where preschool teachers are trained.

TWO VIEWS OF PLAY AND RECESS IN AMERICAN SCHOOLS

The views of G. Stanley Hall and those expressed by Marxist psychologists, such as Vygotsky, and of policy makers represent, at some level, different portrayals of the role of play and recess in American and British schools.

School Play and Recess as Liberation

Consistent with Hall's view that play is unfettered expression of individualism, some scholars consider play in schools as a liberating, or creativity generating, process (Sutton-Smith, 1997). That is, play is viewed as a way in which individuals take an extant situation and transform, or change, it in creative and innovative ways. A paradigm example of this process, of course, involves children taking a conventional prop, such as a broom, and transforming it into a horse. From this view, play (especially pretend play) leads individuals to act more creatively.

When this notion of play as creativity generator is embedded in schools, the implication is that schools bring together children into a central location where they actually have time and opportunity to express their playful ways. These opportunities are thought to result in children generating alternative cultures to those espoused by teachers.

Schools as gathering places for children are typically contrasted historically with children being situated in factories. In contrast to factories, children in school are able to use free-play time and recess not only as a time to simply enjoy themselves but also as a time to subvert the order of school. Advocates of this position mean by this that children can be disorderly in an orderly way and in an orderly place. Correspondingly, the recess period and play time can be venues where children generate and re-generate their cultures in relation to what they are getting in the classroom. For example, in a hypothetical classroom a teacher may remind children to wait their turns in line. On the playground this may be mimicked, parodied, and disregarded in a playful way.

All of this presumes, of course, that children are given the opportunity to first play and second to do so on their own terms. As we saw in the case of Chinese schools (and as advocated by some American superintendents of schools), outdoor play is very structured and more resembles physical education than it does true play.

Furthermore, it seems to me that a basis for considering schools as places for children to be creative is based on an incorrect comparison. Recall, historians often suggested that school play was liberating because it was more so, historically, relative to when children worked in factories (Finkelstein, 1987). A more relevant comparison might be to compare children's play and expression at home or on a community playground when their behavior is not closely scrutinized and regulated.

The idea that play and recess generate creativity draws much of its currency from Sutton-Smith's colorful recollections of play in early 20th-century New Zealand. The vivid images of rebellious children are reminiscent of Breughel's painting of children engaged in various sorts of naughty play. Violent and sexual themes saturate much of these images. For example, he describes how children played on the way to school, wandering through farm fields. As their play spilled over into the school classroom when they arrived at school, it was discouraged by teachers. Flogging was a common method of discouragement. Interestingly, teachers allowed boisterous, and sometimes coarse, behavior on the playground. Sutton-Smith paints a vivid picture of how the rural New Zealand countryside merged with what passed for playgrounds—often just school yards. The school play yards were the domains of the children where they had their own culture and rules, which were very different from those of the class-room. On the playground, they invented games, like shinty (or hockey), where sticks or curtain rods were used as hockey sticks and cigarette tins were used as pucks. By contrast, in the classroom, proper language and behavior were required; the norm was to follow teachers' directions—not to be innovative or questioning.

In addition, the work in the folklore tradition by Iona and Peter Opie (1966) and Peter Blatchford (1998) support the idea that the recess period may be a place of innovation. Specifically, both scholars have studied the origins and transmission of children's games and they have found that children often take games they've learned from an older sibling to school. Thus, the school playground may act as a mixing pot of new forms of play, as long, of course, as they are given free license to play those games.

As noted earlier, in evaluating the extent to which play is an innova-tion generator, it may be more relevant to contrast the play of children in school with their play at home rather than the play of 19th vs. late 20th century school children. From this view, we have some data suggesting that children's play at home is less stereotypical than the play of the same children at school. Specifically, John Gottman (1983) found that young children were more likely to have opposite-sex playmates at home than at school. These playmates seemed to be clandestine to the extent that these same children did not interact with each other at school. This implies that they recognized the social pressures to conform to sex-role stereotypes (that is, of playing only with same-sex peers) at school. This view assumes, however, that the pressure to conform to social pressures comes from children's peers, not the school authorities.

School Play and Recess as Controlling

There is a second view that the school controls children's play. This view holds that school authorities try to control children's play as a way to socialize them to some ideal forms. Typically, historians who take this tack see the control coming from larger socialization agencies. For example, Dom Cavallo's (1981) excellent history of the playground movement in the United States documents the ways in which the emergence of the playground movement corresponded to the massive immigration waves of the early 20th century. He suggests that a child-saving movement existed among the ruling classes in American cities to socialize children to become good Americans.

Part of the orientation of this group of reformers was to minimize the influence of parents on children. After all, this group believed that immigrant ghettoes in American cities were a "malaise" that threatened the order of American society. Recall, at this time Saco and Venzetti, two Italian immigrants, were labeled by a Massachusetts judge, Webster Thayer, as anarchist bastards, falsely accused of murder, tried, and then executed!

The playground movement can be seen as a way order was brought to the perceived pathology of immigrant children. Playgrounds were built in inner cities and staffed with play supervisors to teach young children the proper ways of playing and supercede parental influence on children's emerging social skills. For example, at the end of the 19th century in Boston, sand gardens were built in the middle of urban ghettoes. These play areas served as a precursor to later playgrounds. At this time Boston, New York City, and Chicago all had trained social workers to staff these play areas. So, like the Chinese and Soviet models of play, educators in early 20th-century America thought that play could be used instrumentally, to help socialize children to societal norms, and this was best accomplished by having adults guide children's play.

The way in which play got incorporated into school and the emergence of recess period is more speculative, but most explanations follow some sort of control argument. Specifically, Cavallo (1981) suggests that playgrounds and play workers may have been incorporated into school as part of an effort to have a broader base of control. That is, schools had a broad reach and reformers encouraged cities to construct playgrounds on school grounds so that they could be used during vacations. At the same time the kindergarten movement was developing in the United States, with its stress of using play as a pedagogical tool (Cavallo, 1979). Thus, recess may have originated as a result of the interrelations between the playground and kindergarten movements. Both viewed play instrumentally—it was a way in which children could be shaped into adults according to the views of the social reformers of the time. From this view, children's development could be placed in the hands of experts. It was a needed antidote to the perceptions of "disorganized and unhygienic" working-class families.

It may have been the case that recess and play were seen as ways in which to not only socialize children but also as ways in which to maximize the effectiveness of education. Recess was seen as a break from the stress of instruction. A break would make education more efficient (Aronowitz, 1973; Finkelstein, 1979).

It was also at this time that the view of treating physical games as an appropriate form of recess began to take shape. For example, in 1913, both the Chief Medical Inspector and the Assistant Superintendent of Schools in Cleveland defined play for children in terms of physical education (Finkelstein, 1979; Mergen, 1995).

A related, and perhaps compromise, view might hold that children's playground behavior does relate to their conforming to societal norms, but those norms are not transmitted directly by adult school authorities. Instead, it may be, as Andrew Sluckin (1981) suggested, that the playground affords opportunities for children to learn social skills and adult roles, but these are learned and practiced in the context of peer interaction—not transmitted directly by adults to children. This is a more likely interpretation of the ways in which children learn social roles and skills.

CONCLUSIONS

The history of recess and play in American schools seems intertwined. I say "seems" because there is no authoritative discussion on the history of recess in American schools. Indeed, there does not seem to be even an informal discussion of the origins of recess.

My reading in the area, granted not as a professional historian or in an exhaustive fashion, led me to construct the following scenario. At the turn of the 19th to the 20th centuries, there was a confluence between the Child Study, the Kindergarten, and the Playground Movements, on the one hand, and the movement to get public schools to help socialize children, from both middle- and working-class backgrounds, on the other hand. Schools either were asked to be or volunteered themselves as a socializing agent. The recess period may have been a way in which the ideals of the Child Study Movement, with its emphasis on play, was expressed as a socialization period. When children play with each other they develop and learn social skills.

These ideals, even if they existed, probably were not universal. The paucity of playgrounds in photos of early 20th-century school yards certainly suggests that organized play was not given much formal expression. Recess in many schools, then, may have been used as a break from work, in much the same way as a break from laboring was a break—a chance to blow off steam, recharge, or whatever metaphor one prefers to use to explain taking a break to maximize school performance. The extent to which physical education classes were, and are, used as recess periods is a paradigm case of this view.

SOME THINGS TO THINK ABOUT

1. Interview some older folks—such as your parents or better still your grandparents. Ask them if they had recess.

Was it supervised?

How often did they have it?

At what grade did they no longer have it?

2. Go to the local school board and ask if there is a record of the curriculum guides for the district.

Try to locate any mention of recess.

When was it mentioned?

Was there a rationale given for it?

Were teachers supposed to supervise it?

Were there guidelines or suggestions for supervision?

3. Go to the state historical society and try to find the school district with the most complete records for the longest historical period. Ask the same questions that were posed in #2 above.

It is often helpful to ask archivists at the historical society if they can provide any guidance in your search. They are usually very helpful.

Chapter 3

The School Playground as a Venue for Children's Social Development

In this chapter I describe what children do on the playground during recess and how this behavior may be important for their social development. By social development I mean, generally, children's ability to get along with their peers, how they solve social problems, and their risks for internalizing disorders, such as neuroticism, and externalizing disorders, such as aggressiveness.

The skeptical reader might ask: How does interaction on the playground relate to social development? And what's more, how is this possibly related to the traditional role of schools—to teach children to read, write, and calculate?

First, the notion that interaction with one's peer is important for social development is axiomatic in the peer development literature (Hartup, 1983; Suomi & Harlow, 1972). Arguably, the skills necessary to interact in the social world and form interpersonal relationships begin with a trusting and sensitive mother–child relationships (Sroufe, 1979). Beyond this, however, children learn and practice the skills necessary to interact in the larger social world from their peers. They do this, not through direct tuition but through ordinary give and take with their peers. As I have pointed out repeatedly, and will continue to do so throughout this book, cooperative interaction is a very complex and demanding enterprise. For example, individuals must learn the formal and informal rules of interaction. In seemingly simple games with rules, children must learn how to subordinate their behavior and wishes to the rules of the game. In informal interaction, they must learn to take turns and to be polite (Grice, 1975). Furthermore, they must learn to monitor the interaction for ambiguities and breakdowns of agreement and to compromise their views and wishes to the larger goal of interacting with a peer. To do this requires that individuals have a varied repertoire of social behaviors and the verbal skills to negotiate the compromise.

Indeed, certain peer-interaction regimens can provide opportunities that individuals never learn in their interactions with their primary care givers. Specifically, research by Steve Suomi and Harry Harlow (1972) showed that rhesus monkeys reared in unhealthy mother–child relationships were able to learn skills, such as cooperation, compromise, and the ability to inhibit aggression, when paired with a younger, less skilled, and less threatening peer. This procedure has also been used successfully with young children (Ramey & Campbell, 1987).

Why are children willing and able to learn such difficult and demanding strategies in the context of peer interaction? The answer may lie in the motivational dimension of peer interaction (Waters & Sroufe, 1983). That is, children usually enjoy interacting with their peers, and thus, they have a vested interest in maintaining those interactions. When they are required to invest high levels of mental resources, they willingly do it, because they enjoy it. This combination of high levels of sophistication necessary to interact with peers and high motivation means that peer-interaction contexts are powerful venues for skill learning and development.

So we can safely conclude that interacting with peers is good for children's social development. But there is the troubling fact that the typical primary school day is devoid of much peer interaction (Pellegrini & Blatchford, 2000). Indeed, in much of the school day peer interaction is either prohibited or frowned upon. Well, you might say, there's probably a good reason for this—kids are in school to learn to read and write—not how to learn to get along with their peers! In short, concern with kids' social lives should not be the charge of the school.

My response to this is as follows. First, the worlds of academic achievement and that of peer relations are not separate. Indeed, the two are interrelated. By that I mean that if children do well in one area, they tend to do well in the other, and conversely, if they do poorly in one area, they do poorly in the other. There are a number of reasons for this interdependence. First, as noted above, engaging in cooperative interaction requires cognitive skills.

Second, peers provide the social and emotional support necessary to negotiate especially stressful academic experiences. For example, we know that when children move from preschool to primary school, a very powerful predictor of their adjustment to school is the extent to which they have friends from preschool in the primary school (Ladd, Kochenderfer, & Coleman, 1996). So, for example, during the small-group time that typifies most kindergarten and first-grade classrooms, friends can interact with each other, rather than having to negotiate with an unfamiliar peer and risk being rejected or ignored. The end result of having a friend is that children may actually look forward to school because they have a good time there, in part, because they have a mutual friend.

Third, peers are both models and reinforcers of each other's behavior. For example, a child who is aggressive will imitate and affiliate with other aggressive youngsters (Coie & Dodge, 1998). These children inevitably run into difficulty with school authorities and become disaffected from school. So their negative behavior leads them to negative peer groups, bad grades, and eventually dropping out of school.

The opposite case seems also to operate. Children who are cooperative affiliate with like-minded peers. They bask in their success in school by getting teacher reinforcement, feeling competent, having fun while interacting with their peers, and identifying with the school ethos (Pellegrini, Kato, Blatchford, & Baines, 2002). In short, the peer group is important for academic achievement!

Finally, there is clear evidence that some children need to learn social skills. We have recently, and all too frequently, heard about cases of extreme violence in schools. These cases involve students shooting teachers, peers, or both. The most visible cases make headlines on the national news, such Columbine, Colorado. But there are numerous other cases that do not get such national attention. For example, even in rural Minnesota, in October, 2003, a student shot and killed one of his classmates and wounded another. These are obviously cases of antisocial behavior in school.

If we question the role of social development in schools, would we consider schools successful that had very high graduation rates and high achievement test scores but witnessed frequent bouts of serious aggression? I would hope not. After all, a very basic goal of schooling is to educate citizens in the values of that society. That's the reason we require civics, U.S. history and, more recently, having students recite the Pledge of Allegiance to the flag.

Most of the students who commit these horrendous acts have been rejected and victimized by their peers. Their response to this treatment is to react violently against the perpetrators. Other rejected and victimized children respond very differently. Some tell their parents and teachers while others may get their friends to help them out. This latter group of children possesses the social problem-solving skills that highly emotional and aggressive children do not, and they probably learned those skills by interacting with peers.

Of course I'm not saying that by having recess, we'll eliminate school violence. What I am suggesting is that it is important for children to have time to interact with their peers because it is this time when they learn social skills. School and the school recess period are important venues for peer interaction. Schools, after all, are places where large groups of same-age youngsters are concentrated. Furthermore, children are rapidly losing opportunities for peer interaction, and school may be an ideal place to stage these events.

To illustrate ways in which children are losing opportunities to interact with peers, I point out the fact that there is a whole class of children, latch-key children (Steinberg, 1986), who return home from school every day to empty homes. There they wait until their parent, typically mother, returns home from work. In other, more impoverished neighborhoods, parents forbid children from going outdoors because it is too violent (Guerra, Husemann, & Spindler, 2003).

Finally, a recent survey of London families found that children did not ride the bus to school as frequently as they did 10 years ago. Their parents drove them now instead (Pellegrini & Blatchford, 2000). The school bus ride to and from school is, as most of us remember, a place where children interact. In short, children's opportunities for meaningful interactions with peers are diminishing. Recess is one place that we think it should take place. There are large concentrations of children, it provides opportunities to learn valuable social skills and to establish emotional ties that bind children to school.

In the remainder of this chapter, I present some very general and pre-liminary finding documenting the types of behavior that children exhibit on different types of school playgrounds. I then show how these behaviors relate to the development of social skills. I present contemporaneous correlations, or measures taken at the same time, between playground behavior and dimensions of social status with peers and psychopathology, as well as predictive relations.

Contemporaneous correlations are indicators of current status, for example, social behaviors that can be used to diagnose current perceptions of peer status. They might provide some insight that a child is having difficulty with peers or is having internalizing problems.

Predictive relations, on the other hand, tell us the extent to which a behavior, or set of behaviors, measured at Time 1, predicts social status or achievement at Time 2. These sorts of antecedent-consequence relations are necessary, but not sufficient, to make causal inferences about the effect of one behavior on another. Consequently, predictive relations provide important, preliminary information on the influence of one set of behaviors on another.

WHAT SORTS OF BEHAVIOR DO WE SEE ON THE PLAYGROUND AT RECESS?

With few exceptions, social scientists, such as psychologists, sociologists, and anthropologists, have not studied children on the playground, thus we do not have many good descriptions of what goes on out there. This may be due, as I discussed in chapters 1 and 2, to the fact that most scholars do not think that this sort of work is rigorous or serious enough to deserve their attention.

Scholars from other fields, however, have spent considerable time describing children's behavior on playgrounds, both in and out of school. Landscape architects (e.g., Moore, 1988), environmental psychologists (e.g., Hayward, Rothenberg, & Beasley, 1974), some pioneering developmental psychologists (e.g., Sluckin, 1981), and folklorists (Sutton-Smith, 1990) have provided excellent descriptions of the forms of play that children exhibit on different types of school playgrounds. This work generally has described children's playground preferences and relations between types of playground design and forms of children's behavior.

One of the first studies of children's playground behavior that I am aware of was conducted by a group of environmental psychologists led by Geoffrey Hayward (Hayward et al., 1974). Because this was the pioneering study in the field, even though it examined neighborhood, not school playgrounds, I will discuss it in some detail. In this report three types of playground environments were compared: traditional, contemporary, and

FIG. 3.1.   Adventure playground.

FIG. 3.2.   Contemporary playground.

adventure playgrounds. Traditional playgrounds are probably most familiar to us; they are composed of fixed structures, for example, swings, see-saws, and jungle gyms, on asphalt surfaces.

Contemporary playgrounds are aesthetically pleasing to look at (to adults at least), as they are often designed by architects. They are typically composed of stone, culverts, railroad ties, and so forth, of the sort illustrated in Figs. 3.1 and 3.2.

Adventure playgrounds are composed of a variety of materials that children can use to build their own play environments. This type of playground originated in Denmark after the Second World War where playgrounds where made out of scrap materials, such as tires and building materials. Not surprisingly, Hayward and colleagues found different playground types were related to different play behaviors.

Generally, traditional playgrounds were attended by children least frequently and were least likely to sustain play. It was suggested that the functional diversity of adventure and contemporary playgrounds was responsible for their popularity with children and for their ability to sustain play. This finding was replicated in the United Kingdom (Naylor, 1985).

These studies, though interesting and pioneering, have several important limitations. The first and most obvious limitation is self-selection. That is, different types of children may have chosen to go to specific playgrounds. As such, differences in the behaviors exhibited on each of the playgrounds probably reflect differences in the personalities of children who chose to go to those specific playgrounds as well as differences due to playground type. More basic, different types of playgrounds tend to be built in different neighborhoods; consequently, the behaviors children exhibit on playgrounds are also influenced by personality and socioeconomic variables.

A second and related limitation of these free-selection public playground studies is the age differences of children observed on the different playgrounds. Specifically, in the Hayward et al. study, the percentage of preschool-age children observed on traditional, contemporary, and adventure playgrounds was 29.5%, 25.2%, and 1.8%, respectively; while the percentage of school-age children on these different types of playgrounds was 20.8%, 22.2%, and 44.6%, respectively. Observed behavior differences on the three playgrounds, then, may have been due to the age of children, the type of playground, or a combination (or statistical interaction between) age and playground type.

These limitations should in no way devalue the importance of this work. It was pioneering in the early 1970s for social scientists to study children on playgrounds. Furthermore, the descriptive information of children attending neighborhood playgrounds is certainly valuable in and of itself. As descriptive data, however, they do not inform us as to the "effects" of playground designs on children's behavior.

Some of these limitations can be and have been remediated by observing children's behavior in other naturalistic settings: playgrounds during their school recess periods. The differential age effects are controlled in these natural experiments because all children of a particular, often uniform, age range are required, weather permitting, to be on the playground for the daily recess period. Important work in this area has been conducted by Joe Frost and colleagues (e.g., Frost, 1986; Frost & Sunderlin, 1985).

These researchers examined various social and cognitive aspects of the behavior of pre- and elementary school children on different playgrounds. The social dimensions of play are based on the seminal work of Mildred Parten (1932), who suggested that children's social participation (which is more general than play, per se) went through the following stages: solitary (playing alone), parallel (playing next to but not with another child), associative (playing with others but group composition changes frequently), and cooperative (sustained interactive play).

The cognitive dimensions of play are based on the work of Sara Smilansky (1968). She, like Parten, posited a hierarchy of play forms. The behaviors in Smilansky's cognitive model include functional (repetitious actions), constructive (making things), dramatic (make-believe), and games with rules. A matrix of these two schemes, of the sort presented in Table 3.1, is typically used to categorize children's playground behavior.

Using these separate cognitive and social dimensions of behavior, Frost (1986) examined the effects of different types of playgrounds (i.e., traditional contemporary, and adventure) on preschool and elementary school children's play. Generally, his results suggest that functional play occurred on traditional playgrounds while dramatic play occurred on creative playgrounds. Children tended to engage in cooperative interaction on all playgrounds. For example, Simon and Jack cooperate as they help each other climb up a playscape.

Though this body of research provides interesting data on the relations between types of playgrounds and children's behavior, questions arise from the ways in which children's play was categorized. Most basically, the observational system used by Frost was developed by Kenneth Rubin to categorize the interactions of *preschoolers inside their classrooms*. (See Rubin, Fein, & Vandenberg, 1983 for a thorough discussion of findings derived

TABLE 3.1
Smilansky–Parten Matrix

	Solitary	Parallel	Associative	Cooperative
Functional				
Constructive				
Dramatic				
Games-with-rules				

from this matrix.) It was not designed for older children playing outdoors. Consequently, much of what children do on the playground—run, climb, chase, and play ball games—is not captured by the system. The results are that behaviors may be *forced* into categories in which they do not belong. For example, about 15% of the behavior of primary school children is rough-and-tumble play, a playful form of wrestling or fighting that is not accounted for in the Parten–Smilansky model (Pellegrini & Smith, 1998).

To remedy this problem, I (Pellegrini, 1988) developed a behavioral inventory, or ethogram, of children's behavior on the school playground, following up on the work of a group of human ethologists. Ethologists study animal behavior, Jane Goodall being a notable example, and human ethologists use detailed direct observations to study human behavior (Blurton Jones, 1972, 1976; Humphreys & Smith, 1984). This approach, following an ethological model, initially describes children's behaviors at a microlevel (e.g., clenched-hand beat). These micro-behaviors then become the basis for more inclusive, macrolevel categories (e.g., clenched-hand beat is part of a category called aggression). This ethological approach results in behavioral categories that are age and context appropriate, as well as categories that are exhaustive and mutually exclusive.

AN ETHOGRAM OF PLAYGROUND BEHAVIOR

The categories I used to study children on the playground in my initial studies were intended to form a behavioral index of children's behavior. That is, I intended to generate a category system that accounted for most of the behaviors that primary school children generated on the school playground. This "ethogram" is a useful and necessary first step in scientific studies of humans in their natural environments because it indexes all the behaviors exhibited in specific contexts. From this information, we can later make inferences about the extent to which these behaviors are important in individuals' development.

The ethogram I developed is displayed in Table 3.2 and was based on my observations of children for one year, as well as other peoples' observations of children on playgrounds (e.g., Humphreys & Smith, 1987; Pellegrini, 1988). The more specific details of the methods used to collect the data I discuss in this chapter can be found in the appendix at the end of this chapter.

The children we observed were primary school boys and girls who were enrolled in grades kindergarten, second, and fourth. This school was in a

TABLE 3.2
Inventory of Children's Playground Behavior

Category	Example
1. Passive-noninteractive	Leaning against wall, looking at others
2. Passive interactive	Sitting down, talking with peer
3. Observer directed	Talking with observer
4. Adult organized	Teacher lead game
5. Aggressive	Kicks a peer
6. Rough-and-tumble play	Play wrestling
7. Vigorous play	Chasing a peer
8. Games w/ rules	Kickball
9. Object play	Building a fort with sticks
10. Role play	Super hero play

Note. From Pellegrini, 1988.

university town in the rural southeastern United States. Children were required to go outdoors for their morning recess period and for their after-lunch recess period (both 25 minutes). Children were observed on a playground similar to that shown in Fig. 3.1.

Not surprisingly, results from the earlier studies conducted, as well as my own work, suggest that children's behavior varied according to gender and according to the type of playground on which they were playing. Furthermore, their behavior varied depending on what part of the playground they were observed.

In terms of gender differences, boys more than girls engage in vigorous behavior, such as running and chasing (Pellegrini et al., 1998; Pellegrini, 2004b), rough-and-tumble play (Pellegrini & Smith, 1998), aggression and games with rules (Pellegrini et al., 2002). Girls, on the other hand, are more sedentary, and when they play games, those games tend to be verbal and clapping games, such as jump rope (Pellegrini et al., 2002; Sutton-Smith, 1981).

Two important points are related to aggression and vigorous activity. Aggression, in my own work and in numerous other studies, is a very low-occurrence phenomenon, accounting for only 1% or 2% of all behavior. Correspondingly, rough-and-tumble play does not escalate into aggression (Pellegrini, 1988), except in cases involving aggressive children. For most children, rough-and-tumble play leads to games, such as chase, not to aggression. In short, aggression does not happen much, and consequently, it is a questionable strategy to try to minimize aggression by eliminating recess.

In terms of vigorous activity on the playground, we find that primary school children expend moderate levels of energy (Pellegrini et al., 1998). The importance of this level of physical activity is important to today's youth, especially in light of recent claims of the epidemic levels of childhood obesity and inactivity. It has been suggested that physical strength and endurance can be built and maintained if youngsters engage in this level of activity for one hour per day (Byers & Walker, 1995). As is the case with children's experiences with peers, so too with exercise—they are losing opportunities for exercise for a variety of reasons, such as unsafe neighborhoods and the allure of different forms of screen entertainment (TV and computers). The school recess period is a reasonable place for this to get done.

Gender also relates to the parts of the playground in which children choose to play. Boys self-selected themselves onto the playscape and engaged in vigorous and rough behavior there. For example, as two boys ran out of the school and onto the playground at the beginning of the recess period, they immediately headed to the playscape. They jumped up on to the structure and chased one another around the structure.

Girls, on the other hand, spent more time on the blacktop, engaged in relatively sedentary social interaction with other girls. For example, a pair of girls chatted with each other as they left the school and enter the playground. They waved to and approached another girl eating her snack. The three of them spent most of their recess period standing, talking with each other.

By way of qualification, I must note that we cannot attribute causality to these findings; that is, we can not conclude that different types of playgrounds or different parts of a playground caused a child to behavior in a particular way. In each of the cases discussed so far, different types of children may have chosen to play on different parts of a playground. In fact, this is quite likely. Thus differences in behavior could reflect the sorts of children who choose to play on those playgrounds—not the playgrounds per se.

The only way we can make causal inferences about the type of playgrounds on behavior is to randomly assign children to playgrounds (so that individual differences are randomly spread across the different types of playgrounds and thus, should not have a systematic effect). To my knowledge, only one study, conducted by Craig Hart (Hart & Sheehan, 1986), is capable of making a causal statement about the effects of playgrounds on behavior because in this study children were randomly assigned to environments. Their results, unlike the findings of Frost (1986) and his colleagues, suggest that preschool children exhibit more advanced behavior, such as cooperative relative to solitary play, on *traditional* playgrounds than on contemporary playgrounds. The contrasting results of Frost and Hart and Sheehan may be due to the fact that the nonrandomized studies confounded playground type with other variables; for example, there may be systematic differences between the schools that choose to have different types of playgrounds.

There are other factors that influence children's behavior on the playground, and they include the time of the day in which recess is held, the duration of the recess period, and the weather. Regarding the time of the day, a number of studies have found that the longer preschool and primary school children were deprived of exercise the more active they were on the playground (see Pellegrini & Davis, 1993; Pellegrini, Huberty, & Jones, 1995; Smith & Hagan, 1980). With the passage of time on the playground, however, levels of physical activity declined (Pellegrini & Davis, 1993).

The influence of weather on playground behavior is obvious. In extreme temperatures, children spend less time engaged in physical play than children in more temperate environments (Naylor, 1985). Within a temperate environment, school children at recess seem to engage in more exercise play (e.g., running, chasing, and climbing) on sunny, warm days than on cold, rainy days (Smith & Hagan, 1980).

To conclude this section, children's playground behavior is varied indeed and is affected by a number of child-level variables, such as gender, as well as the type of playground equipment available, the daily schedule, and the weather.

THE DEVELOPMENT OF SOCIAL SKILLS IN SCHOOL

The argument that I have been advancing is that peer interaction is helpful in the learning and development of social skills. Learning and practicing social skills with peers result in children having friends and being popular with peers (Coie & Dodge, 1998). Deficits in social skills lead to being rejected by peers. In this section, I show how different behaviors observed at recess relate to children's social status and social skills.

Developmental psychologists have studied peer relations for many, many years (e.g., Hartup, 1983; Thompson, 1944, 1960), and they generally agree that a very powerful indicator of social skills is the degree to which a child is popular with or rejected by his or her peers. Peer popularity and

PLAYGROUND BEHAVIOR AND SOCIAL DEVELOPMENT

peer rejection are typically measured by asking youngsters to nominate, respectively, the classmates that they like most and like least. A popular child has more "like most" nominations than "like least" nominations. A rejected child has more "like least" than "like most" nominations.

A major difference between popular and rejected children is aggression. Popular children, relative to rejected children, are more cooperative, less aggressive, and able to see different points of view. They also have better language skills and have a greater repertoire of social problem-solving strategies. In contrast, rejected children are either aggressive or withdrawn. There are high risks associated with being rejected (Parker & Asher, 1987). These youngsters are more likely to get into trouble in school, do poorly in school, and have a variety of social/emotional problems.

The ability to solve social problems is widely recognized as an important social skill. Children are faced with numerous social problems during their day. For example, they want a toy that a peer is playing with. Different children respond to these problems in different ways. For example, rejected children often have a more restricted repertoire of social problem-solving skills. To get a toy they may ask for it directly, for instance, "I want that." If that fails, they may just take it. A more competent child has a wider repertoire and uses different strategies in different situations and with different children. He may ask, either directly or indirectly, for instance, "*Please* can I have it?" He might suggest that they take turns, for example, "Can I go after you?" Or he may offer a trade, for example, "If you let me play with that, you can play with my truck." In my work (Pellegrini, 1988), I asked children to generate a variety of social solutions to a series of different social problems. For example, when Frank is pres:nted with the social problem of Peter playing with a toy that he wants, Frank suggests that he can: ask Peter to share the toy; offer to trade one of his toys for the one Peter is playing with; ask the teacher for help. I was also concerned with children's risk of two aspects of psychopathology—internalizing disorders, such as neuroticism, and externalizing disorders, such as antisocial personalities. All these measures were collected across a 2-year period so that we have a longitudinal picture of children's social competence across the elementary school years. Now let's take a look at the results of this study, looking at girls and boys separately.

First, girls' playground behavior did not correlate significantly with any of the measures of social skills I used. This may be because, as I will discuss in the next chapter, the playground is a male-preferred venue. Specifically, it is a place that affords high levels of physical activity, and boys are much more active than girls (Eaton & Enns, 1986). Simultaneously, girls are socialized not to exhibit these sorts of vigorous behavior. As we will see in the chapter on playground games, girls also exhibit lower levels of game sophistication relative to boys. Indeed, other research (e.g., Lockheed, Harris, & Nemceff, 1983; Pellegrini & Perlmutter, 1989) suggests that girls actually suppress their exhibition of competence in male-preferred situations.

Boys' playground behaviors, on the other hand, related to a number of aspects of social competence. Specifically, boys' vigorous and rough-and-tumble behavior (R&T) was positively and significantly correlated with "likes most" nominations (a measures of being popular) and variety of social problem solutions. That is, boys who engaged in more R&T on the playground received more "likes least" nominations and generated a greater variety of solutions to hypothetical social problems children learn and practice the skills necessary to be popular. We know, for example, that in order to be popular with their peers, children must learn to take the perspectives of their peers and to take turns. These skills are learned in play. For example, during R&T, children alternate between subordinate and superordinate roles and learn to differentiate between playful and aggressive play signals. Thus, it is not surprising that there is a relation between the frequency with which boys engage in R&T and popularity with peers. In short, boys' R&T is a form of affiliative behavior that related to their popularity and to their social problem-solving abilities. Aggression, in comparison, related to being disliked by peers—no big news here.

When we look at longitudinal relations, or the extent to which behaviors observed on the playground during Year 1 predicted social skills during Year 2, we find that for boys R&T predicted boys' social problem solving. That is, boys who engaged in high levels of R&T at Year 1, were, on average, more skilled social problem solvers a year later. It may be the case that in R&T, children learn and practice a variety of different strategies for keeping their peers engaged in play. For example, it is well documented that bigger and stronger children often "self-handicap" when they are playing with a smaller peer. For example, they may wrestle from a kneeling rather than a standing position, or they may switch from a superordinate to a subordinate role. This sort of behavioral flexibility is an important skill in children's peer relationships. Importantly, the games that children played were significant predictors.

We begin with boys. The relative frequency with which boys in Year 1 engaged in cooperative games predicted *negatively* their number of "likes least" nominations and their being rated by their teachers as antisocial.

The results for girls' were similar to that for boys to the extent that girls' games predicted "likes most" nominations. Put another way, children who did not engage in games were rated by their teachers as more neurotic and unpopular.

By way of qualification, I must note that the magnitude of these statistical relations was modest. That is, the relations were statistically significant (that is, the relations observed occurred at a level that was greater than chance), but they did not explain most of the variation in the outcomes. For example, girls' engagement in games explained only 9% of the variation in the "likes most" nominations.

The category of games is, obviously, a gross category to the extent that lots of very different games are included. In order to make clearer implications here we need to know more about the games. For example, some games, like tag, are of low cognitive level, while others, like hide 'n' seek, are more strategic. Children engaging in the low-level games would be expected to be low achievers while higher achievers probably engage in the latter types. This issue will be addressed in much greater detail in a subsequent chapter.

CONCLUSION

To conclude this chapter, we have seen how children's behavior on the playground varies considerably by gender and playground location. These behaviors, in turn, have interesting correlations with aspects of children's social competence. That significant relations exist between aspects of playground behavior and measures of social competence is very interesting. Does it mean that children are actually learning something out there? Or, more conservatively, does it mean that they are practicing something important? In either case, these results suggest that recess behavior has important implications for both social competence and, as we will discuss later, cognitive performance. It is perhaps less surprising that children's playground behavior is related to aspects of social competence, such as popularity, social problem solving, and personality factors. After all, recess is, or should be, a time for children to interact among themselves. It is relatively easy, though very labor intensive, to identify children who do that well, as well as those who don't. If educators think it is important to educate the "whole child," then these social concerns also become educational concerns. Following this view, educators should think it important to educate the social, as well as the cognitive.

SOME THINGS TO THINK ABOUT

1. Go to a neighborhood playground and observe what children do in different areas.

Are there areas where more cooperation occurs?

Why?

What about aggression? Are there areas that seem to elicit it?

Why?

2. Go to a park or a playground and watch either children engaged in playfighting, or animals, such as squirrels, playing "chase" up and down a tree.

Do they self-handicap?

What behaviors would you consider self-handicapping?

3. Identify a child whom you know who is either withdrawn or aggressive. If the opportunity presents itself, observe that child with another child who is younger than he or she.

Do they seem to get along?

Play together?

What sorts of roles and behaviors does each of the children enact?

Why do you think their interactions are successful?

Or not?

APPENDIX

Pellegrini, A. D. (1988). Elementary school children's rough-and-rumble play and social competence. *Developmental Psychology, 24,* 802–806.

METHODS USED TO COLLECT THE DATA

Procedures

Children were observed during their daily recess period from October through May. Recess lasted for 25 minutes and was situated immediately following the lunch period for each grade. There were about 120 to 150 children on the playground at any one time and they were supervised by three to five female teachers' aides.

The children had free access to all parts of the playground, which included the following components: a blacktop area of about 1000 sq yds, a contemporary playscape situated in a pine forest, about 350 sq yds, and a grassy area, of about 200 sq yds, separating the playscape from the blacktop. Children's behavior was recorded by four observers using scan sampling and instantaneous recording techniques. Observers recorded the following information by whispering into a small audio-recorder: the name and behavior of the focal child (from the listed behaviors in Table 1 on p. 54), playground location, number of boys and girls in the immediate vicinity of the focal child, and the reactors' behavior. Each child was observed at least 100 times across the school year.

Measures

Popularity.   Children's popularity was assessed using sociometric nomination procedures pioneered by Coie and Dodge (1983). Individual children were seated at a table before a display of individual pictures of all their classmates. They were first asked to point to and name each child, then they were asked to nominate three children they liked best and three they liked least. This procedure, in addition to yielding "likes least" and "likes most" scores, also yields social preference scores (likes most − likes least) and social impact scores (likes most + likes least).

Hypothetical Social Problem Solving.   Children's ability to generate a variety of solutions for hypothetical social problems was used. In this procedure an experimenter presented individual children with five separate pictures of a child trying to get a toy from a peer and five separate pictures of a children trying to avoid being reprimanded by his/her mother. Children were asked to generate as many different solutions to the problems as possible. Children's responses were audio recorded and variety of different responses was scored.

Teachers' Ratings of Children.   The children's behavior questionnaire was developed by Rutter (1967) as part of his studies of children's adjustment in schools. This teacher-completed questionnaire has 26 items scored on a likert scale from 0 (doesn't apply) to 2 (certainly applies) and yields to factors: an antisocial factor and a neurotic factor.

TABLE 1

Results of Analyses for Effect of Playground Location
(Playscape, Blacktop, Soft, Grassy) and Gender
on Children's Playground Behavior

Behavior	Location*		Gender	
	F**	Contrast***	F	Contrast
Passive-noninteractive	33.27++	ps > sf	.22	ns
Passive interactive	9.85	ps + sf > bt	.77	ns
Observer directed	1.30	ns	.83	ns
Adult organized	.72	ns	.42	ns
Aggressive	2.61	ns	.10	ns
R&T	9.81++	sf > bl	3.55+	boys > girls
Vigorous play	34.60++	ps = sf > bt	3.27+	boys > girls
Games w/ rules	1.50	ns	.16	ns
Object play	.01	ns	.01	ns
Role play	.14	ns	1.19	ns
Variety of different behaviors	56.14++	ps > sf > bt	.01	ns

Note: $df = 1,87$ for gender and $2,87$ for location. *Ps = playscape; sf = soft, grassy area; bt = black top; b = boys; g = girls. **F is statistic used in the analysis of variance to detect differences among group means or averages. ***The Contrasts are between group comparisons; $^+p < .05$, $^{++}p < .01$.

Chapter 4

The Two Worlds of the Playground: Gender Segregation at Recess

It is a truism in childhood that boys and girls do not interact with each other frequently or freely during their free times, whether that free time is on the elementary school playground at recess or during free play at day care. This is observed across all regions of the United States as well as in many human societies that have been studied (Maccoby, 1998). If this were not enough to convince you, it is also observed across most vertebrate species (Ruckstuhl & Neuhaus, in press)! Thus, gender segregation (zoologists refer to it as sexual segregation) appears to be a basic component in the social organization of many species. (See Ruckstuhl & Neuhaus, in press, for a whole volume on this.)

Indeed, some of the arguments made for gender segregation among human children are similar to those made for gender segregation in adults of other mammalian species (Ruckstuhl, 1998; Ruckstuhl & Neuhaus, 2002). For example, theorists suggest that male and female humans (Maccoby, 1998), like adult ungulates, such as red deer (Ruckstuhl, 1998), segregate due to differences in behavioral styles. This means that males interact with each other because their behavior is physically vigorous and rough. Females, being more sedentary, or less active, avoid these physically active behaviors to interact with each other.

In this chapter, I discuss the various explanations proffered for this phenomenon. The reasons responsible for children's gender segregation, in turn, are responsible for the different types of behavior that they exhibit on the playground.

Biological explanations are often tendered for phenomena that are observed cross-culturally and across different species. In the world of gender differences in behavior, this sort of dichotomy is typically presented: It's either biology or socialization. By *biological* I mean that some form of deterministic argument is typically made to suggest that our biology determines our behavior. Biological determinism can be presented in terms of genetic determinism, or being trapped by one's evolutionary history. Genetic determinism can be best captured by the "gene for this and that" stance. Scientists, especially with the decoding of the genome, have suggested that specific gene expressions are responsible for certain traits such as alcoholism (see Bateson & Martin, 1999 for a critique of this view).

Socialization is at the other end of the spectrum from genetic determinism. Differences are due, according to this view, to the varying rewards and models presented to boys and girls. It is as if they are born blank slates and their socialization histories determine the differences in behavior of boys and girls. Boys play rough because they have models for this sort of thing at home and on TV, and they are reinforced for exhibiting these behaviors. Similarly, girls' play is nurturing and revolves around domestic themes for the same reasons.

Of course, these represent extreme positions on the nature–nurture continuum, and no serious scholar these days would admit holding such one-sided views. Yet, it is not much of an exaggeration to say that many scholars hold opinions that, practically speaking, are not far removed from one or the other extreme positions.

My orientation is that both the biological and the socialization model as presented are too simplistic. Human development, indeed the development of all animals, is the result of a complex interplay between one's biology and one's environment. I will specify the details of this view below, but before I do that I'd like to define what it is we are talking about when we say "gender segregation."

GENDER SEGREGATION

What Is It?

Gender segregation in children has been defined often in terms of the separation of boys and girls in social groupings. Gender segregation in children begins around 3 years and peaks at 8 to 11 years (Maccoby, 1998). It is also very difficult to change; that is, it is very difficult to get boys and girls to play with each other consistently. When efforts have been made to encourage preschool children to engage in crossgender play, they did so only as long as they were reinforced for doing so (Serbin, Connor, Burchardt, & Citron, 1979). When the reinforcement to play together was removed, children went back to playing in segregated groups. Thus, gender segregation is robust. So robust, in fact, that some have suggested that it is more difficult to change than children's playing in racially segregated groups (Maccoby, 1998). Groups do become less segregated but only as boys and girls approach adolescence and become interested in heterosexual relationships (Pellegrini & Long, 2003).

Gender segregation in childhood is, generally, influenced by differences in behavior of boys and girls, the different roles they enact, as well as immediate environmental factors. As I discussed in the previous chapter and illustrate later, boys are more physically active and rough and enact more competitive roles than girls (Pellegrini et al., 1998; 2002). In terms of environmental factors, children are more likely to segregate when similar age peers are present and adult supervision is minimal, such as play time on school playgrounds (Maccoby 1998). Children are also more likely to play with opposite-sex peers at home and in their neighborhood relative to school, possibly due to there being less peer pressure to conform to segregation norms at home (Gottman, 1983).

There are varying degrees of segregation (Conradt, 1998), but it is most commonly defined in terms of the frequency with which boys and girls are found in separate groups. This method of defining segregation (i.e., the group is either totally segregated or not) has been used by Richard Fabes and his colleagues with elementary school children (Fabes, Martin, Hanish, Anders, & Madden-Derdich, 2003).

Partial segregation is another way of defining segregation, and it is a proportional measure; it indexes the degree to which each group is segregated. The partial metric of gender segregation is typically assessed by the proportion of males or females in a group (e.g., Pellegrini & Long, 2003). For example, in a study of middle school students observed in a variety of unstructured venues (e.g., hallways, cafeteria, dances), the proportion of males to all children in a focal group (that is, number of males/number of males + females) ranged from .92 to .77 across two years of observation (Pellegrini & Long, 2003).

From these studies, it seems that a proportional measure is the most sensitive as well as the one yielding the most realistic picture of the peer group. By this I mean that most groups are not usually totally segregated

FIG. 4.1. Sexually segregated female group, mostly males.

FIG. 4.2. Sexually segregated female group, mostly females.

and that the proportional measure tells us more precisely the degree to which segregation occurs.

So even within specific locations, such as a playground, we have children segregating themselves, as illustrated in Figures 4.1 and 4.2. Note that in the first picture there are three males and one female (.75 segregated), and in the second, we have three girls (1.0 segregated).

In this chapter, I examine two explanations, or hypotheses (given to explain the existence of gender segregation in children: energetics and social roles). This involves documenting (a) the energetic costs (in terms of calories) of the behaviors and (b) the social roles in boys' and girls' groups during those years when segregation is most pronounced—3 to 11 years of age.

But before you start thinking that I am one of those biological determinists that I damned at the start of this chapter, let me specify how I view the interactive role of one's environment and one's biology from the perspective of our species' evolutionary history.

AN INTERACTIVE VIEW OF BIOLOGY AND ENVIRONMENT

While I think that evolutionary history *does* influence human development, I also recognize that the environments in which we develop *interact with*, or affect, the ways in which this evolutionary history is expressed and, in turn, the course of human development. That is, I do not take a deterministic view of phylogenetic history (i.e., the evolutionary history of our species) and the effects of genes on human behavior, even if continuity across common ancestry is found in dimensions of social behavior and organization. As noted above, the ubiquity of gender segregation cross-culturally, and the stability of these patterns may lead to the assumption of a biological deterministic position. My orientation leads, however, to the position that genes, environments, and behavior dynamically influence each other (Archer & Lloyd, 2002; Bateson & Martin, 1998; Bjorklund & Pellegrini, 2000; Gottlieb, 1998; Stamp, 2003).

By way of analogy, this orientation is akin to recognizing evolutionary history as another, more distant, influence on development—in addition to the more immediate influences of factors such as the family or the peer group. Take the example of the well-recognized and relatively distal effects of social economic status (SES) on children's behavior. Just because we recognize this effect, it *does not* translate into our accepting the notion that SES has a similar effect on all people in all circumstances (Bronfenbrenner,

1979; Bronfenbrenner & Ceci, 1994). Instead, SES influences *and is influenced by* subsequent layers of context.

This dynamic relation is nicely illustrated in the work on resilient children (Masten & Coatsworth, 1998). Resilient children are those children growing up to be successful and well adjusted, despite the fact that they experienced very difficult circumstances in childhood—circumstances that result in poor social, emotional, and/or intellectual adjustment for most children. Aspects of children's temperament (they could be easygoing and very sociable kids) and family (positive mother–father relationships) influence the effects of deleterious environments associated with poverty and low social status.

The same seems to be true of the influence of including an evolutionary layer in our explanation of gender segregation. I am assuming that evolution by natural selection, rather than other explanations, such as that given in the Book of Genesis, is responsible, at a distal level, for our current status as humans. This status is, however, dynamic and interacts with more proximal (immediate) aspects of children' lives.

Specifically, the environment in which an individual develops, starting with conception, influences the ways in which evolutionary history is expressed. Patrick Bateson and Paul Martin (1999) use a jukebox metaphor to describe this process. Individuals within each species have a genetic endowment that can be realized through a wide variety of options (similar to the collection of records in a jukebox) but the specific developmental pathway taken (similar to the specific record selected) by an individual is influenced by the perinatal environment (i.e., from conception through early infancy) of the developing organism. Thus a number of developmental pathways are possible, but the environment in which the organism develops determines which one is selected (Archer, 1992; Caro & Bateson, 1986).

For the purposes of this chapter, perhaps the most relevant aspect of the environment is nutrition as it affects sexual dimorphism in size (i.e., males in most primate species, including humans, are physically larger than females), which, in turn, affects physically vigorous behavior, sexual segregation, and types of social behavior, such as rough and vigorous play and different forms of aggression. Specifically, the nutritional history of a human mother impacts the physical size of her offspring and especially that of males (Bateson & Martin, 1999). First, males are physically larger than females by about 10% to 15%, similar to chimpanzees (Alexander, Hoogland, Howard, Noonan, & Sherman, 1979; de Waal & Lanting, 1997). Males' larger size relative to females' (i.e., sexual dimorphism) may be one of the factors responsible for sex differences in vigorous behavior and in competitive behavior where males are more vigorous and more competitive than females (Pellegrini, in 2004b, in press). Larger bodies need more vigorous exercise, relative to smaller bodies.

Consistent with my view, the availability of resources affects human sexual dimorphism and, consequently, gender differences in physical activity. The interactive nature of this system is illustrated by the fact that height is highly heritable, yet this relation is influenced by the fetus' perinatal environment; pregnant mothers who experience nutritional stress have relatively smaller offspring. This is especially the case for male offspring (Bateson & Martin, 1998a).

An example of this phenomenon can be found in the anthropology literature. Both ecological abundance and stress affects mating patterns such that in severe ecological niches (e.g., high Arctic), monogamy among humans is ecologically imposed as it requires both parents to provision the offspring. This in turn attenuates sexual dimorphism (Alexander et al., 1979).

In short, in ecologically stressed environments, such as the Arctic, the size difference between men and women is smaller. Differences in body size are antecedents to differences in physical activity and associated with physical vigor, competitiveness, and aggressiveness, such that males and females view themselves differently very early in development and then segregate (see Pellegrini, 2004b, for a fuller discussion). Later, these differences are translated into different social roles (where males are more competitive), social behavior (where males are more physically aggressive), and differences in levels of physical activity (Pellegrini & Archer, 2005).

In short, the developmental option taken is related to the environment in which the individual develops. Given the vastly different environments into which individuals with the same genetic history are born, a single genetic program would not be equally effective across these different niches. This model is displayed in Fig. 4.3. In the next section, I suggest that gender segregation is due to differences in energetic (or levels of activity) and social roles.

ORIGINS OF SEXUAL SEGREGATION

Differences in Energetics

This explanation suggests that males and female segregate because of differences in size where larger males are more energetic than females.

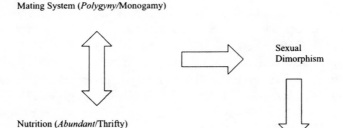

Mating System (*Polygyny*/Monogamy)

Nutrition (*Abundant*/Thrifty)

Sexual
Dimorphism

Gender Segregation

Male Groups	*Female Groups*
Active	Sedentary
R&T/Competitive	Nurturant/Social Dramatic Play
Physical Aggression	Relation Aggression

FIG. 4.3.   A sexual segregation model for sex differences in behavior.

Metaanalyses (i.e., a quantitative comparison of a wide variety of studies available from published and nonpublished sources) of sex difference in physical activity showed that males are indeed more active than females, with differences being observed *prenatally* as well as during childhood (Eaton & Enns, 1986). That differences appear prenatally suggests that differences in activity are not primarily due to socialization. Instead, prenatal exposure to androgens (a class of male hormones, of which testosterone is a member) is probably the mechanism by which natural selection pressure is exerted resulting in the initial sex differences in physical activity (Archer & Lloyd, 2002). These differences, in turn, may be responsible for male infants' preference for high energy behaviors (Campbell, Shirley, Heywood, & Crook, 2000).

If energetic expenditure motivates sexual segregation, we would also expect sex differences in caloric expenditure in physical activity during those periods when sexual segregation is most apparent, beginning at 3 years and peaking at 8 to 11 years of age (Maccoby, 1998). I present three sets of data to support this argument: First, naturalistic descriptions of children's activity during free play, comparing the caloric expenditure of the activity of primary school boys and girls on the playground during school recess. Second, I present data from experimental studies where children were deprived of opportunities for physical activity and then observed after that point. The methodological details of these studies can be found in the appendix at the end of this chapter. And third, I examine the related explanation that boys play with boys and girls play with girls because of behavioral compatibility. That is, they play with each other because they play in similar ways.

Naturalistic Studies of Boys' and Girls' Energetics.   In this study, I (Pellegrini et al., 1998) assessed energetics in the form of caloric expenditure using three types of measures: a behavioral checklist (originally developed by Eaton et al., 1987) and validated against aggregated actometer, or accelermoter (a mechanical device measuring the movement of arms and legs) and heart rate scores. In one study, boys and girls in two age groups (6.8 years and 9.9 years) were studied and the results revealed a sex by age interaction for all three types of measures. Our data showed, across all three measures, that with age the play of boys, relative to girls, became more costly (in terms of calories), whereas girls' caloric expenditure remained flat or did not change.

We also looked at two other groups of children (mean ages of 7.3 and 9.5), but in this case, children's resting caloric expenditure was subtracted from the caloric expenditure during play. The logic here was that to assess the expenditure of energy during play we should do that by subtracting the amount of energy required just to be awake (the resting measure) from the activity during play. The greater the difference between children's caloric expenditure during group activity and while resting, the more calories they consumed during the group activity. Similar to the first study, and as displayed in Fig. 4.4, a sex by age interaction was observed: Boys were

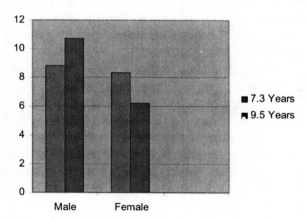

FIG. 4.4.   Caloric expenditure in play and activity, resting rate by sex and age.

more active than girls; boys became more active with age, and girls stayed the same (or actually showed a slight, though nonsignificant decrease).

These data show that there were activity differences for both boys and girls *and* for children of different ages. There was, however, interactive effect between age and gender on physical activity. That is, with age, gender differences became greater. This difference may have been due to differences in maturation where males, relative to females, mature slower. So gender differences at these ages may merely reflect this difference. However, when these differences are statistically controlled, the gender differences remain; boys are more active than girls.

Deprivation Studies. The energetic explanation can also be tested with deprivation studies. The logic behind deprivation studies is that if there is a need to engage in exercise play, then depriving individuals of opportunity to engage in it should result in an observed "rebound" during postdeprivation opportunities to exercise (Burghardt 1998; Bateson & Martin 1999). Higher levels of physical activity should be observed after periods of long, relative to short, deprivation. This rebound may be indicative of the functional importance of those behaviors during specific developmental periods. More specific to segregation, we would expect boys to be more active after deprivation than females.

In the first study of its kind, Peter Smith and Theresa Hagen (1980) measured postdeprivation frequency of exercise play. The children ranged in age from 34 to 57 months, with a mean age of 46 months. Results indicated that children did indeed engage in higher rates of exercise play following long (90 minutes), relative to short (30 minutes) deprivation, but no gender differences were observed. Given that sex segregation is in its earliest stages during the preschool years, we should not be surprised that no gender differences were observed.

My colleagues and I conducted a second series of deprivation experiments with older children (Pellegrini, Huberty, & Jones, 1995). Again, the details of the procedure for this experiment can be found in the appendix at the end of this chapter. In all experiments, the difference between long and short confinement was 30 minutes. Activity was measured behaviorally using the empirically validated rating scale (described in Table 4.1 of the appendix to this chapter) in both studies, and in the second experiment, by scoring the quadrants covered in a classroom. (The floor of the classroom was marked into four relatively equal spaces and the number of spaces crossed during the observation served as the measure of activity.)

In the first experiment three age groups were formed (5.6, 7.5, and 9.7 years of age). Males were more active than females after both short and long confinement conditions, especially in the oldest group where males' activity after the long deprivation (Mean rating = 8.02) was 20% greater than females' (Mean rating = 6.66).

The second experiment, with 7.3- and 9.5-year-olds, used the same deprivation conditions and detected no statistically significant sex differences: Activity was equal for younger and older males respectively, after the long deprivation. In the third experiment, two groups of 10-year-olds were observed during indoor playtime using the same deprivation conditions. Boys' (Mean rating = 5.70) were more active after the long deprivation than were girls (Mean rating = 4.70), again by 21%; the means were in the hypothesized direction, but the difference was not statistically significant (boys = 5.2 and girls = 3.15) between boys and girls. To summarize, results from deprivation studies provide support, albeit equivocal, for the energetics explanation. In all but the youngest group (i.e., the 4-year-olds in the Smith & Hagen study and the 5.6-year-olds in my studies), the mean comparisons within the long confinement condition favored males, although they were not always statistically significant. The duration of the deprivation period may have been responsible for these equivocal results, where I expected statistically significant differences between boys and girls after the long deprivation condition. A longer deprivation period may have exerted a more reliable effect.

At this point it is important to short-circuit any misinterpretation of the theory guiding these deprivation experiments. I am NOT applying a "surplus energy" or "blowing off steam" metaphor to our work. Each of these two hydraulic-like explanations suggests that with rest, energy or pressure accumulates and must be released occasionally. There is no scientific evidence to support the idea of surplus energy or blowing off steam (see Evans & Pellegrini, 1997). Instead, what seems to be operating is the fact that the body's muscle and skeletal systems are especially in need of exercise during childhood, as they are developing rapidly. When they are deprived of opportunities to exercise, they overcompensate, or rebound, when given opportunity. This need seems to be greater for boys than for girls.

Behavioral Compatibility

To be a member of a group requires synchrony of individuals' behavior. That is, the group members should, to a degree, behave in a similar fashion. Level of energetics is an example of behavioral compatibility. Boys play with boys because they all enjoy highly vigorous behavior, and girls often find this unpleasant and, perhaps, counter to sex-role expectations. However, when boys are in the minority in a group, they may change their behavior toward a more sedentary style so as to be more compatible with the group's style.

Consistent with this view, Eleanor Maccoby (1998) showed that there are minimal sex differences when preschool children are playing alone, but when children interact with same-sex peers (boys with boys and girls with girls) reliable sex differences are observed. Perhaps more impressive evidence to support the behavioral compatibility hypothesis has been presented in studies where preference for playmates was examined in relation to the sex of the child (boy or girl) and to the behavioral style being exhibited. Gerianne Alexander and Melissa Hines (1994) showed that boys (4 to 8 years of age) expressed a preference to play with girls with a masculine play style compared to a boy with a feminine play style. Similarly, girls (at 8, but not 4 years) expressed a preference for playmates based on play style rather than sex.

Studies of girls with congenital adrenal hyperplastia (CAH) are also relevant here. CAH is a syndrome where fetuses are exposed to excessive amounts of male hormones. As a result, these girls display higher levels of activity, more similar to that of boys. Results indicated that CAH girls, between 3 and 8 years of age, were more likely than controls to choose males as playmates (Alexander & Hines, 1994).

To conclude this section, the evidence supports the position that males are more active than females from the prenatal period through childhood and that they play so as to be compatible with their peers. These differences result in boys enjoying vigorous behavior. In contrast, girls enjoy the company of other girls while actively avoiding boys, especially in the absence of a potentially protective adult. From this difference in activity, boys and girls choose peers with whom to interact based on both behavioral and dispositional similarities (Hartup, 1983). Boys find their groups rewarding because they are similarly matched in terms of strength and activity levels, and this match maximizes exercise training. Girls find this level of vigor aversive and seek out other girls to learn and practice maternal roles (Pusey, 1990).

That sexual dimorphism is minimal during childhood, when segregation and differences in activity are observed, requires explanation. It may be that energetic behavior is especially important for young boys because it is occurring at a sensitive period for the development of brain and muscle systems implicated in actions associated with later fighting, at least in more traditional cultures (Byers & Walker, 1995). Specifically, the energetic behavior characteristic of young boys may help them develop cerebellar synapse distributions and muscle fiber differentiation important in economical and skilled movements associated with vigorous behavior and fighting and game playing (Byers & Walker, 1995).

Different Social Roles of Males and Females

The social-roles explanation suggests that adult reproductive sex roles are responsible for segregation during the juvenile period. Specifically, the energetic bias of males, with development, takes the form of learning and practicing roles associated with dominance and fighting. In contrast, the more sedentary style of girls is associated with their learning and practicing maternal roles. These sex-specific roles are learned in segregated groups by observing adults and older peers and practiced by playing with peers. Males, for example, segregate around dominance-related activities, such as rough-and-tumble play and aggression (Pellegrini, 2003). These behaviors are related to affiliation with a variety of peers and physical conditioning during childhood (Pellegrini & Smith, 1998). These rough-and-tumble play and dominance-related behaviors relate to early teenage boys being popular with their female peers and being invited to hypothetical dates (Pellegrini & Long, 2003).

Females segregate in the service of forming close bonds with other females to learn and practice nurturing skills, as well as avoiding aggression. Consequently, selection pressures could exist for these behaviors during both the juvenile and adult periods.

Groups of young boys, as just noted, are very high-energy and competitive. These specific behaviors, besides having energetic antecedents and consequences, are related to reproductive roles. Specifically, the quasi-aggressive behaviors, such as rough-and-tumble play, observed in male groups may have their origins in their ancestral roles as hunters (Smith, 1982).

Further, males are socialized to express their physical activity in the form of rough play and aggression, often by their fathers. Fathers of young boys spend significantly more time with sons relative to their daughters (Parke & Suomi, 1981). During this time, fathers often engage in R&T and other forms of vigorous play with their sons (Carson, Burks, & Parke, 1993).

These rough and competitive behaviors exhibited by boys in their groups have implications for their peer-group status. Male groups are hierarchically organized in terms of dominance status. Dominance in male groups is determined by a combination of aggressive and friendly cooperative strategies used in the service of resource acquisition. Thus, in male groups, juveniles use rough-and-tumble play, aggression, reconciliation, and facility in competitive games as means of achieving status (Pellegrini, 2003). Males tend to use aggressive strategies when their social groups are in the formative stages. For example, when children first enter a new school they tend to be aggressive. After status is achieved, instances of aggression decrease and dominant members use more cooperative and friendly strategies to reconcile former foes (Pellegrini & Bartini, 2001). Similar patterns are even seen in preschools (see Hawley, 1999, 2002).

Following a social dominance argument, we would expect more sexual segregation at transition points between social groupings, such as when youngsters change schools. Specifically, male groups should be segregated as dominance issues are being sorted as males enter a new school. Our observational data of youngsters interacting with each other during non-structured time (e.g., in the lunch room and in hallways) across the first two years of middle school (13–15 years of age) showed that both boys' *and* girls' groups remained segregated (Pellegrini & Long, 2003). These results, of course were counter to our prediction. It may be that the demands of the school setting were such that it forced segregation. To support this point, we found that segregation did indeed decrease among these same youngsters when they were observed at a school dance.

Girls' interactions with their peers after the second year of life also reflect their roles in adult society. Specifically, the literature on children's pretend play is unequivocal in documenting sex differences in themes enacted in fantasy. (See Power, 2000, for an exhaustive review.) When fantasy play begins to emerge, at around 18 months of age (Fein, 1981a), girls' play reflects domestic and nurturing themes (McLoyd, 1980). For example, in a classic study of preschool children's fantasy, Eli Saltz and colleagues (Saltz, Dixon, & Johnson, 1977) labeled the sorts of fantasy play that girls enacted as "social dramatic" and boys' play as "thematic fantasy." In social dramatic play, domestic and familial themes are enacted, with girls "mothering" or teaching younger children. Thematic fantasy, on the other hand, is rooted in the world of superheroes and has themes associated with dominance, fighting, and competition. An example of thematic fantasy would be two boys pretending to be engaged in a Star Wars sword battle. In such cases, it is also likely that they would take turns being the winner and the loser.

These biases are reinforced in numerous ways by parents and teachers (e.g., in the toys provided for each and the style of interactions), though fathers seem to be most concerned with shaping sons' actions and choices (Power, 2000). Additionally, children themselves, but especially boys, are reluctant to cross sex-role stereotypic boundaries (Gottman, 1983). For example, in an experimental study of preschoolers' play with sex-typed toys, older boys' play with female-preferred toys was *less* sophisticated than younger boys' play with the same toys (Pellegrini & Perlmutter, 1989).

Females may avoid males because they represent threats in the form of general aggression to themselves (Hrdy, 1976). Consistent with this idea that females segregate due to their need for protection from males is the finding that adult presence is likely to increase the likelihood of girls interacting with boys (Maccoby, 1998). Young girls may see adults as protectors from aggressive and boisterous boys. While male children seem to be more concerned than females with maintaining segregated groups, at least during childhood, females actively withdraw from interactions with males, often to seek the protection of their parents. For example, in experimental studies of unacquainted toddlers where children were observed in mixed-sex dyads, girls often withdrew from the interaction to stand next to their mothers (Maccoby, 1998). This sort of withdrawal was not observed in female dyads. Similar findings are reported for older children (5- and 6-year olds). When quartets were observed in an experimental playroom, girls tended to stay near an adult when in mixed-sex quartets but not in all-girl groups (Greeno, 1991, cited in Maccoby, 1998).

In short, boys' and girls' peer groups are segregated beginning in preschool, their interaction is organized around different activities and toys by both adults and peers. These themes, in turn, reflect males' bias toward competitive and dominance-oriented roles and females' toward nurturing and domestic roles. It may be the case that the energetic dimensions of behaviors initially bias males and females to seek out same-sex peers. Then, with subsequent social cognitive development, children learn the social roles associated with males and females in their society. The roles associated with these behaviors, in turn, predict heterosexual relationships.

CONCLUSION

There is clear evidence for gender segregation of youngsters in most human societies, as Maccoby (1998) has documented in her integrative review. As Maccoby acknowledges, however, socialization theories alone cannot account for the origins of the behaviors associated with segregation. Evolutionary theory can be used to extend this analysis (Pellegrini,

2004b, in press). Branches of evolutionary theory (e.g., Tinbergen, 1963) suggest that if aspects of behavior are observed across a variety of related species, they may have been subjected to similar selection pressures and have a common phylogenetic origin.

The evidence I reviewed supports the claims that energetics and reproductive social roles contribute to sex segregation. Males segregate because their reproductive roles bias them to high energetics, relative to females. This is reflected in higher activity levels, and their very early preference for more active props and different social roles.

Role enactment in segregated groups may provide opportunity to practice and refine skills. That these specific male and female skills are related to fighting and maternal skills, respectively, suggests that they are best practiced with same-sex children. For example, skills related to dominance, such as detecting weaknesses and coordinating skilled movements, may need extensive practice, perhaps through play with peers, given their variety and complexity (Alexander, 1989).

SOME THINGS TO THINK ABOUT

1. Observe young children in different settings: A public playground or a school playground and in a more private setting, such as in the home.

Is gender segregation more evident in one setting than the other?

Is this more characteristic of boys or of girls?

Why do you think this is so?

2. Look at groups of children in a public play space.

Are the groups totally or partially segregated?

3. In totally segregated groups, list the behaviors and roles enacted by boys and girls.

	Boys	Girls
Behaviors		
Roles		

4. Now look at partially segregated groups—first when girls are in the majority—and list behaviors and roles.

	Boys	Girls
Behaviors		
Roles		

5. Now do the same for partially segregated groups where males are in the majority.

	Boys	Girls
Behaviors		
Roles		

APPENDIX

NATURALISTIC STUDIES

Pellegrini, A. D., Horvat, M., & Huberty, P. D. (1998). The relative cost of children's physical activity play. *Animal Behaviour, 55*, 1053–1106.

METHOD

Participants

There were two separate samples of children in this research. In the first sample, there were 15 males and 15 females ranging in age from 5.4 years to 11.5. They were primarily of European origin (85%), with 15% being African-American. In a second sample, there were 38 males and 39 females and they ranged in age from 7.0 years to 9.9 years. The sample was 66% European American and 34% African American. They attended a public elementary school in Athens, Georgia.

Procedures

Children were observed on their school playgrounds during their recess periods and during after-school day-care programs held at the schools. The playgrounds on which they were observed were all spacious places, between 3- and 10-acre sites. Children were observed according to focal child sampling, continuous recording rules (Pellegrini, 2004) for sampling intervals varying from 30 seconds to 16 minutes. In the latter cases, children were observed with heart-rate monitors and actometers, as well as with a behavioral checklist.

Acotmeters measure body movement and provide estimates of caloric expenditure. We used Caltrac systems, placed on children's waists, in conjunction with Polar Vanguard XL Heart Rate monitors, placed around their chests. The behavioral checklist, depicted in Table 4.1, scores children's activity on a 1 to 9 scale and provides an estimate of caloric expenditure.

The three measures of movement were all significantly intercorrelated. The heart rate monitor and the actometer were correlated .45, $p < .01$ so they were aggregated. The aggregated heart-rate monitor and actometer scores were correlated significantly, .44, $p < .01$.

TABLE 4.1
Behavioral Checklist for Caloric Expenditure

Level	Posture	Intensity	Value	Example
1	Lying	Low	1.9	Lying motionless
2	Lying	Medium	3.7	Slow crawl
3	Lying	High	4.5	Rapid crawl
4	Sitting	Low	7.6	Sitting still
5	Sitting	Medium	27.9	Swinging with arm movement
6	Sitting	High	57.5	Vigorous cycling
7	Standing	Low	8.9	Standing still
8	Standing	Medium	34.5	Walk
9	Standing	High	75.0	Running

DEPRIVATION STUDIES

Pellegrini, A. D., Huberty, P. D., & Jones, I. (1995). The effects of recess timing on children's classroom and playground behavior. *American Educational Research Journal, 32,* 845–864.

Participants

In the three deprivation experiments reported in Pellegrini et al. (1995), the children all attended a public elementary school in Athens, Georgia. Children were in grades kindergarten through 4, with 68 males and 75 females ranging in age from 5.6 to 9.7 years. As in the naturalistic work, most children were of European origin.

Procedures

In all experiments children were "deprived" of recess for 30 minutes. By this, I mean that on experimentally varied days children would have recess at a specified time or 30 minutes later. During this time, they were exposed to standardized, sedentary tasks, such as being read a story, in their classrooms.

During recess, children were free to play on a large and varied playground having blacktop, a basketball area, climbing structures, and a field. Children were observed for 30-second intervals, using the 1–9 behavioral checklist described on page 72.

Chapter 5

Gender Differences in Preference for Outdoor Recess

In the preceding chapter, we discussed the fact that boys like to interact with each other because they tend to be more physically active than girls. Correspondingly, girls prefer to interact with each other, rather than with boys, because they are less active. An important implication of these differences in physical activity for our examination of children's recess and playground behavior is that boys, more than girls, seem to prefer to play outdoors. This is probably due to the fact that in the outdoors, relative to indoors, they run, jump, and swing; in short, the outdoors affords opportunities for the expression of boys' high levels of physical activity. It is also in these contexts where boys and girls learn and practice the social roles and skills needed to negotiate the remainder of childhood and into adulthood.

In this chapter, I examine the research evidence for boys' preference for the outdoor recess. As part of this discussion, I will talk about boys' more general preference for outdoors derived from observations at home and at school, relative to girls, from the preschool through middle-school periods. I should note that this research base is very thin indeed. Because of the limited empirical data base in this area, we should be very cautious in our conclusions. We have only a few studies of children at home and in preschool and middle schools, as well as only one crosscultural study, to my knowledge, of young children's play preferences.

The relative dearth of studies in this area may reflect two biases. First, this may be part of the same bias that has virtually ignored the study of recess. From this view, where kids choose to play does not seem important. Second, and less cynically, it may be the case that in most schools children are not given a choice of going out or staying in for recess. Most schools have a policy, either written or unwritten, that all children will go outdoors for recess, weather permitting, unless they have some sort of formal excuse from a parent or physician.

I begin with the home-based studies of preschool and primary school-age children for two reasons. First, studying children's preference for indoor or outdoor activity at home, rather than school, tells us about these preferences independent of school regimens. That is, children may feel less social pressure and more freedom to choose at home than at school. Second, in one case, I present a crosscultural comparison of home preferences, between American and Senegalese children, so the crosscultural comparison provides yet more insight into preferences independent of school culture.

HOME-BASED STUDIES

Boys' and Girls' Preferences for the Outdoors: USA and Senegal

Marianne Bloch (1989) studied the play behaviors of two groups of children—one group from suburban Madison, Wisconsin, and one from a village in Senegal, West Africa. In both cases, two age groups were studied: 2 to 4 years of age and 5 to 6 years of age. Let me provide a brief description of the ecology of the Senegalese group, the Lebou. They are traditional farmers, Moslems, polygynous, and live in extended patrilocal families. The extended families range in size from 4 to 15 people. Men work in agriculture, petty trade, and some commute (60 miles) to Dakar for employment. Women spend about 2 hours/day in agriculture and petty trade. In terms of education, most of the men and women never attended Western schools.

With the Madison sample, Bloch used a technique called "spot sampling" to gather information on the children. The spot sampling strategy involved telephoning the homes of the children for two months during summer, across all seven days of the week (8 A.M. to 8 P.M.). Children's

TABLE 5.1
Proportion of Time Spent Indoors and Outdoors,
Madison Sample

	2–4 Years		5–6 Years	
	Boys	Girls	Boys	Girls
Indoors	.70	.68	.63	.65
Outdoors	.13	.14	.06	.10

TABLE 5.2
Proportion of Time Spent Indoors and Outdoors,
Senegal Sample

	2–4 Years		5–6 Years	
	Boys	Girls	Boys	Girls
In house	.12	.13	.13	.12
In yard	.49	.64	.51	.50

locations were coded as "In house," "In yard," as well as other categories, such as at a friend's house. In Table 5.1 the percent of time spent indoors or outdoors for different age children is presented. Interestingly, the results are surprisingly equal. Though boys spent more time indoors than girls and girls spent more time outdoors than boys, the small magnitude of the differences makes any assertion about their meaningfulness questionable.

For the Senegal sample, children were followed around by observers and their locations were coded. Their times spent in the house and in the yard are presented in Table 5.2. As with the American sample, the results are close to equal. This pattern was reversed with the older sample, though still nearly equal.

So what do we make of this near equality in boys' and girls' preferences for the outdoors when the research literature suggests that boys should favor the outdoors more than girls? This probably has something to do with the fact that these observations were conducted at home, not school. It may be, as Gottman (1983) found, that at home there is less pressure to conform to sex-role stereotypes, and children are freer to express themselves. At home, they are free to interact with whom they please in relative privacy. At school, their choice and availability of a playmate is up for public scrutiny—viewed by one's whole classroom (at least) and then discussed by them!

Additionally, the close to equal distributions may reflect the ages of the children. Children who are this young are probably closely supervised by their parents or other caretakers. This seems to have been the case with Bloch's Madison sample. This may have resulted in the children having little choice of separating themselves from their caretakers, to go outdoors. This restriction may have been exacerbated by the fact that caretakers are typically females, thus restricting boys' ability to choose the outdoors.

Primary School Children at Home

In an early but ground-breaking study, Janet Lever (1975–1976) studied 181 fifth graders from urban and suburban schools in Connecticut. She gave children diaries for every day of their school day across the winter and spring terms and asked them to record what they had done the previous day after school, with whom they had done it, and where it was done; more than 2,000 diary entries were recorded. She found that boys play outdoors "far more" than girls. Forty percent of the girls, compared with 15% of the boys, spent less than one quarter of their time outdoors.

For both boys and girls, the most frequent indoor activities included doing household chores and homework. Indoor activities preferred by girls included playing board games and playing with dolls, and these activities tend to be private—played in small groups and behind closed doors. Boys' outdoor play was most frequently spent in organized sports and in fantasy "war game" activities. Where girls played in small groups, boys played in larger groups of peers.

In another study of American children's daily habits, Jan Carpenter and her colleagues (Carpenter, Huston, & Spera, 1989) had children from 7 to 11 years of age keep diaries of their daily activities. The children were from a small midwestern city and kept diaries for seven consecutive days. In Table 5.3, I extracted the following activity categories: In-home organized, Out-home organized, In-home unorganized, Out-home unorganized. Looking at the two "in-home" categories, you can see that girls chose such categories more often than boys did, though no statistical significance tests were presented. This, of course, is consistent with the hypothesis that boys are more "outdoorish" than girls.

Regarding the out-of-home activity categories, things are not so clear. Girls more frequently chose organized activities than boys, but boys engaged in more outdoor unorganized activities than girls. Again, home

TABLE 5.3
Number of In-home and Out-home
Activities Chosen by Boys and Girls

	Boys	Girls
In-home organized	1.50	1.88
Out-home organized	2.90	3.96
In-home unorganized	4.30	4.90
Out-home unorganized	9.91	7.65

TABLE 5.4
In-home and Out-home Activities, Adults and Peers Present

	Boys		Girls	
	Adults Present	Peers Present	Adults Present	Peers Present
In-home organized	1.39	.30	1.67	.44
Out-home organized	2.56	1.96	3.69	3.05
In-home unorganized	2.81	1.45	2.61	1.86
Out-home unorganized	3.65	7.00	2.82	5.11

activities may afford children more choice and less stereotypic choices than other settings, like schools, as we discuss later. I should note here, however, that the extent to which these children actually chose their activities is questionable; they were probably at least partially chosen by a parent.

One reason sometimes given for girls choosing the indoors, relative to the outdoors, is that adults (both parents and teachers) are more concerned with supervising girls than boys (Fagot, 1974). Consequently, adults keep closer tabs on girls, and keeping them indoors is one way of doing this. In Table 5.4 data are presented that address this issue at some level. In that table we see that for in-home organized activities, adults are present for girls more than for boys, but the opposite is true for in-home unorganized activities. When we look at the adult presence for out-of-home activities, we find an equally unclear picture: In the unorganized activities, boys had adults present more often than girls but the opposite was true for the organized activities! I must note that the results of this study are very complicated to interpret, so I'm unclear as to what they really mean. These results become even more complicated and difficult to explain when we begin to ask some basic questions, like "What are kids doing outside alone?"

To conclude this section, it seems then that at home the gender differences for preference for the outdoors is not supported unequivocally. The mixed results reported by Lever and by Carpenter and colleagues seem to suggest that differences may be due, in part, to methodology. Specifically, the difference may be due to the fact that Carpenter and colleagues sampled children only for 7 days, whereas Lever spent half a year. Further, in the Carpenter study there were different rates of peers available in the different settings.

The equivocal findings by Carpenter and colleagues about adults supervising girls more than boys also merits discuss. We should interpret these results with caution as this was only one study conducted for only one week with a methodology (self-reporting) that is prone to bias. That is, on self-reports, informants, or their parents, often report what they think the researcher wants to hear, rather than what actually is going on. Through the work of Lever, we know that asking children to complete these forms numerous times, across a long time span, may attenuate the bias. Add to this the fact that other researchers, such as Fagot (1974) and Patterson (1986), have found that girls, both during toddler and adolescent periods, respectively, are more closely supervised. This, as researchers are fond of saying, suggests that we need much more research before we can make any conclusions.

SCHOOL-BASED STUDIES

Outdoor Preference in the Preschool

In a pioneering but very short (1 page) study, Larry Harper and Karen Sanders, (1975), observed preschool boys' and girls' preferences to go outdoors during their free-play periods across a school year. This sort of situation represents a natural experiment of sorts as children had free choice regarding venue: They could have gone out or stayed in. When children have free choice and no requirements imposed by the school, we can observe their natural choice for the outdoors without having to experimentally manipulate exposure to outdoor or indoor recess periods.

Children attended a laboratory preschool in Davis, California. Harper and Sanders reported that boys preferred to go out more than girls. So, unlike the home-based studies of similarly aged children (Bloch's study), boys chose to play outside more than girls.

Outdoor Preference in Middle School

Children's entry into and passage through middle school presents a particularly interesting opportunity to study children's choice of activities and peer groups. They, as early adolescents, are entering a new institution at a time when they are simultaneously spending more time with peers in school and less time with peers in their neighborhoods and with members of their families; consequently, children's choice of middle school-based activities and peer groups represent important points in the social development of early adolescents (Brown, 1990).

Young adolescents differ reliably in their choices of free-time activities from younger children. Most notable are the gender differences between the childhood and adolescent periods. Children's preference to spend free time indoors or outdoors seems to be a particularly important choice marker. Perhaps boys of this age prefer the outdoors so they can play the sports they enjoy, such as basketball or soccer. Relatedly, there are reliable gender differences in levels of physically vigorous play from infancy through adolescence, as I outlined in the previous chapter, such that boys are more active than girls (Eaton & Enns, 1986).

Outdoor play spaces, compared with indoor play spaces, are typically more spacious and preferred by boys, relative to girls (Harper & Sanders, 1975); more space per child is, in turn, positively related to vigorous play (Smith & Connolly, 1980). These results are often interpreted as supporting the hypothesis that boys, more than girls, have a biological bias towards "outdoorishness" (Money & Ehrhardt, 1972; Ehrhardt, 1984). Outdoor behavior of adolescents in schools has not been thoroughly studied, primarily because schools make little or no provision for such activities.

The composition of the affiliative groups in which children spend their free time also differs systematically by gender. These differences, in turn, probably provide important differences in boys' and girls' socialization experiences. In terms of size of peer group, boys congregate in larger, more extensive peer groups than do girls. As I discuss in chapter 7, boys' larger groups are often centered around the playing of vigorous games and girls' smaller groups reflect closer relationships.

The outdoors also supports this type of social grouping. Quite simply, outdoors is more spacious than indoors, so it can accommodate larger groups (Fine, Mortimer, & Roberts, 1990; Hartup, 1983). That boys tend to congregate in public places and girls in private places (Fine et al., 1990) may also be related to the outdoor/indoor choice issue to the extent that outdoor places also tend to be more public than indoor spaces.

So far I have conjured a picture of the ways in which children spend their free time in school, living in gender-segregated worlds where boys spend time in large groups of running around the playground while girls interact in small groups in more private, typically indoor, places. This picture is especially incomplete at the point when young adolescents enter middle school. In the remainder of this chapter, I broaden the picture to include young adolescents just entering middle school.

At the descriptive level, direct observational studies of middle-school boys' and girls' preferences for outdoor/indoor play are limited. Most studies of this age group's indoor/outdoor preferences have used question-naires (e.g., Garton & Pratt, 1987) or self-report methodologies (e.g., Kleiber, Larson, & Csikszentmihalyi, 1986). This may be because older children are not given many opportunities for leisure, or recess, periods during school time.

Questionnaire-based data (Garton & Pratt, 1987) suggest that boys, more than girls, continue to prefer outdoor play and play outdoors for longer periods because of boys continuing interest in sports. Sports, such as basketball and football, are often played outdoors at recess by middle school boys (Pellegrini, 1992). Further, this preference does not change during the middle school period because of the important place of sports in adolescent boys' lives (Fine et al., 1990). In this chapter I present data on the degree to which preference for the outdoors varies by both gender and age during the middle school years in a school that allowed youngsters to choose freely whether to go outdoors or stay indoors for recess.

I will also examine possible precursors to the outdoorish bias, as currently little data exist to explain why children choose indoors as opposed to outdoors. As noted above, one level of explanation derives from a biosocial perspective where boys' preference for the outdoors and vigorous play are determined by a predispositional bias for such environments (Ehrhardt, 1984).

I choose temperament as a proxy for youngsters' biological predisposition for physical activity. Temperament can be defined as a behavioral predisposition, such as active/passive and inhibited/bold. The physical activity dimension of temperament is considered to have a significant biological/hormonal component and it is stable from childhood through adolescence. That is not to say that biology, at birth, predisposes children to certain temperamental categories. It does suggest that specific biological processes are implicated in temperament and that these are stable over time.

As noted earlier, there are also social explanations for preference for the outdoors/indoors. Children who are considered good at games should prefer outdoors because that is where these skills can be exhibited for their peers to observe. Many of the games played on the middle school playground, however, are also rough and involve children exhibiting physical dominance over their peers as well (Pellegrini, 1992). If these dominance-related behaviors were observed in large peer groups of other boys, the dominance-exhibition explanation for choosing outdoor play would be supported.

I (Pellegrini, 1992) examined the degree to which these factors (temperament/activity, number of female and male peers observed with focal subjects on the playground, total number of peers in the group, dominance status, passive and rough social behavior, and frequency of times observed outdoors) co-occurred, using factor analysis. Factor analysis is a statistical technique that examines the degree to which individual behaviors or test items co-occur or group together. Details of the factor analyses are presented in the appendix.

Briefly and in terms of method (more detail is provided in the appendix at the end of this chapter), students in a middle school (Grades 6 and 7) in rural Georgia had two breaks each day, and they had choice as to whether they went outdoors for the break or stayed inside. We observed the extent to which boys and girls stayed in or went out and their behaviors while outside. Additionally, teachers completed a battery of questionnaires on each youngster. More specifically, teachers rated students in terms of their achievement, facility in games, and physical attractiveness. These items should reflect teachers' positive or negative attributions of children. I expected variation on these items to be indicators of children's accommodation to the institutional demands of the school.

I also expected to find that males would exhibit high levels of activity and dominance, be observed outdoors, and play in large groups. On the other hand, I expected female peers, passive interaction, and small numbers in groups to co-occur, reflecting more sedentary, female preferred social activity.

It is also interesting from a developmental perspective to determine the extent to which these gender-segregated and dominance-related factor patterns persisted across youngsters' middle-school experience. Do they change or do they remain the same with grade level? Youngsters of this age are becoming increasingly interested in heterosexual relationships (Maccoby, 1998), and they might use their recess to explore these relationships. In my research with another sample of adolescents (Pellegrini & Long, 2003), I found that youngsters of this age were ambivalent about cross-gender interaction. They cling to their gender-segregated groups while also making efforts to integrate with the opposite sex. Free time during school seems to be an especially good time to explore relationships with the opposite sex (Maccoby, 1998). Accordingly, I expected youngsters' cross-gender interaction to increase across the first two years of middle school. The specifics of the methodology and the statistical analyses used to address these questions are presented in the appendix at the end of this chapter.

In terms of results, I found, like the results reported in preschool, that boys preferred to go outdoors more than girls but this only occurred during the first year of middle school. Further, the sixth graders, relative to the seventh graders, spent more time outdoors; this was especially true for boys.

These results show that gender segregation at recess decreases with time as youngsters move across middle school. It is probably the case that as youngsters enter and move through an institution like middle school, their identity changes from children to adolescents. For children, gender-segregated groups are appropriate. Adolescents, on the other hand, have emerging interest in heterosexual relationships and, consequently, they are more interested in gender integration than segregation. Thus, as they move through middle school, they self-select themselves less frequently into such stereotyped environments, such as the outdoors.

I also examined the factor structure of measures related to children's outdoor play and how these factors varied by grade and gender, respectively. One factor, which was more frequently observed for girls than for boys, is typified by relatively small female peer groups (indicated by the negative loading of Number of Peers and positive loading of Female Peers), that exhibit both rough and socially active behavior (indicated by the positive loading of Rough Social Behavior and negative loading of Passive Social Behavior, respectively) when they are on the playground. Further, teachers consider these children to be temperamentally active. That frequency of play outdoors did not load on this factor further suggests that these children did not choose to go outdoors frequently, but when they did, they were active. This group seems to be composed of high-energy girls who chose to go outdoors only when they are feeling particularly active, which does not seem to be that often. The grade effect for this factor may indicate that as these active girls felt more comfortable being in middle school, they more freely expressed their propensity towards activity.

Another factor was characterized by boys who exhibited rough behavior in large groups. These boys were considered by their peers to be dominant, or tough, and frequently chose to play outdoors. This group seemed to be composed of children who choose to engage in rough behavior outdoors in order to exhibit dominance.

More specific to boys' peer groups, adolescence is a time when their dominance status in groups is in flux (Zakriski & Wright, 1991). Dominance status during the period of early adolescence moves from a physically aggressive basis to a more affiliative base. The sixth-grade boys I studied were new to the middle school at a time when they were also in this transitional phase of peer/dominance relationships. As a way of trying to establish their dominance in a new situation they relied on exhibitions of quasi-aggression, or rough play. They used their recess time to exhibit dominance. As they became socialized to the school setting in seventh grade, this reliance on rough play and dominance declined.

CONCLUSION

Research generally supports the idea that boys prefer the outdoors more than girls, but these findings need to be qualified at many levels. First, preference for outdoors has not been extensively studied and where it has there are often methodological problems that prevent us from having full confidence in the findings. We need much more study, particularly observational studies of children of different ages in different settings. The setting issue is especially important as boys' preference for the outdoors is found more frequently in school-based studies than in home-based studies.

Age is another important variable to consider. We'd expect gender differences in preference for indoor versus outdoor play for children during the ages in which they segregated from each other—roughly from the preschool through the elementary school years. As youngsters hit adolescence and their interests turn to heterosexual relationships, they want to spend time with members of the opposite sex, so gender differences in preferences that separate them tend to diminish.

SOME THINGS TO THINK ABOUT

1. Observe groups of boys and girls in a home setting. Other things being equal (such as weather), do boys go outdoors more than girls?

2. Does this happen with equal frequency when boys are alone? In groups?

Why?

3. In mixed-sex groups in home settings, do boys or girls make initial suggestions to go out?

What's the reaction of the kids of the opposite gender?

4. Do mothers and fathers differentially suggest that kids go play outdoors?

Why?

5. Do mothers and fathers react differently when kids say they want to go out?

How?

Why?

APPENDIX

Pellegrini, A. D. (1992). Preference for outdoor play during early adolescence. *Journal of Adolescence, 15*, 241–254.

METHOD

Participants

The site of this study was a rural public school in the northern part of the state of Georgia. The total sixth and seventh grades of the middle school were recruited for the research. The population of these grades was 138 in the sixth grade (73 males and 65 females) and 167 in the seventh grade (83 males and 84 females), for a total of 305. From this population, parental consent forms were returned from 133 children (71 sixth graders with 36 males and 35 females with a mean age of 12.4 years; 62 seventh graders with 32 males and 30 females with a mean age of 13.8 years).

Procedures

There were two outdoor periods available daily. One period was in the early morning and the other after lunch; each lasted between 15 and 20 minutes. Children were free to go outdoors for recess or to stay indoors. Children who stayed indoors could sit in rooms and talk with friends and/or walk around the corridors. Children who chose to go outdoors were observed in the school courtyard located in the middle of numerous school buildings and bordering asphalt walkways. The grassy courtyard area was of rectangular shape, measuring approximately 25 meters × 35 meters; walkways bordered the courtyard.

There were two observers of children's behavior. Focal children were observed, in counterbalanced order, for 3-minute periods. Their rough and game behavior as well as their social interaction was recorded continuously for 3 minutes. Additionally, children's group size (the number of children in the focal child's immediate vicinity at the start of the recording) and gender of *playmate* were described. The *number of observations* (the frequency of separate focal samples conducted on each child outdoors) and duration of observations (the number of 5-second intervals/observation) were also recorded.

Dominance. Children's dominance was assessed by asking them to rate "Kids in their class who are tough."

Physical Activity. Children's physical activity was assessed by having teachers rate them on Keogh's (1982) measure of temperament (e.g., child has difficulty sitting still).

RESULTS FROM STATISTICAL ANALYSES

Factor analyses were conducted to determine the extent to which theoretically relevant variables formed reliable factors. The variables chosen were: Teacher ratings of physical attractiveness; teacher ratings of games skills; teacher ratings of temperament/activity; teacher ratings of achievement; social/passive interaction on the playground; rough games on playground; number of peers in playground groups; male peers in playground groups; females peers in playground group; frequency of times observed on playground; peer ranking of dominance. Principal components analysis procedures, with a varimax rotation, were utilized and factors were limited to those with eigenvalues greater than 1.0. Loadings of .35 and above were considered necessary for inclusion in a factor. Three factors emerged. The factor structure is displayed in Table 1.

The factors were labeled: Teachers' Choice, Active Female Oriented, Outdoor Male Oriented. They each accounted for the following amounts of variance: 2.40, 2.17, and 1.64, respectively. Notable in the factor struc-

TABLE 1
Results of Factor Analyses

	Active	Outdoor
	Active Female Oriented	Male Oriented
Active	.46	
Female peers	.60	
Passive social behavior	−.79	
Rough social behavior	.70	.49
Number peers	−.55	.57
Dominance		.52
Male peers		.75
Frequency outdoors		.78

tures is the overlap of rough social play and number of peers in both factors two and three. Both factors are characterized by rough behavior, while the positive and negative values assigned to number of peers indicates different ends of a continuum.

Chapter 6

Children's Play
and Rough-and-Tumble Play
on the Playground

The controversial nature of recess in schools, as I have argued throughout this book, may be part of a larger debate about the role of more divergent, play-like activities in schools. In previous chapters, I generally discussed the role of play in children's development and potential gender differences in various forms of play. In this chapter, I discuss, in much more depth, a form of play commonly observed on elementary school playgrounds at recess: Rough-and-tumble play (R&T). R&T, like the greater debates over the roles of play and recess in schools, is controversial. It is viewed as a disruptive and antisocial form of behavior that is antithetical to the traditional goals of schooling. If this indictment sounds familiar, it is. Recall the views expressed in chapter 2, on the history of playgrounds and recess in school, where some viewed playground behavior as rebellious and the antithesis to the order required in the classroom.

A discussion of R&T is important in the context of this book because it is frequently observed on the elementary school playground, especially among boys. Generally, R&T for boys is related to good things, such as being popular and being flexible in solving social problems. Despite these findings, teachers frequently discouraged or prohibited it. Consequently, a discussion of the roles of R&T is crucial, in keeping with the orientation of this book, that theory and data guide playground and recess policy.

In this chapter, I discuss children's play, generally, in terms of definition, development, and possible functions. Then I discuss R&T in light of these definitional criteria and speculate about possible functions of R&T.

A general discussion of play is important, I think, to understand R&T in its larger context. The debate over the role of play in educational settings is still controversial for many reasons I discussed early on in this book. If forms of play, such as fantasy, are controversial, R&T should be more so because of its resemblance to aggression. A disciplinary and historical overview of play, generally, should help us to understand these issues more clearly, and the role of play and R&T in schools. But before we proceed, it is important to define what it is we mean by "play."

WHAT IS PLAY?

Observers can reliably recognize play when they see it but have difficulty in finding satisfactory operational definitions. Given the complexity of play, it is generally considered that no one definition of play is necessary or sufficient (Martin & Caro, 1985; Pellegrini & Smith, 1998; Rubin, Fein, & Vandenberg, 1983), thus definitions are typically multidimensional. For example, in a review of the child development literature by Kenneth Rubin and his colleagues (1983), children's play is defined according to three dimensions: psychological disposition, behavior, and contexts supporting (or preceding) play. Ethologists also advocate defining play along a number of dimensions (Bateson, 2005; Martin & Caro, 1985, p. 62; Pellegrini & Smith, 1998), suggesting structural (behavioral), consequential (those behaviors following play), and contextual (where it is observed) criteria. In this section, I briefly review these two sets of definitions, noting cases where similar labels are used to describe different phenomena.

One of the most widely agreed upon criteria for defining play is that it does not seem to serve any apparent immediate purpose. More specifically, play behaviors resemble "serious" behaviors, but they do not serve their "serious" purpose. Additionally, exaggerated motions and vocalizations often typify play behaviors, relative to their nonplayful counterparts. A common example from children's pretend play would involve the exaggerated walk and voice of a child pretending to be flying, as illustrated in Fig. 6.1, with the girl's extended arms. In Rubin, Fein, and Vandenberg's

FIG. 6.1.   Exaggerated movements are typical of play.

(1983) scheme this immediate "purposelessness" criterion also corresponds to the "means over ends" dispositional criterion. Attending to means over ends assumes that children are less concerned with the outcome of their behavior than with the behavioral processes per se. Ethologists also have noticed the importance of means over ends for a definition of animal play (Martin & Caro, 1985). For example, in the case of two lion cubs playing with captured prey, they do not kill it but chase and gently pounce on it (Caro, 1995).

Besides defining play along dispositional dimensions, play has also been defined according to contexts that support it. Rubin et al. (1983) considered these contextual factors antecedents to play, and they include: (a) an atmosphere that is familiar (in terms of props and people), (b) safe and friendly, (c) a minimally intrusive adult, and (d) children who are free from stress, hunger, and fatigue. Paul Martin and Patrick Bateson (1993) invoked a similar method in their use of spatial relations to categorize behaviors; that is, behaviors can belong to the same category if they co-occur in a specific setting or among a certain group. For example, behaviors on the playground could generally be considered play. Ethologists commonly define play as juvenile behaviors mainly because adult animals (other than humans) rarely play (e.g., Hinde, 1982). Correspondingly, play can be defined in terms of its immediate consequences, or the behaviors that follow play. This strategy has been used in the child development literature to define specific dimensions of play, such as rough-and-tumble (Pellegrini, 1988) and parallel play (Bakeman & Brownlee, 1980). A behavior can be categorized as rough-and-tumble play, not aggression, if, along with other criteria, children stay together after the conclusion of the bout; if they separate, it is defined as aggression (though see de Waal, 1986, for an alternative view). Similarly, parallel play, or behavior that has children interacting next to, but not with each other, can be defined as social, rather than solitary, behavior because the cooperative interaction follows parallel behavior at a greater than chance rate (Bakeman & Brownlee, 1980).

Such a multidimensional approach to defining play is useful, and some studies have examined how observers combine information from a number of cues to decide whether an activity is playful or not (Costabile et al., 1991; Smith & Vollstedt, 1985). However, the antecedents and consequences of behaviors should be considered as elicitors and outcomes, respectively, of those behaviors, rather than as components of the behavior per se. Thus, it is important to keep these dimensions conceptually distinct, especially when we consider the role of play as serving a developmental function.

THE DEVELOPMENT OF PLAY AND INFLUENCES ON ITS DEVELOPMENT

The fact that play has been described along a number of different dimensions is evident when its different forms are examined during childhood and from our earlier discussion of definitions. Ethologists and psychologists have divided the different forms of play that occur primarily during childhood differently.

Ethologists, or biologists who study animal behavior, including play, generally consider three forms of play, all of which have the common attribute of purposelessness: locomotor play, social play, and object play (Bekoff & Byers, 1981). Locomotor play involves exaggerated and repetitive movements, which often occur in novel sequences. These movements are the sorts of behaviors described by Piaget (1952) and Jerome Bruner (1972), which very young children engage in as they are beginning to master the functions of their bodies and the objects that furnish their world.

Social play refers to the seemingly goalless behavior that involves a peer or an adult. In the nonhuman literature, most social play occurs among juveniles (that corresponds to "children" in our language!), while in the literature on humans, social play first appears in adult–infant play and later in peer play (Haight & Miller, 1993; see Pellegrini & Smith, 1998, for review). Object play can be solitary or social and involves manipulation of the material environment.

These types of play are not considered to be hierarchical, and they often occur together; for example, rough-and-tumble play involving two children is both social and locomotor. Further, most mammalian species exhibit these forms of play (Bekoff & Byers, 1981; Fagen, 1981). Extensive reviews of the literature on animal play suggest that play accounts for about 10% of juvenile animals' time and energy budgets (Byers & Walker, 1995; Fagen, 1981; Martin & Caro, 1985). Estimates of children's play similarly suggest that play accounts for about 10% of their energy budget (Pellegrini, Horvat, & Huberty, 1998).

Children's play, on the other hand, is more differentiated than that of nonhumans, to the extent that developmental progressions of different forms of play have been documented. One of the earliest differentiations in children's play begins in infancy where play is differentiated from exploration: Exploration is *epistemic*—in which objects are manipulated so as to gain information, while play has no goal as such.

Exploration

Children spend much of their time exploring their environment rather than playing with it, particularly in the period of infancy, though the exact amounts of time and energy spent in exploration have not been documented. Exploration is an information-gathering activity and is evident, in its earliest forms, by mouthing and simple manipulation of objects (Belsky & Most, 1981; Hutt, 1966). When exploring, infants are thought to be guided dispositionally by the question: "What can it do?" This object orientation is different from the more person-centered orientation guiding play "What can *I* do with it?" (Hutt, 1966). Through exploration, children come to know their environments. It is this knowledge that provides the basis for play. As such, exploration must be considered separate from play.

Exploration precedes play in the course of children's development and in the course of their encountering new objects. Within children's development, observations of infants interacting with their mother in a laboratory suggest that exploration dominates infants' behavior for the first 9 months of life; by 12 months, play and exploration co-occur; and by 18 months, play accounts for more of the child's interactions with the environment than does exploration (Belsky & Most, 1981). During late infancy and early childhood, boys, more than girls, engage in exploration (Bornstein et al., 1999). Exploration also precedes play to the extent that children of all ages explore an object, or learn its properties, before they play with it (Hutt, 1966).

FIG. 6.2.   Child in pretend play.

Developmental Sequences in Play

Piaget (1952) described a developmental sequence of play, starting with practice play or sensorimotor play, including the circular reactions that embrace the transition from exploration to play in infants' interactions with objects in their environment. He documented the origins of pretend play from 15 months onward, as characterized by nonliteral actions, object use, and vocalizations (e.g., his daughter Jacqueline putting her head on a cloth, sucking her thumb, blinking her eyes, and laughing, "as if" going to sleep).

The picture of the little boy in Fig. 6.2, engaged in pretend play is one of the most commonly recognized, and valued, forms of play. Piaget argued that from 6 to 7 years, children left behind the more private worlds of symbolic play and engaged in games with rules—such as hopscotch, football, marbles—in which playful actions were coordinated within a publicly agreed framework of constraints.

Sara Smilansky (1968), as I discussed earlier, began with this view of play and further developed a four-fold sequence of functional play, constructive play, dramatic play, and games with rules. The distinctive new element here is the postulation that constructive play—making things with objects—is a transitional phase between the functional (sensorimotor) play of infancy and the dramatic (symbolic role play) of 4- to 6-year-olds, while allowing some overlap between these stages. This was in opposition to Piaget (1952), who had said that construction was not a form of play, but midway between play and games. However, a number of North American researchers took up Smilansky's scheme and combined it with Mildred Parten's (1932) categories of social participation to create a sociocognitive "nested play hierarchy" (e.g., Rubin, Watson, & Jambor, 1978).

Although such sequences have attractions for applied, descriptive purposes (e.g., estimating the maturity of children's play in different nursery environments), the approach has definite shortcomings (Takhvar & Smith, 1990). As Piaget and Smilansky defined, practice or functional play could occur well beyond infancy and would seem to include play-fighting or rough-and-tumble play in middle childhood and adolescence. The special role of constructive play in Smilansky's scheme is even more dubious; constructional and overtly pretend play seem to coexist through the pre-school years, and apparently constructive play may have fantasy elements (as becomes obvious when children are asked about their play). Language play, or play with words (Weir, 1962), also does not fit into this scheme.

Fantasy Play

Fantasy, or pretence, is perhaps the most widely recognized form of play during childhood. Fantasy involves an "as if . . ." orientation to the world and involves actions, the use of objects, verbalizations, and nonliteral meanings; often, it involves playing a distinct pretend role such as mummy, fireman, or doctor. Because of its representational nature and its reliance on language, fantasy play is practically unique to humans.

Fully developed pretend play, including role play, seems universal in human societies, as witnessed in anthropological accounts. It is seen in hunter-gatherer societies (Konner 1972; Eibl-Eibesfeldt, 1989), where pretend play occurs in mixed-age peer groups (e.g., children using sticks and pebbles to represent village huts, herding cows). A review of pretend play in non-Western societies by Schwartzmann (1978) mentions more than 40 articles describing pretend play. There are certainly variations in the amount and type of such play, and it can appear "impoverished" in some societies (Smilansky, 1968), but its presence is ubiquitous. Diane Slaughter and colleagues (Slaughter & Dombrowski, 1989) suggest that in the light of the anthropological evidence "children's social and pretend play appear to be biologically based, sustained as an evolutionary contribution to human psychological growth and development. Cultural factors regulate the amount and types of expression of these play forms" (p. 290).

The great majority of studies of children's play, including fantasy, have been carried out in preschool classrooms in Western societies. This research suggests that fantasy begins during the second year of life, peaks during the late preschool years, and declines during the primary school years. Estimates of time and energy budgets are limited, but it has been found to account for over 15% of the total in school time budget (Field, 1994), and for 10% to 17% of preschoolers' and 33% of kindergartners' play behaviors, and subsequently declining into the school year (Fein, 1981a).

Although most studies of fantasy play have been made in peer groups in school, an intensive observational study in homes of young children shows the important supportive role of mothers in early pretend play interactions (Haight & Miller, 1993). Based on these in-home observations, rates of pretend play began at .06 minutes/hour (that is, fewer than 4 seconds per hour) for 12- to 14-month-old children, increased to 3.3 minutes/hour at 24 months, and 12.4 minutes/hour at 48 months. Thus, there is convergence between the observational data from the preschool and the home indicating that pretend play accounts for 12% to 15% of children's available time.

There are robust gender differences in fantasy play during the preschool period. Girls engage in fantasy play both more frequently and at more sophisticated levels than do boys. Mothers tend to engage in symbolic play with daughters more frequently than with sons (Bornstein et al., 1999). While the pretence of girls tends to revolve around domestic, dramatic themes, the pretence of boys tends to be more fantastic and physically vigorous, often co-occurring with play fighting and super-hero themes (Fein, 1981; Pellegrini & Perlmutter, 1987; Smith, 1974).

Social variables as well as play materials influence fantasy play. Children who are securely, compared to insecurely, attached to their mothers engage in more sophisticated pretend play. By securely attached I mean, very generally, that these children feel safe in the presence of their mothers, and their mothers are responsive to the needs of the child. This results in children's willingness to explore their environments. For example, securely attached children initiate more play interactions and the tenor of their interactions with their mother while playing is more positive than that of insecurely attached children (Bretherton, 1984; Roggman & Langlois, 1987). Further, children's pretense is more sustained and complex when they are playing with friends compared with acquaintances (Howes, 1993). The mutuality and emotional commitment of friends may motivate children to sustain cooperative interaction (Hartup, 1996).

Play themes generally follow those inherent in the materials available (Pellegrini & Perlmutter, 1989; Smith & Connolly, 1980). For example, when presented with doctor props, children engage in play around medical themes. Furthermore, the sex role stereotypicality of the materials influences boys' and girls' play. Boys' play with female-preferred toys, such as dolls, is less sophisticated than it is with male-preferred toys, such as blocks. Correspondingly, girls show higher levels of sophistication with female props than male props (Pellegrini & Perlmutter, 1989).

Besides giving an authoritative description of sociodramatic play, Smilansky (1968) argued that the play of children from culturally deprived backgrounds was impoverished in terms of content, duration, and complexity. This led to a body of research suggesting that children from lower socioeconomic-class backgrounds showed less fantasy play. These studies were criticized by Vonnie McLoyd (1982) for poor methodology. Some failed to define social class adequately or confounded it with other variables such as race or school setting. For example, Black children studied are often poor Black children, thus the influence of both race and poverty are influencing the observed forms of play. When middle-class Black children are observed, their behavior is more similar to middle-class White children than to poor Black children.

In summary, fantasy play accounts for 12% to 15% of preschool children's time at home and at school. Both gender and social partners in play, in turn, affect these rates. As I will discuss later, gender differences in time spent in different forms of pretend play as well as social partners in play should also have implications for function.

Locomotor Play

Locomotor play is physically vigorous behavior, such as chasing, climbing, and rough-and-tumble play, which does not appear to serve an immediate purpose. Peter Smith and I (Pellegrini & Smith, 1998) argued that there are three distinctive forms of locomotor play: rhythmic stereotypies, exercise play, and rough-and-tumble. Each of these forms of play have distinct inverted-U age curves, such that rates of play start low early in life, peak in frequency sometime during early childhood, and subsequently fall in frequency later in childhood. It is also possible that different forms of locomotor play serve different developmental functions. Each is discussed in turn, as well as associated gender differences. (Gender differences are discussed in some detail in the last chapter.)

Rhythmic stereotypies are gross motor movements without any apparent function and occur in the first year of life, for example, body rocking and foot kicking (Thelen, 1979, 1980). The very beginnings of rhythmic stereotypies are probably controlled by neuromuscular maturation: They are first observed at birth and peak around the mid-point of the first year of life (accounting for about 40% of a 1-hour observational period, Thelen, 1980), averaging about 5.2% of the waking time during the first year of life. There are no apparent gender differences in rhythmic stereotypies.

Rhythmic stereotypies can also occur in the context of adult–child interaction. For example, Jaipaul Roopnarine and colleagues (1993) described instances of parents bouncing children on their knees and throwing them in the air. This sort of activity accounted for 13% of all the play activity of 1-year-olds; object play accounted for another 80%. Esther Thelen (1980) reports similar level of parent–infant physical play in the form of vestibular stimulation, or when parents throw a child in the air and catch them.

Exercise play is gross locomotor movement, such as running and climbing, in the context of play. It is physically vigorous and may or may not be social. Exercise play can start at the end of the first year, and initially much of it (like later aspects of rhythmic stereotypies) takes place between a child and an adult. Though adult–child exercise play peaks at around 4 years of age (MacDonald & Parke, 1986), there are cases where the adult role is to encourage young children to engage in exercise. For example, Melvin Konner (1972) observed that adults in a Botswana foraging group encouraged infants to chase after and catch large insects.

Exercise play is common during the preschool period, though many studies do not differentiate exercise play from rough-and-tumble or pretend play, with which it co-occurs (Pellegrini & Perlmutter, 1987; Smith & Connolly, 1980). Thus, it may be underreported in the literature. Where it is reported, like other forms of play, it follows an inverted-U developmental curve, peaking at around 4 to 5 years (Eaton & Yu, 1989).

For example, at 2 years, exercise play accounted for about 7% of children's observed behavior in a day-care center (Rosenthal, 1994), and it increased to about 10% for 2- to 4-year-olds in day care (Field, 1994) and at home (Bloch, 1989). At 5 to 6 years, exercise play accounted for about 13% of behavior in the home (Bloch, 1989) and about 20% of all observed behavior in school (McGrew, 1972; Smith & Connolly, 1980).

There are also reliable gender differences in children's exercise play, with boys engaging in it more than girls (Pellegrini & Smith, 1998). This is probably related to the more general sex difference in physical activity, where differences increase from infancy to midadolescence (Eaton & Enns, 1986).

A clear limitation of this work is that children's exercise play has been studied for the most part in schools, particularly in preschools. However, to better understand the context of play and make accurate estimates of the time and energy expended in play, expanded efforts must be made to study children in their homes and communities (Barker, 1968; Bronfenbrenner, 1979; Pellegrini & Smith, 1998).

One such effort was mounted by Bruce Simons-Morton and colleagues (1990) in a study of children's (aged 9 to 10 years) exercise and physical fitness. Using self-reported frequencies of moderate to vigorous physical activity across a 3-day period, they found that children exercise more before and after school than during school. Over the course of each day, they engaged in one or two bouts of moderate to vigorous physical activity (of 10 minutes or longer).

It is especially important to note that the extent to which children have been deprived of exercise before recess influences their levels and durations of exercise once they do go out onto the playground. When children (Pellegrini, Huberty, & Jones, 1995; Smith & Hagen, 1980) as well as animals such as deer (Müller-Schwarze, 1984) are deprived of an opportunity to exercise and then given an opportunity, the level and duration of exercise increases. It may be the case that, during the period of childhood when skeletal and muscular systems are maturing quite rapidly, the body overcompensates for lost opportunities to exercise those rapidly developing systems. Malnourishment inhibits exercise play (Pellegrini & Smith, 1998). In such circumstances, the body probably uses valuable nutrients for physical growth, rather than exercise play. As I will discuss in the final chapter, providing opportunities for recess may be very important in stemming the tide of childhood obesity.

ROUGH-AND-TUMBLE PLAY

Rough-and-tumble play (R&T) is especially important to consider because it is commonly observed on the school playground at recess and especially by boys.

What Is It?

To my knowledge, "R&T" was first used in the social and behavioral sciences by Harry Harlow (1962) in his discussion of the social play of rhesus monkeys. For Harlow, R&T resembled play fighting. In preschool children this often takes the form of superhero play (Saltz, Dixon, & Johnson, 1967).

Based on Harlow's work, and on the subsequent work with children by Nick Blurton Jones (1972), R&T has been characterized by positive affect,

FIG. 6.3.   Play face in child.   FIG. 6.4.   Play face in chimpanzee.

or a "play face"; high energy behaviors; exaggerated movements; and soft, open-handed hits or kicks. The play faces of the child and the chimpanzee displayed in Figs. 6.3 and 6.4 clearly signal that the intent of these acts is playful, *not* aggressive. The exaggerated movements and gestures, as demonstrated by the child in the figure, further helps signal the playful, not aggressive, intent to other players.

Often R&T is confused with aggression because at some levels they resemble each other. Upon close inspection, however, they are clearly different. In this section I briefly explicate those differences. Categories of behavior, such as aggression and R&T, can be defined along the following dimensions: individual behaviors, consequences, structure, ecology, and developmental trajectories.

Behaviors. Beginning with individual behaviors, numerous studies have differentiated R&T and aggression (e.g., Blurton Jones, 1972). The assumption here is that behaviors with similar meaning will co-occur and form a meaningful category. By this, I mean that when children are engaged in R&T, they will display many of the behaviors in this constellation. R&T is typically composed of run, chase, flee, wrestle, and open-hand hit. Aggression is typified by closed-hand hits, shoves, pushes, and kicks. Also a quite simple, yet reliable, way in which R&T and aggression differ is in terms of expression of affect. Generally, smiles (or a play face) accompany R&T, whereas frowns, or crying, accompany aggression. Note the play faces in the boy and the juvenile chimp in Figs. 6.3 and 6.4 serve as clear signals that the intent of the behavior is not serious and certainly not aggressive.

Consequences.   Classes of behavior can also be differentiated in terms of consequences, or those behaviors immediately following the target behaviors R&T and aggression. As in the case of co-occurring behaviors, we assume that behaviors that follow a focal behavior systematically are related to that antecedent in a meaningful way. In many cases, we can make assumptions about the meaning, or function, of an antecedent behavior based on its consequence. For example, when R&T bouts end, children often stay together and begin cooperative social games (Pellegrini, 1988). Aggression, on the other hand, often leads to one of the participants trying to separate from the other (McGrew, 1972a). Thus, R&T may have peer affiliative functions whereas aggression does not. More will be said about consequences of R&T in the section of this chapter on function.

Structure.   The structure of R&T is also different from aggression. By structure I mean the roles that typify each class of behavior. In R&T, youngsters alternate roles, such as chaser and chasee. In some cases, stronger or bigger players self-handicap so as to sustain play. For example, an older child may fall to the ground at the slightest touch of a younger playmate. Such handicapping enables children of different levels of strength and physical prowess to play together.

Role alternation is a hallmark of other forms of play, such as dramatic play, where children often change, or negotiate, roles repeatedly in the course of an episode. Role alternation seems to serve an important purpose in children's social perspective taking; taking different play roles, both in fantasy (Garvey, 1990) and R&T (Pellegrini, 1993), enables children to take different perspectives. Aggression, on the other hand, is typified by unilateral roles: Aggressors don't switch roles with their victims.

Ecology.   Ecologically, R&T tends to occur in spacious areas, such as the outdoors (Smith & Connolly, 1980), and on those parts of playgrounds with soft, grassy surfaces (Pellegrini, 1990). That R&T is physically vigorous and involves running, falling, and wrestling means that it is more likely to occur in areas supportive of this sort of behavior, compared with more confined areas.

Aggression does not, however, vary according to playground location (Pellegrini, 1990); it is equally likely to occur anywhere. Among preschoolers, where toys are present, however, aggression is likely to result from children's disputes over objects (Smith & Connolly, 1980).

For most children, R&T and aggression are not significantly correlated (Blurton Jones, 1972; Fry, 1987; Pellegrini, 1988). That is, children who show high (or low) levels of aggression do not necessarily show corresponding levels of R&T. Additionally, these differences have been observed crossculturally, for example, among foraging bushmen (Konner, 1972), indigenous Mexican people (Fry, 1987), and in India (Roopnarine et al., 1993). As we see in the next section, R&T leads children into a very positive developmental trajectory; this is not the case for aggression.

Interviewing Children and Adolescents: Differences Between R&T and Aggression

R&T is also considered playful by children when they are interviewed. These interviews are typically conducted by showing children and adolescents a series of videotapted bouts of R&T and aggression enacted by actors other than themselves. After the presentation of each bout, a child is asked to say or mark a sheet to indicate if the bout was real fighting (mark the sad face) or play fighting (mark the happy face). In these cases, children shown videotaped R&T and aggressive bouts clearly differentiated between the two and consider R&T playful (e.g., Costabile et al., 1991; Pellegrini, 1988; Smith, Hunter, Carvalho, & Costabile, 1992).

Interpretations in Childhood

In the first study of its kind (to my knowledge, anyway), Peter Smith, Rebecca Smees, and I (Smith, Smees, & Pellegrini, 2004) presented young primary school children in Sheffield, England, with videotaped bouts of play fighting and aggression in which they were both participants and nonparticipants. The children's responses to videotaped bouts in which they had taken part themselves—the participant condition—was contrasted with responses to bouts in which their peers, not themselves, took part—the nonparticipant condition. We compared their responses after a short interval (about 2 hours) and a longer interval (about 1 week). The details of the methodology are presented in Appendix A at the end of this chapter.

Not surprisingly, participants appear to have a better understanding of an episode than nonparticipants. They were able to give more criteria to explain their judgments as to why an episode was playful or not. They also cited criteria that are likely to be useful and to which participants have more privileged access—whether a hit or kick really hurt and whether an apparently aggressive act was within a pretend or game framework previously agreed by those involved. In addition, they gauged enjoyment, friendship, and the likelihood of someone being hurt, in ways that more clearly discriminate playful and real fighting.

In short, the results of this study suggest that participants have unique insights into the nature and motivation of play fighting and real fighting bouts. This insight is best tapped shortly after the incident, but is still partially available after a 1-week period. Nonparticipants fall back on less useful cues for their judgments about episodes and are less accurate in assessing motivation and intention, as judged by their discriminatory responses to playful, ambiguous, and real fighting episodes. The obvious reason for the more insightful responses obtained from participants is that they have personal knowledge of actions and agreements among those involved, not available so readily to nonparticipants. In addition, participants may feel more involved and interested in watching episodes that they are taking part in; and, as children tend to play with friends (Humphreys & Smith, 1987; Smith & Lewis, 1985), they may make more accurate judgments based on friends whom they know better than nonfriends.

The difference between participants and nonparticipants also has implications for playground supervision. Specifically, children are often disciplined by their teachers or playground supervisors for perceived infractions of the playground. These results clearly show that not all children's opinions are equally accurate. The opinions of participants should take precedence over nonparticipants.

The content of the responses suggested that to participants, compared with nonparticipants, play fighting is seen as friendly and not involving hurt or showing off. The great majority of such bouts (85%–89%) were seen by participants as enjoyable and between friends. Although some episodes were classified as ambiguous, in most cases (75%), participants felt that no one was being hurt in these encounters, which they may accurately interpret as part of a more complex game. Although many participants felt that someone was "showing off" in real fights (75%), few did so in play fights (17%). In general, this supports the view that most, though not all, play fights are friendly and not hurtful. The responses of the children did not give much reason to hypothesize that some children were cheating on others by manipulating the play convention to cause deliberate hurt; the protocol that came closest to this was Mark, who said of one episode in which Duane and Mark are playing "police,""Duane's dragging me—watch Nicky now. It is a game, but I don't like Nicky and Adam kicking me. They were my friends, but they're not now." Nicky described this as "just play kicking," but it could be interpreted as deliberately taking advantage of the play convention to join in and hurt Mark.

This was the closest example to cheating in this data set. However, these findings apply only to 5- to 8-year-old boys. Besides bearing in mind sample limitations (of number, school, gender, and culture), this picture will change in older children and especially as adolescence is reached, when children are becoming more consciously sophisticated in their social thinking and strategies and when dominance assertion is becoming more salient as a social goal (Humphreys & Smith, 1987; Neill, 1976; Pellegrini, 2001). Evidence from adolescent boys has suggested a stronger involvement of showing off or display and dominance in play fights.

Interpretations in Adolescence

During adolescence, youngsters are increasingly concerned with their status among their peers and they are becoming interested in heterosexual relationships. Indeed, early adolescence and the middle schools that house them are primary venues where boys and girls negotiate early heterosexual contact, after spending their childhoods in relatively segregated peer groups (Maccoby, 1998). It seems as though adolescent boys use R&T to dominate their male peers and, later, to engage in playful forms of heterosexual interaction.

Unlike the finding with children that I presented in the preceding section, where R&T is not related to aggression or dominance, theory and research (Fagen, 1981; Humphreys & Smith, 1987; Pellegrini, 1988, 1995, 2002a, 2002b; Pellegrini & Smith, 1998) suggest that R&T for adolescent males is related to physical aggression and may be used as a way in which to establish peer status in the form of dominance with other boys. This status, in turn, results in their being viewed as attractive dates for girls (Pellegrini & Bartini, 2001). Furthermore, it may be that after dominance is established between boys, boys may then use it in more playful ways to initiate heterosexual contact.

Dominance is a construct referring to the social ordering, from toughest to least tough, at least in male groups (Maccoby, 1998; Strayer, 1980). This ordering prioritizes access to resources where the most dominant gets first priority to resources. Dominance is established through a series of *intra*sexual agonistic (aggressive) and affiliative behavioral strategies. That is, boys interact with each other in aggressive and competitive ways. When individuals first encounter each other, such as when they first enter a new school, agonistic strategies (such as threats and physical aggression) are used to establish status (Pellegrini & Bartini, 2001). Results of aggressive bouts, perhaps most clearly, indicate winners and losers of contests. R&T, especially during adolescence, may also be used as a way to gain access to resources. Typically this is done by cheating at R&T, or exploiting the playful tenor of R&T for dominance-exhibition ends (Fagen, 1981; Smith & Boulton, 1990). For example, two boys may begin what appears to be a playful R&T bout, and one boy "pins" the other. This can be exploited if the boy doing the pinning violates the playful tenor and refuses to let up the pinned boy, thus exhibiting his dominance.

In keeping with dominance theory, male-to-male aggression tends to decrease across the first year of middle school. According to this theory, boys should use aggression against other boys as one of their strategies to establish dominance when they first enter a new social group, in this case, a new school. Once dominance is established in the middle of the year, aggression should decrease, the argument here being that once dominance is established, there is little purpose served by being aggressive. Youngsters can typically predict who will win, in advance, so with this knowledge they should they should avoid aggression.

The data presented in Fig. 6.5 show this developmental course and come from a study I did with Maria Bartini (Pellegrini & Bartini, 2000). By way of explaining this figure, the x-axis, labels each of the grade levels at which youngsters were asked to refer to those same questions being asked during the fall (e.g., 6.1) and the spring (e.g., 6.2) of the sixth and seventh grades. The y-axis refers to the students' average responses, on a 1–7 scale, in the degree to which they engaged in bullying.

Self-reported aggression increased from fifth to sixth grades as boys moved from primary to middle school, and declined across the first two years of middle school, Grades 6 and 7. The methods and data for these findings are presented in Appendix C at the end of this chapter. Indeed, one of the major functions of dominance hierarchies is to minimize aggression within a group (Dunbar, 1988). Specifically, aggression is minimized after dominance is established because members of the group recognize who the leaders are and to challenge them would, in all probability, result in their defeat, with little gain. Furthermore, leaders have little need to be aggressive as long as their status is secure.

In the cases of R&T and aggression, we would expect boys to use both of them more frequently with other boys, relative to girls. Additionally,

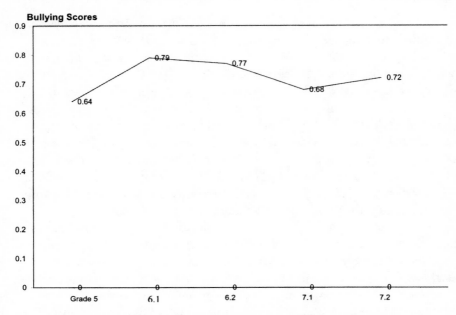

FIG. 6.5. Developmental path of aggression from primary through middle school, Grades 5 through 7.

most aggression and male-male R&T should take place in the beginning stages of group formation and wane as group structure is established.

The data presented in Fig. 6.6 show this pattern. Boys are aggressive with other boys, not with girls. Also note that there were no cases of girl-girl or boy-girl aggression in the seventh grade.

In the second half of the year, however, we expected intersexual (i.e., between boys and girls) R&T, initiated by both boys and girls to increase, relative to the first half of the year. That is, boys and girls should start to engage in R&T together but not for aggressive purposes. Quite the opposite: Though boy-boy R&T will remain higher than boy-girl R&T, by the second half of the year, both boys and girls should use R&T with each other as a playful way in which to initiate heterosexual contact. Use of such playful strategies to establish heterosexual relationships has been labeled "poke-and-push courtship" (Schofield, 1981). In contrast to male-male R&T, male-female R&T is typically more affiliative, perhaps reflecting a playful form of early heterosexual contact. As shown in Fig. 6.7, boys move from targeting other boys to targeting girls during the sixth grade.

Such playful, and indirect, strategies to initiate cross-sex contact seem appropriate given risks to participants associated with initiating public

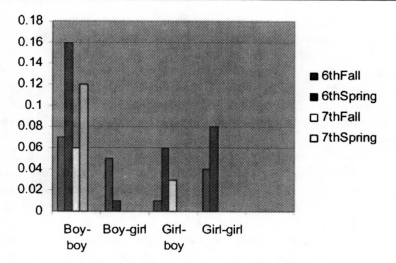

FIG. 6.6. Gender of initiators and targets of aggression in middle school.

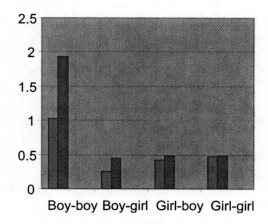

FIG. 6.7. Gender of initiators and targets of R&T in sixth grade.

heterosexual contact. Initial cross-sex contacts are quite risky to initiate in that they break the well-established patterns of sex segregation, entrenched since early childhood that I discussed in earlier chapters (Maccoby, 1998; Serbin, Tonick, & Sternglanz, 1977). Further, there is a real likelihood that one's overtures to opposite-sex peers will be publicly rejected.

One way in which youngsters can minimize risks associated with public rejection is to use overtures that are playful and ambiguous in their intent.

Specifically, youngsters of this age sometimes resort to poking-and-push-ing courtship behaviors; for example, playfully hitting, pushing, grabbing, and teasing an opposite-sex peer. These R&T-like behaviors can be inter-preted as courting, or affiliative overtures, by the recipient and reciprocated. Alternatively, they can be rejected. In the former case, cross-sex contact has been successfully initiated and in the latter case, the initiator saves face for an unsuccessful attempt because the bout can be dismissed as playful and not serious.

With all of this said, there are sometimes cases where it is difficult to differentiate R&T from aggression. For example, aggressive children have more difficulty discriminating R&T from aggression than nonaggressive youngsters. Video playback methodology can be useful here in getting closer insights into the ways in which boys and girls use R&T. Asking them directly, though it has limits, approaches this goal, and when used in conjunction with the observational data, converge on a common interpre-tation: Adolescent boys used R&T for dominance and aggressive ends.

In my research with middle school youngsters, I filmed them inter-acting with each other at different points in the school day, such as in between classes, in the lunch room, and at school dances (Pellegrini, 2003). Individuals viewed R&T bouts in which they were participants and nonparticipants. Responses in the participant condition were contrasted with responses to videotaped bouts in which their peers, not themselves, were participants.

The assumptions guiding the questions I posed to these youngsters were as follows. We assumed that boy-boy R&T would be aggressive and used to serve a dominance function, so boys who participated in R&T bouts, relative to nonparticipating boys, would say R&T was aggressive and used for dominance. Nonparticipating boys, on the other hand, should see R&T as playful. This may be based on their memories of R&T during childhood when R&T is playful and not aggressive.

Female participants, relative to female nonparticipants, should see it as playful because they realize that they do this with boys as a form of early "courting behavior." Nonparticipant girls, on the other hand, should see it as aggressive, relative to participating girls. This is essentially what we found.

Though these analyses suggest that boys' R&T with other boys does relate to dominance, Donald Symons (1978) is critical of this hypothesis. As counterevidence, he notes that in primate and child research on R&T self-handicapping occurs; blows are not forceful, and individuals take turns to gain or cede the upper position in wrestling. However, subsequent findings counter this argument in two ways that I review in more detail later. First, children can often evaluate the strength of others from R&T bouts, despite self-handicapping and restraint. Second, in some youngsters (and especially by adolescence), it now appears that subtle or not so subtle forms of "cheating" may occur, demonstrating clearly to opponents and to onlookers that one participant is in fact stronger (Smith & Boulton, 1990).

This argument is also consistent with the gender differences in R&T. Children establish and maintain dominance in different ways. Girls primarily use verbal, rather than physical, means to gain and keep resources (Charlesworth & Dzur, 1987). Boys, on the other hand, use a variety of skills, some of which are related to physical prowess to regulate access to resources, for example, struggling over access to a toy. Fighting skills, or toughness, when used in conjunction with more affiliative skills, is an important dimension of boys' peer group status and popularity (Pellegrini & Bartini, 2001). It may be the case that dominant individuals reconcile (e.g., shake hands, offer gifts, etc.) after their aggressive acts as a way in which to maintain group harmony (de Waal, 1982, 1986). Additionally, leaders may use aggression to stop fights or to help their allies (Strayer & Noel, 1986).

CONCLUSION

While I have talked about different forms of play across childhood, I focused on R&T because it is very common on the school playground at recess—especially for boys. I suggest that the primary function of R&T through the primary years is to provide a way in which boys assess the strength of others for dominance purposes, possibly in addition to providing practice in fighting skills, for which, however, little direct evidence exists. Good evidence shows that in early adolescence (and perhaps earlier for rejected children) R&T functions to actually establish dominance status in boys' peer groups. The contemporaneous correlations between R&T and dominance and R&T and popularity for adolescent boys suggest that R&T is only one behavioral strategy used by boys to gain and maintain status.

APPENDIX A

Smith, P. K., Smees, R., & Pellegrini, A. D. (2004). Play fighting and real fighting: Using video playback methodology with young children. *Aggressive Behavior, 30*, 164–173.

METHOD FOR THE VIDEO PLAY-BACK STUDY OF PRIMARY SCHOOL CHILDREN

Participants

The sample comprised all the boys (except one who had a low attendance rate) at one primary school in a northern urban city in England. The school was situated in an area of mixed- to lower-socioeconomic status. Forty-four boys aged 5 to 8 years took part, from four classes; most were White, but 11 were from ethnic minorities (Asian, Black) or of mixed race.

Procedures

The researcher filming the children (R.S.) spent 4 weeks familiarizing herself with the children and carried out pilot work with the filming, editing, and interview procedures. We then obtained videotapes of 42 episodes of what might be either playful or serious fighting over 9 school days in the school playground. Filming took place every day from 12:00 to 12:30 P.M. Immediately following filming on each day, four or five episodes were chosen from the video record on the basis of quality of the record and variety in types of actions and of children involved. These were played back to children individually, on the same day, from 1:00 to 3:15 P.M. (the short-term recall condition). The four or five episodes were shown to every participant in each episode, and therefore children were also nonparticipants in several episodes. The same video clips were shown to the participants (only), for the second time approximately 1 week later (the long-term recall condition).

During the individual interviews, each child was asked a series of questions including:

1. *Who is taking part in what you saw?*
The child named the other children in the episode.
2. *Is it play fighting, or real fighting?*
This was scored as play fighting/real fighting/a mixture/don't know.

3. *How can you tell?*

Responses to this question were content analyzed and coded into 15 categories; 13 categories were identical to those identified and defined in Costabile et al. (1991): length of episode, stay together or separate, facial expression, physical actions, on the ground, presence/absence of crowd, actions of nonfocal peers, inference about affect, inference about action or intent, stereotyped knowledge, knowledge of focal child, other, don't know. The overall level of agreement among the three researchers (averaged over pairwise agreement) in classifying episodes was kappa = 0.89.

4. *Do you think [each participant] is enjoying it, or not?*
Scored as yes/no/don't know.

5. *Is either of them/anyone getting hurt? Who?*
Scored as yes/no/don't know.

6. *Is either of them/anyone showing off? (if so) How?*

A content analysis of "how" answers following a yes response produced categories of: verbal/physical/assertive, other child scared of him/being silly, rude, messing about/other (e.g., showing off to camera)/don't know. The overall level of agreement among the three researchers (averaged over pairwise agreement) was kappa = 0.78.

7. *Are they friends?*
Scored as yes/no/don't know.

APPENDIX B

METHOD USED WITH ADOLESCENTS — OBSERVATIONAL DATA

Pellegrini, A. D. (2003). Perceptions and possible functions of play and
real fighting in early adolescence. *Child Development, 74,* 1459–1470.

Participants

The participants in this study were sampled for one year from two middle
schools (Grade 6) in a rural school system in North America. The sample
of 138 (77 males and 61 females) youngsters had a mean age = 12.8 years
at the start of the school year. Though rural, parts of the county also served
as bedroom communities for a large urban area. The schools were predominantly European American (95%) with the remainder being comprised of
African Americans and even fewer Asian Americans. The schools, though
having a mixed socioeconomic base ranging from professional classes
(physicians, lawyers, etc.) to unemployed, were predominantly middle
class. Youngsters were told that in return for participation, they would be
paid; they were paid $20. All participating teachers were paid $50.

Procedure

For the purposes of this study, we present data collected from students
using direct behavioral observations of peer interaction and teacher ratings
of boys' dominance status.

   Direct Observations.   In the course of the school year (which began in
August and ran through June) focal participants were observed directly at
least once/week for the whole school year. Observations took place across
the school day and at various locations. Morning observations took place
in the hallways and in the cafeteria as youngsters waited to be admitted to
their homerooms. In the late morning and early afternoon, observations
were conducted in the halls and in the cafeteria. Additionally in the late
afternoon, observations were conducted in the hallways and during their
"free time" (sometimes occurring outdoors), which lasted 15–30 minutes.
The specific details of the observational procedures follow.
   Before the school year began, seven research associates attended training sessions. The initial weeks of training involved familiarization with

the observation coding sheets and discussion of terms. Next, observations were made using the coding sheet on videotaped episodes of youngsters' playground and lunchroom behavior.

R&T and aggression were both defined in terms of physical description, affect, and consequence. Specific to R&T, physical description criteria included soft or open-hand hit, push, and teasing; affective criteria were positive and included smiling and laughing; consequences had participants staying together after the rough act. Aggressive physical description criteria included hard, closed-hand hit; kick; and nasty talk. Affective criteria were negative and included frown or cry; and consequential criteria had the participants separating after the aggressive act. The expressed scores represent the number of times a behavior was observed in each month of each of the two 5-month periods.

In addition to coding the behaviors per se, the sex of the initiator and target of each behavior was also coded. Individual *kappas* were computed at the end of this week on training tapes and they were all well above .80, which is considered good (Pellegrini, 1996).

Training observations were conducted in the schools themselves. During the first weeks of school, research associates took individual photographs of students that were then used to aid in the identification of focal children. Research associates also observed informally (ad libitum sampling, Pellegrini, 1996) in the school (mostly in the cafeteria at lunch time) so that they and the participants habituated to each other. During the next two weeks each research assistant conducted focal child samples and continuous recordings (Pellegrini, 1996). At the end of this period, *kappas* were recalculated between each of the seven observers and a checker, and they remained over .80. After this training period, observations to be used in the data analyses began.

Research associates received counterbalanced lists of focal children to observe for each academic quarter; they observed a different set of focal children each quarter. For alternative months, across the school year observers were retrained (on videotapes) or were checked for reliability.

Focal child sampling/continuous recording rules were used (Pellegrini, 1996), yielding information on relative frequency of all behaviors (relative to all coded behavior). Each observer had a counterbalanced list of 17–20 focal participants to be observed. Focal children were observed for 3-minute sampling intervals (marked by a beep using the "count down" function on Timex Ironman Triathlon watches) and the behavior of the focal child was recorded continuously on a check sheet. If focal children "disappeared" during this period (e.g., to go into the bathroom) for 30 seconds or more the observation was terminated and the time was noted; the research associate then moved on to the next focal child.

Direct observational data for sixth grade was divided into two equal five-month periods: Time 1 and Time 2. The choice of dividing each year in half was based on the following. We wanted some metric of change but one with an equal number of valid data points. Dividing the year into halves, rather than quarters, allowed the observational data from five, rather than 2.5, months to be aggregated. Aggregation across a number of data points seemed particularly important in our observing aggression, which occurs relatively infrequently. Scores for individual categories were expressed as frequencies of aggression and R&T per observational session.

Research associates were given a different cohort of focal youngsters to observe every 10-weeks to minimize their becoming too familiar with each other. By the end of each school year, each research associate had observed all participants in a school. Each focal child was observed at least one time/week across the whole school year, for a minimum of 36 times.

Dominance Rating.   During late fall/early winter of the school year (after Thanksgiving and before the Christmas break) teachers were asked to complete for each participant Dodge and Coie's (1987) Teacher Check List. Observers also rated dominance. The teachers' and observers' ratings were significantly correlated, $r = .48$, $p < .0001$. Youngsters were rated, on a 1–7 scale, for constructs related to social competence. We used the Dominance subscale (composed of 6 items, e.g., Wants to be in charge, Shows off, Egotistical), with a .88 *alpha*. The unit of analysis was the aggregated average of the observer and teacher score for the subscale where scores ranged from 1–7.

APPENDIX C

Pellegrini, A. D. (2003). Perceptions and possible functions of play and real fighting in early adolescence. *Child Development, 74,* 1459–1470.

METHOD USED WITH ADOLESCENTS — VIDEO PLAY-BACK

Participants

A total of 95 (54 males, 41 females) youngsters took part in this study. They were part of the group of participants who took part in the previous study I described in Appendix B. The average age at the start of the study was 12 years of age.

Procedures

Students were observed and videotaped, as part of the observational procedure described in Study 1 (see Appendix B) at various locations across the school day, from breakfast in the morning, through changing classes and lunch time, to free time at the end of the day on Fridays. Additionally, youngsters were also observed during a Friday evening dance held monthly.

Event sampling with continuous recording rules were followed for recording R&T. Tapes were reviewed by research associates trained to differentiate R&T from aggression along the criteria established by Costabile and colleagues (Costibile et al., 1991). R&T has positive affect, soft or exaggerate physical contact, and participants stayed together after the bout terminated. Aggression, on the other hand, is characterized by negative affect, hard hits, and separation of peers at bout termination. From the corpus of tapes, a set of six bouts was chosen for each participant.

Participants viewed two sets of tapes. In one set they were participants and in the other they were nonparticipants. They were asked, individually, a series of standardized questions by an interviewer for each of the six bouts. Responses were audiorecorded and later coded. For purposes of this study, only responses to R&T bouts were analyzed. Participants were asked, "Why are you/they doing it?" Responses were coded as: play, tease, retaliate, pick on/victimize, an accident, don't know/can't remember, hurt/aggress against. Next, they were asked, "Is it fun?" and responses included yes, no, and don't know, and "Is he/she showing off?" with yes/no responses.

SOME THINGS TO THINK ABOUT

1. How often do you see children engaging in R&T?

   Are they boys?

   Girls?

   Are boys and girls doing it together?

   Separately?

2. When you observe children engaging in R&T, are there adults around?

   If adults are around, do they seem tolerant of it or not?

   Are male adults more tolerant than females?

   Why?

3. Have you seen adults engage in R&T with kids?

   Are the kids boys?

   Girls?

   Are the adults males?

   Females?

4. If you've observed adults sanction kids' R&T, are the adults more likely to be males or females?

5. Go to a place where you think you can find children engaging in R&T, such as a playground with minimal adult supervision.

   How often do you see R&T escalating to aggression?

Chapter 7

Children's Games on the Playground at Recess

In this chapter, I talk about the games children play on the playground at recess. We're all familiar with these games—basketball, tag, hopscotch, and so forth. Games, like play, are not taken very seriously in the context of schooling. In this chapter, I hope to convince you that games, like play, are important for children in school. Where play is important for preschool children, I think that games are more important for primary school children.

It is important, however, to differentiate games from play as they clearly are different constructs (Garvey, 1977). As discussed in chapter 1, in Piaget's theory (1983), play is best understood in terms of *preoperational intelligence,* where children cannot subordinate their behavior to sets of abstract rules. Recall that two forms of play, fantasy and rough-and-tumble play, were defined and discussed in an earlier chapter. Games, of course, are governed by such rules and thus are characterized by *operational intelligence* and characteristic of older children. Play and games were very different constructs for Piaget. Play reflected the preoperational thought of the child who could not take multiple perspectives on a person or an event. Instead, the young child is centered on his/her own perspective. From this view, play is mostly assimilative. That is, in play children subordinate the world to their mental state. For example, a stick becomes a horse or a rag becomes a doll.

The games of primary school children, on the other hand, reflect the beginnings of operational thought. In this case, the child can handle multiple perspectives on other people and events and subordinate his or her view to preset rules. Thus, in games children are learning to follow established rules. In the course of interacting with peers around games, however, youngsters often disagree with each other, and when they do, they are forced to consider their points of view in relation to their peers' points of view. That they enjoy interacting with their peers motivates them to do the difficult social-cognitive work of considering the perspectives of their peers in relation to their own and coming up with a compromise. These sorts of conflict-resolution cycles have the effect of fostering children's cognitive development.

Play and games are sometimes confused, however, possibly because they share some design features. For example, both play (e.g., fantasy play) and games (e.g., soccer) are rule governed. The rules governing games are a priori and codified, whereas the rules governing play are flexible, negotiated by players in different ways, and not set in advance. For example, in a play episode where two children are pretending to cook a meal, they can negotiate rules and roles regarding what is to be cooked (e.g., "Let's cook *stew*. No, let's make a *cake*.") and how it is to be cooked ("*I* want to be the cook now"). Once these issues are agreed upon, play behavior is consistent with the rules for the theme and the roles, until the rules or roles are challenged. At that time they are typically renegotiated (Fein, 1981a; Garvey, 1977). Indeed, more time is typically spent negotiating and renegotiating roles and rules in play than in play itself (Garvey, 1977).

Games, on the other hand, are guided by explicit rules that are set in advance, and violations of these rules usually results in some form of sanction, not renegotiation (Garvey, 1977). So, for example, in a game of basketball, a child running with the ball without dribbling would be told by peers to forfeit the ball.

Children's games, surprisingly, have not received extended empirical attention from psychologists or educators for a number of years. I say "surprisingly" because at least one influential theory (Piaget, 1932/1965), as discussed above, suggests that games have important implications for children's, and especially boys', social and cognitive development. Correspondingly, there have been repeated calls for more research on games over the last 50 years (e.g., Gump & Sutton-Smith, 1953; Hart, 1993; Rubin, Fein, & Vandenberg, 1983; Sutton-Smith, 1973, 1975; Sutton-Smith,

Rosenberg, & Morgan, 1963). Yet, the latest *Handbook of Child Psychology* volume on social and personality development (Eisenberg, 1998) does not have a single reference in the subject index to games or games with rules, down from the rather sparse six references in the 1983 *Handbook* (Hetherington, 1983).

Though a number of possible reasons exist for the recent neglect of research on children's games, it clearly is consistent with the theme of scholars and educators not taking the play and games of children seriously. Another reason for this neglect may relate to availability of and access to a research sample of young children at a time when they typically engage in games (i.e., primary school). Compare the ease with which infants and preschool children can be observed in university laboratory schools and the massive amount of research on the modal forms of play for children of these ages, sensorimotor and fantasy play (Rubin et al., 1983). Primary-school-age children, on the other hand, are less accessible for study and proffer fewer opportunities for observations of peer interaction, as much of the primary school day is tightly scheduled around regimens of solitary and sedentary academic work (Pellegrini & Blatchford, 2000).

The school playground at recess does, however, provide an interesting and under-used venue for the study of school-age children's peer interaction, generally (Boulton & Smith, 1993; Hart, 1993), and games with peers (Boulton, 1992), more specifically. Further, participation in recess is, by most school standards, required for all children; thus, problems associated with self-selection out of recess are minimal. Also very important is the fact that recess is one of the few places during the mandatory school day where children are free to interact with their peers in games with relatively few restrictions (Boulton & Smith, 1993). From this view, it is an ideal venue for studying a relatively large and diverse sample of children engaging in activities that they enjoy: games and interacting with peers.

Correspondingly, observations of children at recess probably yield valid information on their social competence because interaction with peers at recess is both motivating and demanding for children (Waters & Sroufe, 1983). That is, children typically enjoy recess and games, and to successfully engage in games requires a fair level of social and cognitive sophistication (Piaget, 1932/1965). Indeed, it is not until children first enter school, in kindergarten and first grade, that they possess the requisite skills necessary to begin to play games. For example, children must know the rules of the games and subordinate their personal views and desires to those rules and to the positions of their peers. That they enjoy these interactions motivates them to exhibit the high levels of competence required to participate in the games. Children's engagement in playground games, then, should provide valid insight into their competence.

Competence for young primary school children can be defined in terms of forming and maintaining peer networks (e.g., being liked by peers and having friends) and adhering to group norms within organized peer groups (such as playing games with rules with peers). To these peer competencies, it is also important to add adjustment to the demands of school (Sroufe, Egelund, & Carlson, 1999; Waters & Sroufe, 1983). This definition is derived from developmental theory suggesting that competence is defined differently at different ages and competence can be represented by corresponding developmental tasks, such as games with peers in a school setting (Waters & Sroufe, 1983). Competence with peers, according to this orientation, is rooted in earlier relationships (such as the attachment relationship with mother) and should reflect the confidence and ability to get along with a variety of individuals (peer popularity) and to form close relationships (such as friendships).

Interaction with peers, especially around games in a school setting, is an especially interesting developmental task for studying social competence during middle childhood. Engagement in games with peers requires the sorts of social facility (e.g., cooperation, turn-taking, rule-governed behavior) necessary for competence with peers. Additionally, social engagement with peers during the school day, at recess, should also be indicative of one's efficacy in one dimension of early schooling.

First, I describe the frequency of occurrence of children's games on the school playground during recess across the entire first-grade year. Though there is a general lack of recent descriptive data on children's games, there is information from the more general literature on children's peer relations and older work on games that enables us to generate hypotheses. I expect the frequency with which children engaged in games to vary according to gender and time of the school year.

Regarding gender, it has been clearly documented, and as I discussed in the chapter on gender segregation, that boys, relative to girls, are more physically active (Eaton & Enns, 1986) and correspondingly, they prefer to interact with each other in outdoor relative to indoor play space (Harper & Sanders, 1975) because this venue affords opportunity to engage physically vigorous activity. Consequently, we expect boys more than girls to engage in physically vigorous games, such as chasing and ball games. Further, boys should exhibit a more varied repertoire of games given their preference for games and for the outdoors. Margaret Goodwin (1990), in

FIG. 7.1. An African American urban street game.

her ethnography of urban African American children, reported that boys, relative to girls, are more facile at games. (See Fig. 7.1.)

Girls, relative to boys, however, should more frequently be observed in games requiring verbal facility, such as chanting, hopscotch, and jump rope games (Goodwin, 1990; Heath, 1983; Janikas, 1993; Lever, 1975/1976; Maccoby, 1998; Thorne, 1986), given the reliable gender differences in children's oral language production (Maccoby & Jacklin, 1974). That is, girls' language is typically more advanced than boys' language. Consistent with this view, the ethnographic literature also finds that girls, relative to boys, from both European American (Janikas, 1993; Lever, 1975/1976) and African American backgrounds (Heath, 1983; Goodwin, 1990) spend more time in verbal games. (See Figs. 7.2 and 7.3.)

The frequency with which certain games are observed should also increase as children get older and gain more experience with school, especially during the first years of formal primary school. Specifically, those games requiring the greatest coordination of social, cognitive, and physical skills, such as ball games, should increase as the year progresses. It also requires time and maturation for children to learn the rules of games played at school, which are sometimes idiosyncratic to a specific location

FIG. 7.2. Verbal street games.

FIG. 7.3. Verbal street games.

(Blatchford & Sumpner, 1998). Playing these games requires learning the rules, applying them, and recognizing violations. Correspondingly, children must also learn to subordinate their perspectives to the rules of the games and the perspectives of their peers. Given the finite amount of time at recess, typically less complex games, such as chase, should correspondingly decrease as children spend increasing time in typically more complicated games, such as ball games.

In this chapter, I also examine the role of facility at games in children's social competence and adjustment to very early school, or the first year of mandatory, full-day schooling. Specifically, I document the degree to which children's facility with playground games at the start of school predicts their subsequent social competence with peers in school and to their more general adjustment to early schooling. Results from earlier pilot work (Blatchford, 1989) suggest that children who are facile at games, or game leaders, are the individuals who initiate, maintain, and terminate games. Case studies also indicated that these children are likely to be popular and to be seen by peers as group leaders (Blatchford, 1989).

Being facile with games on the school playground at recess should also predict adjustment to the very earliest school years because game facility is an indicator of children's engagement in one important dimension of the school day. Being engaged in this context with peers should generalize to school adjustment in first grade because it is an indicator of children's sense of efficacy in the very early grades of school. As we all know, children put great importance to having peers with whom to interact at recess. Being good at games at recess seems to be an important part of enjoying school and peers at school.

Specifically, games at recess represent a transition point from the relative unstructured and peer-oriented regimen of most preschools and very early primary school (kindergarten and first grade) to the structure of elementary school. Positive, rule-governed peer interaction is valued by educators on both the playground at recess and in the first-grade classroom (Pellegrini & Blatchford, 2000). From this view, and consistent with ethological models of domain-specific cognition (Bjorklund & Pellegrini, 2000), the playground and the first-grade classroom are relatively similar niches with similar demand characteristics; thus competence in one area (the playground) should relate to competence in the other (school more generally).

A STUDY OF GAMES ACROSS THE FIRST YEAR OF SCHOOL

The complexity of specific types of games that young primary school children play varies from turn-taking games, such as tag and chase, to more complex games with a variety of roles and rules, such as ball games and verbal games (Borman & Kurdek, 1987; Sutton-Smith, 1973, 1975). Though chase games can be complicated, the relative simplicity of most chase games is reflected in the fact that they have been observed among primary school children at the start of the school year (Thorne, 1986). Ball games, on the other hand, often involve a variety of roles. For example, in basketball, there are forwards, guards, and a center, with each of these having both offensive and defensive realizations. Further, a wide catalogue of rules govern ball games. Clapping, jump rope, and hop scotch games, too, have multiple roles, such as jumper and rope spinner, and numerous rules.

Game leadership, or facility, is also defined in terms of the number of children in the focal child's immediate peer group. This idea of facility is derived from the ethologically oriented work on leadership and dominance (Chance, 1967; Vaughn & Waters, 1981). Dominance is an ethological construct indicative of an individual's status in a social group. Dominance is typically achieved by a combination of prosocial and assertive strategies (Pellegrini & Bartini, 2001) with an aim toward accessing some resource, such as access to a toy or a piece of playground equipment. Peer groups have dominance hierarchies that range from most to least dominant. Most dominant individuals are leaders and are sought after and attended to by peers.

Children want to be around leaders for a number of reasons. For example, by affiliating with leaders youngsters may learn valuable social skills from and form alliances with leaders. Alliances with leaders can also protect more vulnerable children from bullying and victimization (e.g., Hodges & Perry, 1999). Thus, number of individuals surrounding an individual is an observational indicator of leadership status.

I suggest that the role of game leadership, or facility, in children's social competence and adjustment to school supports, or scaffolds, initial interactions between children at recess. That is, knowledge of relatively simple and routinized games is probably shared by many children and serves as a way in which children can interact with each other with limited social skills and shared knowledge of basic games.

The use of the term *scaffold* comes from studies of play (Bateson, 1976) and language learning (Snow, 1989; Wood, Bruner, & Ross, 1976) where a behavior is used in the early developmental history of another, more mature behavior. When that stage of development has been reached, the scaffold is disassembled and disappears. For example, the routinized nature of some games, such a tag, provides a readily known repertoire of possible behaviors that can be used to initiate interaction. In tag, a child can initiate interaction with a peer in the context of a game by running up to another child, saying, "You're It," tagging him, and running away. The routinized nature of the game serves as a scaffold for social interaction, making it easy to initiate interaction. After the child masters other peer interaction initiations strategies, he no longer needs routinize games to serve that purpose, thus this scaffold is disassembled.

A final dimension of social competence and adjustment to schooling, especially in ethnically diverse societies, such as the United States and the United Kingdom, involves children interacting in ethnically diverse groups. A basic aim of school desegregation in the USA has been to provide opportunities for students from diverse backgrounds to interact with each other in integrated schools, resulting in fading racial divides (see Schofield, 1981 for a discussion).

The extent to which this ideal corresponds to the empirical record is, however, questionable. In a study of an American middle school, Janet Schofield (1981) observed youngsters at various venues and found that peer groups were, by and large, segregated. In the UK, Mike Boulton and Peter Smith (1993) reported similar results in their observational study of a group of ethnically diverse primary school children on playgrounds in the north of England. Only one study (Blatchford, 1996) found that children's playgroups became more ethnically diverse with time.

In a subsequent study, we examined the extent to which peer groups became more ethnically integrated with time, but in light of the equivocal findings, we did not pose an hypothesis. Ken Kato, Peter Blatchford, Ed Baines, and I (Pellegrini, Kato, Blatchford, & Baines, 2002) conducted a study to examine the games first-grade children play at recess and how those games, and children's facility with them, change over the course of a year. Generally, we studied first-grade children in two Minneapolis public schools. The children in the schools were from a variety of socioeconomic and cultural backgrounds but predominantly lower socioeconomic status, with 40% having Spanish as their first language. The study was conducted across an entire school year, from September through June. More methodological details of this study can be found in the appendix at the end of this chapter.

The number of games per observation across the whole school year (divided into three time intervals: September–November; December–February; March–May) for boys and girls are displayed in separate graphs in Figures 7.4 to 7.7. Some of the statistical analyses are provided in the appendix at the end of this chapter.

We begin by considering gender. Boys engaged in a greater variety of games than girls, as can be seen in Fig. 7.4. Boys were more likely than girls to take part in chase games at each observation interaction (Fig. 7.5) and were much more likely to engage in ball games than girls (Fig. 7.6). In all cases, the figures reflect the number observed in each observation.

This gender difference probably reflects the finding that boys are more physically active than girls as a result of both hormonal and socialization

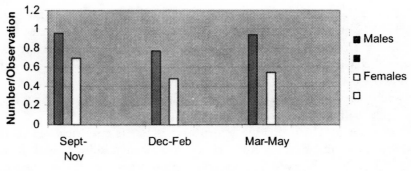

FIG. 7.4.   Variety of games.

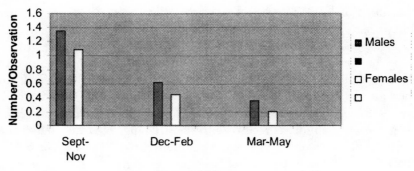

FIG. 7.5.   Chase games.

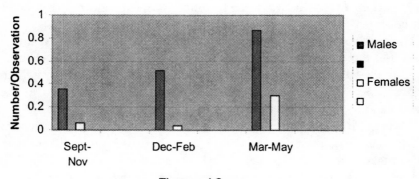

FIG. 7.6.   Ball games.

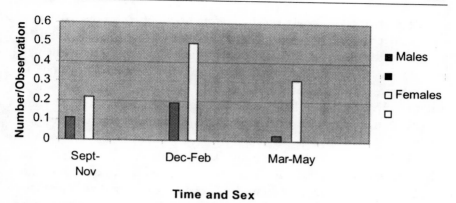

FIG. 7.7. Verbal games.

events (Hines & Kaufman, 1994; Maccoby, 1998). When boys are put into a context that affords opportunities for physically vigorous activity, such as an outdoor playground, predicable and robust gender differences are observed (Harper & Sanders, 1975). The roots of these differences were discussed more fully in the chapters on segregation and rough-and-tumble play.

Not all differences favored boys, however. Girls, compared with boys, were more frequently observed in less vigorous verbal games, such as jump rope chanting and clapping games (Fig. 7.7). This probably reflects girls' verbal facility, relative to boys, as well as girls' adversity to rough and vigorous games. This finding, as discussed in more detail below, is also consistent with ethnographic studies of children from a variety of cultures (e.g., Goodwin, 1990; Heath, 1983; Lever, 1975/1976; Thorne, 1986, 1993).

The gender differences in games may be interpreted in a number of ways. First, it may be that girls are less concerned with games, generally, than boys. This view is consistent with Piaget's (1932/1965) observations of children's games and with some ethnographic descriptions of the games of urban children (Goodwin, 1990). Boys may play games more than girls because the competitive nature of games is more in keeping with the hierarchic and competitive nature of male peer groups (Maccoby, 1998). Indeed, most studies of games find the same thing: Boys play games more and play a greater variety of games (e.g., Goodwin, 1990; Heath, 1983; Lever, 1975/1976; Thorne, 1986, 1993).

We also found that as the school year progresses, gender differences emerged in the occurrence of games. Specifically, no significant gender differences were found in the relative frequency of total games during the first part of the school year, but differences between boys and girls increased over time. Boys engaged in more games and in a greater variety of games at the end of the year, relative to the beginning. Girls' participation in games remained flat across the year—they engaged in games at the same rate at the beginning and at the end of the school year. These results confirm the sex-role expectation that the playground is a venue that affords males opportunities to engage in locomotor and competitive activities.

The observed time changes of individual types of games were consistent with these expectations as well. Chase games decreased across the year and ball games increased. During Time 1, chase games occurred with greatest frequency and declined across the year. This trend in chase may be due to the relative simplicity of the game. The simplest variants involve only the most basic rules: chase and be chased. The simplicity of this game is further evidenced by the fact that most simple variations are commonly observed in even very young preschool children (Pellegrini & Smith, 1998).

Similarly, Thorne's (1986) ethnographic study of primary school children in Michigan playgrounds also found that chase games tended to be observed at the start of the school year and decreased as the year progressed. Children may have used chase games as opening gambits in initiating interaction with new and unfamiliar peers. These games often require little background knowledge or negotiations about interpretations; thus, children can interact with each other in these games from the very earliest phases of social group formation.

The changes we found associated with the passage of time were conflated with seasonal and familiarity variation. That is, the observed time changes may in fact have been influenced by seasonal effects such that in the upper Midwest of the USA, we might expect winter (Time 2 in this study) to inhibit games. Though I recognize this possibility, some of our data support the interpretation that boys' engagement in ball games increased steadily over time. Specifically, ball games (for boys) increased from Time 1 to 2 to 3. This increase in game complexity corresponds to a steady drop as time progressed in the seemingly least complex games observed, chase games, from Time 1 to 2 to 3. To more convincingly eliminate seasonal variation as a confound of time, children should be observed across the school year in a climate that is less variable and less extreme (e.g., San Diego).

Familiarity among peers also contributes to the increase of ball games, relative to simpler games, across time. Familiar peers, relative to unfamiliar peers, engage in more sophisticated and cooperative forms of interaction (e.g., Brody, Graziano, & Musser, 1983; Hartup, 1983). Future research should address the effect of familiarity on game performance by varying individuals' expectation of repeated meetings. Cooperative interaction, including games, should be observed more frequently in conditions where individuals anticipate repeated meetings, compared with expectations of no repeated meetings.

Game Facility, Social Competence, and Adjustment to School

I considered games as an important developmental task for children, and especially boys, entering primary school. Boys used their facility with games as a way in which they could achieve and maintain social competence with their peers and to adjust to very early schooling. This finding is consistent with the theoretical assumption that the social rules and roles that children learn in one niche (with their peers on the school playground) should predict competence in related niches, with their peers in first grade. Both niches are similar to the extent that they encourage rule-governed behavior and cooperative interaction with peers. Social competence in this study (Pellegrini et al., 2002) was defined following Alan Sroufe and colleagues (Sroufe, Egelund, & Carlson, 1999) at both the group (being liked by peers) and close social relationship (reciprocal friends) levels.

Game facility.[1]   As measured by observed games played as well as peer nominations and teachers' ratings of game playing facility, predicted end-of-year social competence and school adjustment, even after we considered children's social competence and adjustment at the start of the school year (the statistical details are available in the appendix at the end of this chapter). These relations, however, differed for boys and girls, especially in the case of social competence. For boys, game facility was a more powerful predictor of social competence than it was for girls. This finding is consistent with the view that male groups are hierarchic and competence in these groups is often judged by ability to compete and lead (Maccoby,

---

[1] To maximize the validity of the construct "game facility," it was defined from a multi-method, multiinformant perspective using peer nominations, teacher ratings, and direct observations (Cronbach, 1971). Children were asked to nominate peers who suggested things to do at recess and were facile at games and sport. Teachers and research associates also rated youngsters on games and sport. Behaviorally, game facility was defined in terms of the relative frequency with which children played games and by the number of peers observed in their immediate group. The details of this measurement are presented in the appendix at the end of this chapter.

1998). The statistical analyses are discussed in the appendix. Similarly, game leadership predicted boys' school adjustment but not that of girls. That game facility predicted boys' school adjustment is a very important finding for educational policy makers. Games probably provide opportunities to learn and practice the skills necessary for effective social interaction with peers in an important socialization context, early schooling.

These results do reinforce earlier research where children's peer relations in school predicted school success (e.g., Ladd & Price, 1987). The results of the present study, however, extend this earlier work in that the majority of the students were low-income children. It is well known that children, and again boys especially, from economically disadvantaged groups have difficulty adjusting to and succeeding in school (e.g., Heath, 1983). We have demonstrated that their success in one part of the first-grade school day (games at recess) can predict more general school adjustment. The mechanisms by which this happens, however, are not clearly understood and are worthy of further study.

Does facility in games lead to children feeling self-efficacious about school? Or is it that having a leadership role in a peer group results in children having sources of social and emotional support from their peer group while adjusting to school (e.g., Ladd & Price, 1987)? We do not know the answer to this educationally important question yet, but future research should also examine the extent to which game leadership predicts school adjustment in later grades, when the niches of the playground and the classroom are more different (i.e., solitary academic work replaces more socially interactive instructional modes).

Finally, we examined inter-ethnic interaction on the playground across the year. The level of ethnic variety in playgroups did not vary by either time or gender. As in other observational research, primary school children prefer to interact with peers of the same race (Boulton & Smith, 1993). It is probably the case that desegregation may actually entrench segregation unless existing stereotypes are changed (Allport, 1954). This seems to be especially true when children are observed in unstructured settings. Integration can be facilitated, however, when adults structure peer interaction around games so that different types of children are encouraged to participate (Serbin, Tonick, & Sternglanz, 1977; Maccoby, 1998).

It would be very interesting, and important, to examine the effectiveness of policies that foster inter-ethnic interaction. Research with adolescents has shown that school policy (e.g., where differences are minimized and similarities are maximized) can increase interaction among different ethnic groups (Schofield, 1981). It is also important, however, to examine the maintenance of effects as these biases—though they are less persistent than sex-segregation biases—can be very difficult to change without adult-provided structure and support (Maccoby, 1998).

In summary, in this chapter, I described a study my colleagues and I did on the occurrence of games with peers across the first year of full-day schooling for a sample of ethnically diverse children. I found that games accounted for a significant portion of boys' recess behavior. Further, and also consistent with expectations, boys' games increased in complexity and variety across the school year.

Boys' facility with games also appears to be an important predictor of social competence and adjustment to first grade. These data support the extant research, which has documented the dynamic relation between peer status and school success. As Gary Ladd and Joe Price (1987) noted, having friends aids in the transition from preschool to kindergarten. We extend this research by suggesting that participating in games with peers is one of the ways in which boys, especially, adjust to school.

POLICY IMPLICATIONS

This work also has educational policy implications. This study suggests that facility with games is implicated in boys' social competence and adjustment to first grade. The finding that competence develops in the context of interacting with their peers is especially important, as children are rapidly losing opportunities to interact with peers. There are signs in both the United States and the United Kingdom that children of primary school age have fewer opportunities out of school for interacting freely with peers and thus developing social skills and competence. For example, a British survey in the early 1990s showed that one important venue for peer interaction is disappearing: English students are now far less likely to walk to school in comparison with 20 years ago (Hillman, 1993). Furthermore, many American children enter empty homes after school, waiting for their parent(s) to return from work (Steinberg, 1986). And as we've seen, there is the trend in both the U.S. and in the U.K. for recess time to be limited or eliminated from the primary school day. Recess may be one of the few times during the day when children have the opportunity to interact with peers and develop social skills.

There are also policy implications for our finding that peer groups are not ethnically integrated. Adult intervention has been used successfully to encourage the integration of peer groups by gender, a task more difficult to accomplish than ethnic integration (Maccoby, 1998). In these cases, integration is facilitated when adults model and reinforce integration. The presence of trained adults in both the classroom and on the playground may result in children choosing to model these adults and integrate their peer groups. The positive role of trained adult models may also point to the importance of having teachers, not aides, on the playground. An additional benefit of having teachers on the playground is that their presence minimizes bullying (Pellegrini, in 2002a).

APPENDIX

Pellegrini, A. D., Kato, K., Blatchford, P., & Baines, E. (2002). A short-term longitudinal study of children's playground games across the first year of school: Implications for social competence and adjustment to school. *American Educational Research Journal, 39*, 991–1015.

METHOD

Participants

Children in this study were recruited from two urban primary schools in a large American Midwestern city and represented the ethnic diversity of the city. The sample consisted of 78 children (30 males and 48 females), and had a mean age of 77 months.

Procedures

A total of four research associates worked on this project, all of whom were female graduate students. Logistically, each of two research associates was assigned to separate schools to conduct behavioral observations. The other assistants alternated between sites. To minimize bias, research associates did not interview children whom they observed.

Behavioral Observations. Observers were trained extensively before data collection began. We chose to use both focal child and scan sampling strategies because they provide complementary data in field studies (Martin & Bateson, 1993).

For the focal child sample procedures, children were observed for 3 minutes (minimally, once per month) and their behavior was continuously recorded on coding sheets. The following information was recorded in the focal child samples. At the beginning of each focal sampling the composition of the focal child's immediate peer group was coded in terms of each child's identity (if he or she was a study participant), ethnicity (African American, Asian American, Latino, European American), and gender. Regarding the ethnic make-up of the peer groups, we were interested in deriving a measure of the ethnic integration of the group. Scores varied from 0 (where the group was comprised of children from the same group as the focal child) to 4 (where there were individuals from each of the four ethnic groups represented in the sample).

Across the 3-minute sampling interval behaviors were recorded in order of occurrence. While we recorded a number of different behaviors (i.e., locomotor behavior, fantasy play, rough-and-tumble play, aggression, submit, unoccupied, and other) into mutually exclusive categories, we will describe only game behavior in this report. The sum of all behaviors coded was, however, used as the denominator to derive the relative frequency of total games played.

Games were coded as interactions following a priori rules and they could be social or solitary. Based on earlier pilot work (Blatchford, 1989) the coded games included: chasing games, ball games, and verbal games. Chasing games were defined as simple games involving alternating reciprocal role taking and locomotion, for example, tag and IT. Ball games were defined as rule-governed activities with a ball as the central object of activity, for example, basketball, soccer, and baseball. Verbal games were interactions that centered on rule-governed interactions where verbalizations were a central part of the interaction, for example, hand clapping games, jump rope games, and hopscotch games.

Observed games were scored at two levels. First, we derived a relative frequency of total games, relative to all other behaviors scored, by dividing the frequency of observed games by the total number of focal behaviors recorded. Second, we derived a frequency score of the types of games observed in each of the three time intervals across the school year.

Children were also observed using scan sampling, instantaneous recording rules. Behaviors recorded instantaneously in the scans were similar to those recorded in the focal samples. Children were also scanned sampled across the whole year. As with the focal sampling data, the number of individual games, relative to all other behaviors scanned, was derived by dividing the observed frequency of games by the total number of scanned behaviors recorded. Additionally, we scored the number of types of games/ scan for each of the time periods across the school year. As noted earlier, scans were averaged with focal samples to yield a frequency/time measure.

A variety-of-games measure was also derived from both focal child and scan data by tallying, 0/1, the nonoccurrence/occurrence of each of the three types of games. For example, if a ball game was observed on one occasion, a tally of 1 would be scored. The same score of 1 would be assigned even if that one game was observed in all 12 observations. If no games were observed in any of the observations, a 0 score would be assigned. Scores could range from 0, where no games where observed during any of the observations, to 3, where each of the different types of games was observed at least once across all observations.

Peer Nominations and Self-Reports.   Children were interviewed twice during the course of the school year: In the late fall and in the late spring. To minimize bias, children were not interviewed by the same researcher by whom they were observed. Children whose first language was Spanish were interviewed by a native speaker of Spanish. The research associate read a list of the names of the children in the classroom to each child. They then asked the child to nominate three peers they like most, who were friends, and who were very good at sports and games, as well as a series of other questions not used in this study.

Children were also asked to rate the extent to which they liked school. Individual children were interviewed and the items were read to them. The school liking measure consisted of 12 items (e.g., Going to school makes me happy. School is boring.), and children were asked rate each as yes, not sure, no (scored 3,2,1).

Teacher and Research Associate Rating Scales.   Teachers and research associates were also asked to rate children's adjustment to school and their facility in games; these scores were aggregated. Research associates rated the children they observed. Adults as informants provide information that complements both the individuals' and the peer groups' perspective to the extent that they too are normative but their ratings are probably more in tune with institutional expectations, rather than peer group expectations.

Teachers and research associates completed the same, well-established, rating scales (Pupil Behavior Scale and Teacher Checklist) for each child late fall and spring. The Pupil Behavior Scale is a 54 item rating scale (1–3) with many questions complied from Ladd and Profilet's (1996) Child Behavior Scale. Five empirically derived factors were used in this study and, for the purposes of this report, we were interested in the school adjustment factor (e.g., Coping well with school; Has friendly and responsive relationship with teacher; with an *alpha* of .95).

They also completed the Teacher Checklist, developed by Dodge and Coie (1987). It has a total of 45 items, scored 1–7. In the present study we utilized the item rating facility in sports and games. Each teacher was paid $50 for participation.

RESULTS

This section is organized around the two general goals of this study. First, we describe the types of boys' and girls' games as they progressed across their first year of full time schooling. Second, we examine the degree to which facility with games forecasted boys' and girls' social competence and adjustment to school.

Occurrence of Games for Boys and Girls Across the School Year

Types of Games. Regarding the frequency of occurrence of individual types of games, we next examined the effects of gender and time on each of the three types of games observed from the combined focal and scan sampling data (chase, ball games, and verbal games) with a repeated measures ANOVA. The values of the dependent measures represent the mean frequencies of types of games observed in scan and focal child samples for each of the time periods across the year.

For chase, significant main effects were observed for both gender, $F(1, 72) = 4.77, p < .03$, and time, $F(2, 144) = 30.43, p < .0001$. Boys engaged in significantly more chase games than girls and there was a significant increase in chase from Time 3 to Time 2 to Time 1. The time × gender interaction was not significant. For ball games, significant main effects for gender, $F(1,72) = 16.04, p < .0001$, and time, $F(2,144) = 8.89, p < .0002$, were observed, as was a significant gender × time interaction, $F(2, 144) = 6.19, p < .002$; boys engaged in significantly more ball games than girls; more ball games were observed at Time 3 than at either Time 1 or Time 2, which were not significantly different from each other. The interaction clarified these main effects to the extent that the frequency of boys' ball games increased from Time 1 to Time 2 to Time 3, but girls' did not vary across time. Verbal games varied significantly by gender, $F(1,77) = 13.60$, $p < .0001$; girls exhibited significantly more verbal games than boys. The time × gender interaction was not significant.

Variety of Games. For variety of games, analyzed with a repeated measures ANOVA, significant main effects were observed for gender, $F(1, 69) = 6.14, p < .01$, and time, $F(2,138) = 2.97, p < .05$. Boys exhibited a more varied repertoire of games than did girls. In terms of time, the greatest variety of games was observed during Times 2 and 3, relative to Time 1; there was no difference between Times 2 and 3. The time × gender interaction was not significant.

Descriptions of Games by Ethnic Group. Inspection of data for variation in total games and types of games observed by ethnic groups and time suggested that ethnicity was not implicated in variation of total games, chase games, ball games, or verbal games.

Game Facility as a Predictor of Social Competence and School Adjustment

Facility with games, or game leadership, was defined using a variety of measures: Peer nominations (being good at games and sports) and adult ratings from the Teacher Checklist (good in games and sports). Both measures were administered during the late fall/winter of the school year. We also included behavioral observations (using the relative frequency of children's engagement in total games and the average size of their playgroups during games across the first two thirds of the year). These measures were standardized and aggregated as the measure of game facility. The behavioral measures for total games and group size at Time 1 (September–November) and Time 2 (December–February) were each aggregated as they were significantly intercorrelated, respectively, $r = .33$, $p < .002$, and $r = .61$, $p < .0001$.

Social competence for this age group was defined in terms of popularity (like-most nominations) and reciprocated friendships nominations. These measures were administered in the fall (and used as a control for stability of social competence) and spring (used as the criterion variable) of the year; these scores were standardized and aggregated. The intercorrelations between these measures in the fall were, $r = .70$, $p < .0001$, and in the spring were, $r = .80$, $p < .0001$.

In light of the consistent and robust gender differences on total games, types of games, and variety of games reported above we adopted the following analytic strategy in game leadership predicting social competence and adjustment to school. First, we tested separate models for boys and girls. In each case, models were tested using hierarchic regression procedures. Control variables were entered first, followed by the game leadership variable. The control variable for the model predicting end of year social competence was beginning of the year social competence and the control variable for school adjustment model was beginning of the year school adjustment. Second, we tested for gender differences within each of the criterion variables by testing the difference in the regression planes across gender.

We tested separate models for boys' and girls' game leadership predicting end of the year social competence and school adjustment. Beginning with social competence we see that game leadership did not predict girls' social competence but did predict boys' social competence. For school adjustment, game leadership did not predict girls' adjustment, but did predict boys' adjustment, though the girls' model was approaching significance with a p-value of .08.

Next, we test for gender differences within social competence and within school adjustment, by fitting regression models with boys' and girls' data combined. Model 1 contains only the control and game leadership variables as in the previous analyses. Each of the models was significant, and the incremental change in R^2 from Model 1 to Model 2, $R^2 = .06$, $F = 12.22$, $p < .0008$, was significant. That the G × GL1 interaction was significant indicates that game leadership was more important in predicting boys' social competence, relative to girls' social competence.

Next, we tested for gender differences between the boys' and girls' models of game leadership predicting adjustment to school. Each of the models was significant, but the incremental change in R^2 from Model 1 to Model 2 was not significant, $R^2 = .02$, $F = 1.76$, $p < 0.18$, indicating no gender difference in games predicting school adjustment.

SOME THINGS TO THINK ABOUT

1. Go to a preschool playground. Do you see children playing games?

What sorts?

How many different roles is it possible for each child to enact? For example, as in the case of "chase," can he/she only chase or be chased? Or can, as in the case of basketball, he/she, shoot the ball, dribble, or pass it?

2. Go to an elementary school playground. Do the same as above.

Do you see children playing games?

What sorts?

How many different roles is it possible for each child to enact? For example, as in the case of "chase," can he/she only chase or be chased? Or can, as in the case of basketball, he/she, shoot the ball, dribble, or pass it?

3. Are the same kids who are leaders in one game also leaders in others?

Why is it?

What is it that they do that makes them seem like leaders?

Are these games leadership skills in any way related to skills needed in school?

In what ways?

4. For a moment, let's suppose that you're a teacher. You have a young child who is very good at games and popular with his peers on the playground. Unfortunately, this child does not seem to be very interested in the traditional school subjects, such as math, reading, and language arts. List five strategies that might engage that child in the classroom. A hint—Try to link his/her skills at motivation for games to traditional academic subjects.

1.

2.

3.

4.

5.

Chapter 8

The Role of Recess
in Children's Cognitive Performance
in Classrooms

In this chapter, I cut to the chase. After all is said and done, the role of recess will probably be judged, for better or worse, on its influence on children's academic achievement—children's scores on measures of reading and mathematics, most likely. The role of children's performance on tests is *the* currency by which schools, teachers, principals, and children are judged. Scores are posted in local newspapers so that families can decide the best school to send their children. In Minneapolis, school test scores are included in packets sent by realtors to potential home buyers. Quality of schools—as indicated by test scores—is an important dimension of location, location, location. Additionally, test scores of Twin Cities schools are published in the Minneapolis *Star Tribune*.

I have argued that using any one indicator of children's competence, whether that measure be a test score or a teacher-rating of a child, is bound to be less valid than a composite of many indicators. This does not, however, mean that I think that schools should relinquish responsibility for nurturing children's academic progress. Granted, there are numerous factors influencing children's achievement in school, including socioeconomic status and parental socialization practices; but schools and their practices must be included in that equation and ultimately held accountable for results.

For that reason, I address head-on the role of recess in children's cognitive performance. If recess does indeed interfere with children's learning, then it should be minimized. Correspondingly, if it facilitates learning and achievement, it should be supported and possibly expanded.

WHAT IS "COGNITIVE PERFORMANCE"?

A primary business of schooling is teaching children skills and strategies associated with literacy, mathematics, and science. These goals are not too far from the traditional holy trinity of schooling—reading, writing, and 'rithmetic. I use the term *cognitive performance* as an umbrella term to cover those skills and strategies associated with school-based learning. From this view, cognitive performance does indeed include performance on standardized tests.

I refer to these measures of performance as *distal* measures because they are somewhat distant from the direct impact of classroom behaviors associated with recess. That is, performance on tests usually represents the culmination of many different processes and forces in children's environments. For example, children's socioeconomic status influences their performance on reading achievement to the extent that presence of books in the home as well as the availability and willingness of adults to read to children all influence these scores, indirectly.

Cognitive performance also includes more *proximal*, or immediate, cognitive processes, such as attention to classroom tasks. By "proximal" I mean more direct and immediate processes that relate to school performance. As I suggested in earlier chapters, recess may maximize children's attention to tasks directly following recess because children's efforts are distributed across a longer time span rather than massed into one longer time period. Attention to tasks should result in more efficient and more accurate learning of the tasks being taught at that time, thus, the proximal nature of this measure. These proximal measures, of course, then relate to the more distal measures: Attention to numerous tasks across time should, cumulatively, result in better test performance. As we know from years of research dating back to the 19th century (Ebinghaus, 1885/1964), distributing practice maximizes cognitive performance across the life span and indeed across numerous species.

For young children, a specific form of break from cognitively demanding tasks may be especially effective in maximizing cognitive performance. As I noted in the introductory chapters, my orientation, developed with Dave Bjorklund (Pellegrini & Bjorklund, 1996, 1997), holds that playful break times may be especially important in maximizing performance to the extent that they reduce the cognitive interference acquired in earlier instruction (Bjorklund & Harnishfeger, 1990).

In the next section of this chapter, I address the ways in which these specific aspects of unstructured peer interaction at recess relate to one aspect of kindergarten and first-grade children's cognitive performance— performance on a standardized achievement test.

THE ROLE OF RECESS IN COGNITIVE PERFORMANCE: DISTAL MEASURES

In this section, I explore the relations between playful, often social, interaction typical of children's recess behavior and traditional measures of cognition. Specifically, I present longitudinal data on the relations between kindergarten children's social behavior on the playground and measures of the peer relations and first-grade achievement.

Furthermore, I explore the idea of the playground as a context for assessment that was introduced in the preceding chapters. Recall, I argued that the playground may provide an interesting assessment venue for young children because it is cognitively and socially very demanding while at the same time very motivating for children. This combination should lead to children exhibiting higher levels of competence than on traditional achievement tests.

I was guided in this area by earlier work I conducted that showed that specific types of oral language preschoolers use with their peers accurately predicted their early literacy status (Pellegrini & Galda, 1998). That is, I believed that the competence used in social interaction with peers was related to skills and strategies tapped by traditional achievement tests. Such qualitative transformations in cognition typically occur when children are 5 to 7 years of age (Kagan, 1971; White, 1966). The kindergarten to first grade transition is a period during which relations between social interaction and cognition may be observed.

The specific types of social interaction on the playground that I examined in my research were: peer interaction, adult-directed behavior, and object play. A number of studies have demonstrated that, when given free choice in a play environment, children who choose to interact with peers are more sophisticated, on a number of social-cognitive measures, than children who choose to interact with adults (e.g., Harper & Huie, 1985; Wright, 1980). These findings are consistent with Piagetian (1983) theory, which suggests that the disequilibration characteristic of peer interaction facilitates development, whereas the typically unilateral interaction characteristic of adult–child interaction inhibits development. That is, and as discussed in chapter 1, when children interact with peers, relative to adults, they are more likely to disagree with each other. When peers disagree, they are confronted with points of view other than their own. If they want interaction to continue, which they usually do, they must incorporate (or accommodate, to use Piaget's term) their peers' points of view into a compromised form of interaction. In short, to engage in sustained social interaction with peers requires a fair amount of social (e.g., cooperation, perspective taking) and cognitive (e.g., ability to communicate clearly) skill. By comparison, when interacting with an adult, the adult will often take over some of this difficult work if the child is having problems (Pellegrini, 1984; Vygotsky, 1978). Furthermore, children do not tend to question adults as they are typically socialized not to challenge grown-ups.

As I have argued throughout this book, the playground should be a particularly good place to study this phenomenon because when young children are put into enjoyable environments with their peers, like playgrounds, they typically exhibit high levels of competence (Waters & Sroufe, 1983; Wright, 1980). Consequently, observations in such a highly motivating context should maximize children's exhibition of competence. As noted in preceding chapters, such playful contexts typically provide an important motivational component in children's learning.

Correspondingly, placing children in such highly motivating, natural situations is also important from an assessment perspective. It may be that the often described difference between children's competence as measured in standardized testing situations and their competence measured in playful situations is because of different levels of motivation to exhibit competence. In the former situation, youngsters may see little reason to achieve while in the latter children typically enjoy interacting with peers, and thus are motivated to do the difficult social cognitive work necessary to sustain interaction (Pellegrini, 1982).

I was particularly interested in examining the kindergarten to first grade transition because this is a period in children's development when social interaction and play may be particularly important. As noted above, qualitative changes in children's development characterize this period. Further, and from a policy perspective, the research for this chapter was conceptualized in reaction to a law in the state of Georgia (where I lived at the time) requiring kindergarten children to pass a standardized paper-and-pencil test in order to be promoted to first grade.

My intent was to show, once again, that standardized achievement and aptitude measures alone have limited explanatory and predictive power for young children. Ed Zigler and Penelope Trickett (1978) made this point a number of years ago in service of a similar cause, that is, to argue against overreliance on standardized measures of cognition, such as IQ tests, in favor of measures of social competence, to assess the impact of early intervention programs, like Head Start. I also hoped to use these analyses to show legislators and people in the state departments of education, like Georgia, that their view of children and ways in which to study them is much too limited.

The methods I used to collect the data used in this section are presented in the appendix, under the heading "Kindergarten to First Grade."

HOW WELL DOES KINDERGARTNERS' PLAYGROUND BEHAVIOR PREDICT END-OF-FIRST-GRADE ACHIEVEMENT?

This section presents the results of a 2-year longitudinal study I conducted in a public school in Athens, Georgia (Pellegrini, 1992). The school catered to a wide variety of children, from very poor to very affluent. There was also a racial mix of children from different economic circumstances. In this study, I observed the same children (at least once per week) across two years on the school playground during their recess periods. I also had information on their standardized, academic achievement test performance. This sort of study, where the same children are followed across a sustained time period, is known as a longitudinal study. The Metropolitan Readiness Test (MRT; Nurss & McGauvran, 1976) was used to assess the general knowledge and early reading and math concepts of the kindergarten children. The measure of academic achievement for first graders was the Georgia Criterion-Referenced Test (GCRT), also a test of general knowledge and early literacy and numeracy concepts.

Here, I demonstrate that what children do on the playground as kindergarteners is a valid predictor of their first-grade academic achievement, as measured by the GCRT while taking their kindergarten achievement into consideration. What this means, without going into the details of the statistical analyses (which are presented in the appendix at the end of this chapter) is that I was able to statistically equalize children's kindergarten academic achievement and use only how their playground behavior predicted first-grade achievement. The measures of playground behavior that I used included: object play, peer interaction, and adult-directed behavior.

The results, first of all, suggest that the kindergarten Metropolitan Readiness Test did indeed predict first-grade academic achievement. However, and most important for our discussion of the point of recess, the behavioral measures collected while children were on the playground at recess were even more predictive of first-grade achievement, even after kindergarten achievement was considered! The important point here is that what kids do on the playground accounts for a statistically significant, and unique, portion of the variation (40%) beyond what standardized tests tell us.

It was interesting that kindergarten achievement as measured by the Metropolitan Achievement Test, while a significant predictor, left much of the first graders' achievement unexplained. Again, this finding supports the criticisms of Zigler and Trickett (1978) that standardized measures of children's cognition have limited predictive value. Substantially more variance in first-grade achievement is accounted for when children's behavior in a naturalistic and motivating environment is considered.

I caution, further, that test scores, though limited in their predictive powers, should not be totally disregarded as they accounted for a statistically significant portion of the variance in first-grade achievement. This "throwing the baby out with the bath water" would limit our understanding of a very complex phenomenon, school achievement.

Another important aspect of the results relates to the developmental nature of the findings. During this period of developmental flux (Kagan, 1971; White, 1966), aspects of children's object play and peer relationships predicted more traditional aspects of school achievement. To illustrate, the object play measure was a positive predictor of achievement. This was a measure of children manipulating sticks, logs, and stones on the playground. It should not be surprising that the cognitive demands of such manipulative play should predict performance on a test with a mathematical thinking component; indeed, object play was a positive, significant predictor of performance on the math portion of the GCRT.

Such a relation between object manipulation and early numeracy is certainly consistent with Piagetian (1983) and the curricular advice of Constance Kamii and Rheta DeVries (1978). Both suggest that logico-mathematical thought has its developmental roots in object manipulation.

Caution must be exercised, however, when interpreting such a correlation. Specifically, just because two things are intercorrelated does not mean that one causes the other. For example, it could be that children's logico-mathematical thought caused them to play with objects, not vice versa. Clearly, more research is needed before we invest too much confidence in these findings. For example, observers might attend more closely to what children actually say and do during object play. That this level of analysis was not included in the present study is clearly a limitation.

Further, peer interaction was positively related to achievement, while adult-directed behavior was negatively related to achievement. That is, children who interacted more with peers at recess tended to score higher on the GCRT than children who interacted less with their peers. In contrast, children who were involved in high levels of adult-directed behavior at recess tended to score *lower* on these achievement tests than children who interacted less with adults. Children who chose to initiate contact with adults in a play arena, rather than peers, may have lacked the social skills to interact with their peers. It has been shown in the social-competence literature that when young children choose to interact with teachers, compared with peers, in play-oriented contexts, teachers do most of the work of maintaining interaction (Harper & Huie, 1985; Wright, 1980). In comparison, when children interact with peers, they must use their own social competence to initiate and sustain interaction (Dodge et al., 1986).

In this situation, more than 100 children were on the playground with three to five adult supervisors. Clearly, the role of the adults here was custodial, not educational. Thus, with such low-quality adult-child inter-action, it is not surprising that a negative relation between adult direction of interaction and achievement was detected. When children and adults were together, compared with when children were with peers, children were passive.

More specifically, when we observed children with adults, the adults were more likely to be talking than children. Thus, when children and adults were together on the playground, adults talked and children listened. On the other hand, when children were in the presence of peers, their likelihood of talking, compared with not talking, was beyond chance. It is important to note that the amount of peer talk was positively related to achievement (i.e., the more one talked the higher the achievement), while not talking was negatively related to achievement (i.e., the more frequently we observed children being silent, the lower their achievement). Although neither correlation was significant, each was in the predicted direction to suggest that social interaction is positively related to achievement while passivity is negatively related to achievement. In short, the nature of the recess period may have constrained the adult–child relationship. In other, more conducive settings, such as small-group teaching sessions, the relation between adult-directed behavior and achievement may be positive.

This interpretation of the varying role of adults in children's cognition in different contexts is consistent with extant research. For example, in free-play situations adults generally inhibit older preschool children's exhibition of complex forms of play, whereas peers facilitate it (e.g., Pellegrini, 1984). However, in a small-group teaching context, such as planning an errand or a classification task, adults are much more effective tutors than are peers (Tudge & Rogoff, 1989).[1]

These results also have important policy implications. Predicting children's achievement is a very difficult enterprise. Use single measures, such as standardized tests, limits our understanding of a very complex process. Even when tests are reliable predictors of achievement for older children, they often are not reliable for young children (see Messick, 1983). The picture they draw is limited; the variance accounted for, though statistically significant, is limited.

THE ROLE OF RECESS IN COGNITIVE PERFORMANCE: PROXIMAL MEASURES

In this section, I address more proximal effects of recess on children's cognitive performance. By this I mean the processes that are probably more directly responsible for the increases in cognitive performance. I

---

[1] While these results are consistent with both Piagetian (1983) theories and theories stressing the social origins of intelligence (e.g., Humphrey, 1976), they are counter to the research of Entwisle and colleagues (Entwisle et al., 1987), who minimized the predictive value of kindergarten social experiences. This inconsistency may be due to the different ways in which social data were collected in the two studies. In the present study, direct observations of social behavior were made in a context that elicited social competence. In the Entwisle et al. (1987) study, teacher ratings of children's social competence were used. These different data sources often do not converge (Cairns & Cairns, 1988; Smith & Connolly, 1980). This discordance may be due to the fact that teacher-rating scales tend to identify individual differences among children and children's relative status to their peers, while behavioral measures identify skills, regardless of children's relative status (Cairns & Cairns, 1988). That our first grade achievement measure assessed individuals' accumulated skills (i.e., mastery of subject matter), not relative standing (i.e., mastery in relation to peer), may be responsible for the predictive power of the behavioral measures in our regression results.

have chosen children's attention to classroom tasks as a proximal measure of cognitive performance because it provides direct, and relatively easy to measure, insight into children's motivation for and attention to the work they are expected to complete.

Furthermore, attention is a measure that is consistent with theories suggesting that breaks from work should maximize performance. Following the notion of massed versus distributed practice (Ebinghaus, 1885/1964), children are less attentive to classroom tasks during longer, compared with shorter, seat-work periods (e.g., Stevenson & Lee, 1990). Children are more physically active and socially interactive on the playground after longer, compared to shorter, confinement periods (e.g., Smith & Hagen, 1980). These breaks and behaviors, in turn, may have implications for children's behavior when they return to the classroom after recess (e.g., Hart, 1993), as well as more distal academic and social cognitive development as I have demonstrated in the previous section.

In this section, I summarize my research into the ways in which recess timing affects children's behavior on the school playground at recess as well as their attention to school tasks before and after recess (Pellegrini & Davis, 1993; Pellegrini et al., 1995). By recess timing, I mean the amount of time before recess that children are forced to be sedentary (or are deprived of social and physical play) and attend to class work. This type of regimen typifies most primary school classrooms (Minuchin & Shapiro, 1983). My studies reported in this chapter involved children in a primary school in Athens, Georgia. I worked with one of my PhD graduate students (Patti Davis Huberty), who was also a teacher there, and some of her colleagues. They allowed me, as I will discuss later in this chapter, to manipulate the times that children went out for recess as well as what they did in their classrooms before and after recess. But before I go into that detail, some theoretical background is necessary in order to understand fully the importance of "depriving" children of recess.

Play deprivation theory (Burghardt, 1984, 1988; Fagen, 1981; Smith & Hagen, 1980) predicts that duration of the confinement period immediately before recess should result in a "rebound" (i.e., increased levels of those behaviors of which children were deprived). Post-deprivation activity "rebounds," as we discussed in earlier chapters, have been observed in the animal literature (with domestic goats *Capra hirus* [Chepko, 1971] and black-tailed deer *Odocoileus hemionus* [Müller-Schwarze & Müller-Schwarze, 1982]) and with small samples of British preschool (Smith & Hagen, 1980) and American primary school children (Pellegrini et al., 1995; Pellegrini & Davis, 1993).

The reasoning behind the play deprivation–rebound hypothesis is as follows. Childhood is a period during which social skills and cardiopulmonary functions are developed and exercised (Fagen, 1981; Smith & Hagen, 1980). Given opportunity, young children engage in social and physically vigorous behaviors that develop these functions (Fagen, 1981; Smith & Hagen, 1980). If deprived of these opportunities, they will later compensate, or "rebound," with increased levels of physical activity and social interaction when given the opportunity.

Extant research, and our earlier discussions of physical activity and gender segregation, suggests that children's gender and grade level may interact with deprivation effects on these behaviors. Boys are, generally, more physically active than girls; however, Peter Smith and Theresa Hagen (1980), in their study of British preschool children, found no gender effects on vigorous playground behavior suggesting that gender differences for this sort of physical activity may appear later during the primary school years. Consistent with this explanation, Patti Davis and I (1993) found gender differences in the vigorous play of a group of American third graders.

Following the Pellegrini and Davis (1993) experiment, Patti Davis, Ithel Jones, and I examined the extent to which short and long deprivation periods before recess affected the playground physical activity and social interaction of boys and girls across the primary school grades in three field experiments conducted in a public elementary school. While the full details of the method are presented in the appendix at the end of this chapter under the heading Recess Deprivation Studies, I very briefly present here what we did.

The children were all enrolled in a public elementary school in Athens, GA. While this was a different school than the one used in Pellegrini (1992), the demographics of the children were similar. They were from varied social economic and racial backgrounds. In all of the cases, the children in each of the grades were systematically exposed to different schedules for recess timing. On some days they went out to recess at 10 A.M. and on other days at 10:30 A.M. Before and after each recess period children were read a male-preferred or a female-preferred book. During this time we coded their attention to the task, we also observed and coded their recess behavior.

By experimentally manipulating recess timing and the tasks on which children worked, we could make inferences about the role of different types of recess timing during the school day on children's classroom attention. If, for example, children were less attentive after recess than before, there would be support for minimizing or eliminating recess. If, on the other hand, attention waned with durations between breaks and attention increased after recess, we could (indeed, *should*) argue that schools need more recess periods as part of their efforts to maximize cognitive performance.

My orientation in studying the role of recess timing in children's attention, and consistent with the literature in massed versus distributed practice, suggests that during the deprivation period, or that period immediately preceding recess, children's inattention to instructional tasks should increase as a function of duration of the deprivation period. Anecdotal evidence from Japan and Taiwan (Stevenson & Lee, 1990) suggest that children's attention to class work is maximized when instructional periods are relatively short, not long, and intense. Specifically, in these countries children are given a break every 50 minutes or so. When children came back from these breaks, they seemed more attentive and ready to work than before the breaks.

We also examined the relation between playground behavior and postrecess behavior in the classroom. This set of analyses addresses fairly directly the degree to which energy, or caloric expenditure at recess, relates to subsequent attention. Recall from our earlier discussions, one of the "folk" justifications for recess is that children get a chance to "blow off steam" during recess and after this is done, they can concentrate on school work. If this is the case, there should be a relation between physical activity at recess and attention to classroom activities after recess.

The one study to address directly this issue of recess activity and postrecess attention (Pellegrini & Davis, 1993) found the opposite: Boys' level of physical activity on the playground was related to postrecess *inattention*. That is, the level of activity observed at recess was negatively related to attention to a classroom task after recess. However, before accepting these findings at face value and assuming that recess causes children to be less focused in their studies, at least one alternative explanation for the results in this study is possible. These results may have been due to the fact that boys were less attentive because they worked on female-preferred tasks. Specifically, in the Pellegrini and Davis (1993) study, children's class work often involved listening to a story. Though we did not systematically monitor the stories read, it may be the case that some of the stories read were more preferred by girls, thus their attention may have been related to the task, not the effect of recess. For this reason, we systematically varied gender-preference of tasks before and after recess.

In Experiment 1 of this series of experiments (Pellegrini et al., 1995), we examined the effects of confinement duration on the playground behavior of boys and girls in Grades K, 2, and 4. The specifics of the study are listed in the appendix, but I briefly describe them here. There were approximately 20 children (about half males and half females) at each grade level. As in all experiments reported in this section, recess timing varied by 30 minutes. Children's attention (assessed by the looking at the book being read to them or at the teacher doing the reading) was assessed before and after recess on male-preferred and female-preferred books.

In Experiment 1, the prerecess results supported aspects research conducted in Asian schools (Stevenson & Lee, 1990), showing that children are less attentive during long, compared with short, work periods. That is, children were generally more attentive during the short deprivation period, relative to the long period, and older children were more attentive than younger children. For example, among fourth graders, children's mean inattention scores (a proportion of time not attending) were greater during the short deprivation time ($M = .49$), relative to the long deprivation time ($M = .67$). It should not be surprising that children are less attentive as the time they spend on a task increases. Nor should it be surprising that their attention to a school task increases with age.

The pre-recess results support earlier work suggesting that attention to school tasks increases with age (Wittrock, 1986). Further, we found that boys' and girls' attention to the book read to them was influenced by the sex-role stereotypicality of the story. For example, fourth-grade boys in the long confinement condition were less inattentive to male-preferred stories ($M = .60$) than to female-preferred stories ($M = .76$), while the pattern was reversed for the girls. For example, fourth grade girls were more inattentive to male tasks ($M = .73$) than to female tasks ($M = .62$). This finding is consistent with the extant literature on gender preference for stories (Monson & Sebesta, 1991).

Regarding the effects of deprivation on recess behavior, children (especially fourth graders) were more socially interactive on the playground after the long deprivation (30 minutes) condition, relative to the short condition. These results can be explained in terms of children rebounding from deprivation through some form of social interaction after a period of being deprived of that sort of interaction.

Regarding levels of physical activity, gender effects were observed on the physical activity measure at recess, replicating earlier studies of elementary school children's physical play at recess (Pellegrini & Davis, 1993), as well as the more general gender difference in activity (Eaton & Enns, 1986).

Results from this experiment should be interpreted cautiously, primarily because of the small sample size (20/grade and 10/sex within each grade) and because there was only one classroom at each grade level. Replication is clearly needed to assure that the results are not aberrational (Lykken, 1968). Replication is also needed to clarify the effect of condition on physical activity at recess; the results from this experiment were not consistent with the one other experiment involving primary school children. With these needs in mind, Experiments 2 and 3 were designed. (See appendix for methods and results.)

In Experiment 2, we used the same deprivation and attention procedures as in Experiment 1. In Experiment 2, 22 second graders and 15 fourth graders (one classroom for each grade) were studied in the same school as in Experiment 1. The results from Experiment 2, like those from Experiment 1, suggest that children's task inattention is affected by recess timing and that timing interacts with dimensions of the task as well as children's age and gender. Children generally, but especially second graders, were more attentive after recess (as measured earlier by the proportion of observations scored as attending or not attending), relative to before recess; a significant difference between pre-recess ($M = 5.66$) and post-recess ($M = 3.88$) was observed for second grade only, not for fourth grade ($M = 6.60$ and 6.20, respectively).

Correspondingly, duration of pre-recess class time affected children's level of social interaction at recess. By this I mean that children were more socially interactive on the playground following long versus short deprivation period. Children's recess behavior, especially boys, tended to be more social and physically active with age. Specific recess behavior was generally not related to post-recess task attention in either experiment. The behaviors that we coded on the playground, such as children's activity level and their social behavior, were not related to their post-recess attention to the classroom task. Again, and like Experiment 1, children exhibited higher levels of inattention before recess than after recess.

In Experiment 3 we studied two fourth-grade classrooms (approximately 20 children in each) and we used the same play deprivation paradigm with two groups of fourth graders; their recess, however, was indoors. (See appendix for methods and results.) We chose this specific design for a couple of reasons.

First, examining the effects of indoor recess on children's attention would provide insight into the role of a relatively sedentary break period on subsequent attention. Thus, these results should provide further evaluation of the blowing-off-steam hypothesis. If children's attention is greater after than before the indoor break, the role of physical activity would be minimal. What this means, of course, is that there does not seem to be a connection between physical activity (associated with "blowing off steam" and cognitive performance). This point, in turn, is relevant to those who advocate substituting physical education for recess. Their assumption is that cognitive performance *is* related to physical activity. In fact, it is not.

Second, and also from a policy perspective, educators sometimes use indoor recess as an alternative to outdoor breaks. Results from this experiment should provide insight into the efficacy of indoor breaks.

We conducted the same experiment with two separate intact classrooms. Such a design was chosen because of the relatively small samples involved in each classroom and because of the interdependence of social behavior within each classroom (Smith & Connolly, 1980). This procedure minimizes the probability of obtaining aberrational results. We can be confident in the results if they are obtained in both samples—thus replicating each other.

The results from this experiment are similar to those from other experiments: Boys ($M = 4.60$), as a measured on a 1–8 rating scale, were more active than girls ($M = 3.86$) and especially after being confined for longer periods. This finding supports the argument we made in the discussions of gender segregation that boys' higher level of activity, relative to girls, may be responsible for the two sexes playing in separate groups. Furthermore, there was no relation between physical activity at recess and post-recess attention. And importantly, attention increased in the post-recess period. In terms of differences in inattention to male- and female-preferred tasks in Experiments 2 and 3, effects were only observed in Experiment 2 where boys were less attentive to female-preferred tasks (second grade $M = .54$; fourth grade $M = .93$) than to male-preferred tasks (second grade $M = .21$; fourth grade $M = .54$). Note that the differences become greater with age, perhaps reflecting boys' increasing sensitivity to sex-role stereotyping with age.

CONCLUSION

One longitudinal study and three experiments were conducted to examine the extent to which recess was related to children's cognitive performance. Basically, children, but especially boys, exhibited signs of inattention as length of deprivation increased. In short, having recess boosts attention. Results from all experiments also implicated the gender-preference of the task in children's waning attention. Simply, and not surprising, children were more attentive to stories that were consistent with their own gender.

Probably most basic to the intent of this chapter, data from the experiments provides empirical support of anecdotal evidence from Taiwanese and Japanese schools and the massed versus distributed practice literature that in order to maintain high levels of attention, children need frequent breaks in the course of the day (Ebinghaus, 1885/1964; Stevenson & Lee, 1990; Stevenson, Stigler, Lucker, Lee, Hsu, & Kitamura, 1987; Toppino et al., 1991). In Japanese schools, primary school children typically have a 10–15 minute break every hour or so (Stevenson & Lee, 1990).

The recess data from all experiments indicate that rebounding from deprivation may involve children sampling varied and interesting stimuli. During class work, they are exposed to specific work for sustained periods. When given the opportunity at recess, they sample more varied environments. David Bjorklund and Brandi Green's (1992) cognitive immaturity hypothesis supports this phenomenon. They posit that children's cognitive immaturity, relative to adults, is characterized by a short attention span and a desire to play after concentrated periods of attention. Such breaks from demanding cognitive tasks may facilitate school learning. It seems to be the case that children's attention to classroom tasks does wane as the duration of the class work increases. This may be a reason for Japanese and Taiwanese primary schools including double the number of recess periods compared with American schools (Stevenson & Lee, 1990).

Children's behaviors at recess, however, did not relate significantly to their post-recess behavior. Future research should continue to examine this issue. It may be the case the recess behavior relates to classroom behavior differently, at various post-recess time intervals. For example, children may enter the classroom after recess in highly excited state; this actually may interfere with attention to sedentary tasks immediately after recess. Similarly, after 40–50 minutes, recess effects may wane. Again, such waning attention may be the reason behind Japanese and Taiwanese recess policies.

Finally, these experiments implicated gender-preference of classroom tasks in children's attention to those tasks. These findings have obvious importance for the design of subsequent studies and for school policy. Regarding the former, researchers must take care not to have gender-preferences for tasks confound their designs. Regarding policy, educators should be aware of the fact that children's ability to attend to tasks is related to a host of factors, ranging from ambient temperature to the sex-stereotypes of the activities. This is clearly important as educators make inferences about certain learning disabilities (Pellegrini & Horvat, 1995).

In short, the research presented in this chapter attempted to contextualize the recess period within the school day. Different school policy variables, such as the timing of recess, play an important role in the behavior that children exhibit on the playground. Given the reliability of the deprivation effects observed in the experiments reported here, it is time for schools to systematically study their recess policies. While it is common for schools, and politicians, to extol Asian educational practices, they should also consider Asian recess practices.

APPENDIX A

Pellegrini, A. D. (1992). Kindergarten children's social cognitive status as a predictor of first grade success. *Early Childhood Research Quarterly, 7,* 565–577.

KINDERGARTEN TO FIRST GRADE

METHOD

Subjects

All children attended a suburban public elementary school in Athens, GA. The kindergarten children, who were part of a larger study, participated in the study for 2 years. There were a total of 24 children (14 males and 10 females) who participated in the study for 2 years; they were 5 years of age ($M = 64$ months) at the beginning of the study.

Procedures

Children were observed on their school playground during the recess period from October to May for 2 years. Between 120 and 150 children (from four to five classes at one grade level) were on the playground during each period. There were three to five adults supervising the children.

Each child was observed at least 112 times each of the 2 years. Behaviors noted in the scan sampling included: *Peer interaction; Object play;* and *Adult directed behavior.*

Measures

Achievement.   Children's achievement was measured in kindergarten with the *Metropolitan Readiness Test* (MRT; Nurss & McGauvran, 1976). In first grade, achievement was measured with the *Georgia Criterion Reference Test* (GCRT). The GCRT test is a reliable (i.e., KR-20 of .92) and content-valid achievement test. For both the MRT and GCRT, the composite achievement and standardized scores were analyzed.

APPENDIX B

Pellegrini, A. D., Huberty, P. D., & Jones, I. (1995). The effects of recess timing on children's classroom and playground behavior. *American Educational Research Journal, 32,* 845–864.

RECESS DEPRIVATION STUDIES

METHOD

EXPERIMENT 1

Subjects

Similar to those described previously and from Grades K, 2, and 4.

Procedure

Four days per week (Monday through Thursday), the duration of children's pre-recess classroom work was manipulated in each of the three grades such that twice weekly children went to recess at 10:00 A.M. (short deprivation) and twice weekly they went to recess at 10:30 A.M. (long deprivation); order of deprivation was counterbalanced across days and grade levels. Additionally, on each day children in Grades 2 and 4 were presented with either a male-preferred or a female-preferred task immediately before recess (i.e., pre-recess) and immediately after recess (i.e., post-recess). Teachers in Grades 2 and 4 read children a male-preferred story before and after recess or a female-preferred story before and after recess. Gender preference was determined by the gender of the main character in the stories. Children were expected to sit quietly in their seats during this time.

Observational Methods

Each child was observed on each of the experimental days (Monday through Thursday) for 2 months during the prerecess, recess, and post-recess periods. Each of the three periods lasted 20 mins. A total of four observers, blind to the purposes of the study, were used; there were three regular observers and one rotating observer whose primary job was a reliability judge.

Observations for Data Collection. Observations followed scan sampling/instantaneous recording rules (Pellegrini, 2004) in each setting. Specifically, each child within a classroom was observed in each of the three periods (i.e., pre-recess, recess, and post-recess) on each observation day. Children were observed an average of 21 times in each of these periods. A different child's behavior was scored instantaneously every 30 seconds across each period.

Two sets of behavioral codes were used: For the indoor observations, inattention was coded. For outdoor behavior, physical activity and social interaction were coded.

Inattention was determined by the direction of the child's gaze (Pellegrini & Davis, 1993). Physical activity was coded along a 9-point ordinal scale developed by Eaton, Enns, and Presse (1987). Social interaction was defined as any instance where communication, verbal or nonverbal, was observed between children; thus, verbal interactions as well as reciprocated gazes were coded as social (Pellegrini & Davis, 1993).

RESULTS

Prerecess Analyses

For the kindergarten prerecess inattention measure, a significant main effect for condition was observed, $F(1,15) = 3.64, p < .03$, such that children were less attentive during the long, compared with the short, confinement period. The effect for gender approached significance, $F(1,15) = 2.49, p < .06$, with boys being less attentive than girls.

For the second and fourth grade pre-recess analyses on inattention, there was a statistically significant main effect for grade, $F(1,41) = 19.11$, $p < .0001$, but it was mediated by a significant condition × grade interaction, $F(1,41) = 4.35, p < .02$; for second graders there was no significant effect for confinement, but for fourth graders, children were less attentive during the long, compared with the short, confinement period.

A significant task × gender interaction, $F(1,41) = 4.86, p < .01$, was also observed; girls exhibited higher levels of inattention than boys in the male-preferred task.

Recess Analyses

Analyses of the recess data were conducted with a grade (3) × gender (2) × condition (2) repeated measures ANOVA, with the last factor being repeated. The dependent measures were physical activity and social interaction. Regarding the physical activity measure, main effects were observed for grade, $F(2,56) = 4.92, p < .0005$, and gender, $F(1,56) = 10.26$, $p < .0001$. Post hoc analyses revealed that fourth graders were significantly more active than other children and boys were more active than girls. For the social interaction category, main effects were observed for grade, $F(2,56) = 18.03, p < .0001$, and condition, $F(1,56) = 44.88, p < .0001$. Additionally, a significant grade × condition interaction was observed, $F(2,56) = 7.30, p < .0001$; within the long confinement condition, fourth graders were significantly more social than were second graders.

Post-Recess Analyses

The post-recess analyses involved correlating recess behaviors with classroom inattention to seat work after recess. Correlation coefficients were calculated between the recess physical activity and social interaction scores and the post-recess inattention measure across the three grade levels; the correlations were not statistically significant (respectively, $r = .05$ and $.01$, N = 62).

To test the massed versus distributed practice hypothesis, we measured the difference between inattention to tasks before and after recess with a 2 (grade) × 2 (pre-recess/post-recess) repeated measures ANOVA. Significant effects for grade, $F(2,32) = 14.47, p < .0001$, and difference between pre-recess and post-recess attention were observed, $F(1,32) = 33.70, p < .0001$, but these were moderated by a grade × difference interaction, $F(1,32) = 13.19, p < .0001$. Inattention to task was also significantly greater before recess than after recess at Grades 2 ($M = 14.83$ and 6.44, respectively) and 4 ($M = 9.15$ and 7.45, respectively) but not for kindergarten ($M = 4.3$ and 3.5). Post-recess analyses suggest that providing a break from seat work maximizes attention. Behavior during the break period, however, was not implicated in post-recess attention.

EXPERIMENT 2

Experiment 2 was designed as a literal replication (Lykken, 1968) of Experiment 1. We attempted to replicate the deprivation effects on Grades 2 and 4 children's pre-recess inattention to classroom tasks and deprivation effects on recess behavior. This study was conducted in the winter, one year after Experiment 1.

METHOD

Subjects and Procedures

The children in this experiment attended the same school as those in Experiment 1. The sample consisted of 22 second graders and 15 fourth graders. As in Experiment 1, children's recess period was manipulated four times weekly, Monday through Thursday.

Scan sampling, instantaneous recording rules were followed for pre-recess, recess, and post-recess periods. Individual children in the class were observed at 30-second time intervals during the recess, pre-recess, and post-recess periods daily. Each child was observed in counterbalanced order such that he/she was observed (on the average of 19 times) in each of the 30-second intervals in each of these periods. The behavioral measures utilized in Experiment 1 were also used in Experiment 2 for the three periods.

RESULTS

Pre-Recess Analyses

The pre-recess analyses tested the effects of grade (2), gender (2), condition (2), and task (2) on children's inattention to a task with a repeated measures ANOVA, where the last two factors were within-subjects variables.

Significant main effects for grade, $F(1,33) = 5.86, p < .01$, and task were observed, $F(1,33) = 4.20, p < .02$. Grade, however, interacted with condition and gender, $F(1,33) = 2.66, p < .05$, such that fourth grade boys', not girls', inattention scores were higher in the long, compared to the short, condition. Grade and condition also interacted with task, $F(1,33) = 18.27$, $p < .0001$, indicating that the female-, compared with the male-, preferred task elicited higher levels of inattention except for fourth graders in the long confinement condition.

Recess Analyses

The next series of analyses examined the effects of grade (2) × gender (2) × condition (2) on children's physical activity and social interaction at recess. Separate repeated measures ANOVA were calculated for each of the dependent measures; the last factor was a within-subjects variable. For the physical activity measure, grade, $F(19,33) = 49.19$, $p < .0001$, and condition effects were observed, $F(1,33) = 3.21$, $p < .04$. Fourth graders were more physically active than second graders and children after the long, compared with the short, periods were more physically active. Regarding social interaction, grade, $F(1,33) = 7.93$, $p < .0001$, and condition, $F(1,33) = 12.30$, $p < .0001$, again, had significant main effects. Social interaction increased with grade level and with length of previous class work periods. Grade, however, interacted with gender and condition, $F(1,33) = 3.68$ $p < .03$. Social interaction increased across grade for boys in the long, not short, condition; for girls, too, the grade-related increase was only observed after the long condition.

Post-Recess Analyses

Post-recess analyses involved correlating post-recess task inattention scores to levels of recess social interaction and physical activity. The relation between physical activity was not significant while the relation between social interaction and inattention was positive and significant, $r = .39$, $p < .005$ ($N = 37$). The difference between pre-recess and post-recess inattention was examined at each grade level with a repeated measures ANOVA. A significant difference, $F(1,15) = 3.35$, $p < .04$, between pre-recess ($M = 5.66$) and post-recess ($M = 3.88$) was observed for second grade only, not for fourth grade ($M = 6.60$ and 6.20, respectively).

EXPERIMENT 3

METHOD

Subjects and Procedures

Children in this experiment were drawn from two fourth-grade classrooms in the same school as children in Experiments 1 and 2. In Classroom 1, there were 10 boys and 11 girls, and in Classroom 2, there were 7 boys and 16 girls. The average age of the children was 10.1 years.

Exact procedures were followed in each classroom. Children's recess period was manipulated four times weekly, Monday through Thursday. Recess periods were held at either 10:00 A.M. or 10:30 A.M. in counterbalanced order for the entire experimental period. Children's recess periods, however, were held indoors; the average room temperature was 69°F.

During this 20-minute recess period children could move freely around the room and interact socially with peers. Observations were conducted as in Experiments 1 and 2. Physical activity and social interaction, as in Experiments 1 and 2, were coded; additionally, the variety of physical locations in the classroom sampled by each child during the entire 30-second period was scored. The variety of location measure was derived by dividing the classrooms into six equal space units. The unit of analysis was the average number of locations visited/observation period.

RESULTS

Recess Analyses

First, regarding the effects of gender and condition on physical activity for Classroom 1 a significant effect for gender was observed, $F(1,19) = 3.83$, $p < .03$, with boys being more active than girls. Gender, however, interacted significantly with condition, $F(1,19) = 3.86$, $p < .03$, such that boys were more active than girls after the long period. Regarding Classroom 2, main effects were observed for gender, $F(1,21) = 2.82$, $p < .05$, such that boys were more active than girls, and condition, $F(1,21) = 4.96$, $p < .01$: children were more active after the long condition. Thus, in both experiments children's physical activity was greater after long confinement and boys were more active than girls.

For the social interaction measure no effects were observed in either Classroom 1 or 2. Regarding the variety of locations measure in Classroom 1, a main effect for condition was observed, $F(1,19) = 9.54$, $p < .003$, with more locations being visited after the long confinement period. In Classroom 2, main effects for gender, $F(1,21) = 3.23$, $p < .04$, and condition, $F(1,21) = 9.06$, $p < .003$, were observed with more locations being visited by boys and after long confinement. Condition effects on location were thus replicated in this experiment.

The relations between recess behaviors (i.e., physical activity, social interaction, and locations visited) and post-recess inattention were assessed. No significant correlations were observed in either classroom. Lastly, separate repeated measures ANOVAs were calculated for differences between pre-recess and post-recess inattention. A significant effect was observed for Classroom 1, $F(1,19) = 3.66$, where inattention was higher before recess ($M = 6.65$) than after recess ($M = 5.40$). The effect for Classroom 2 was not significant, $F(1,21) = 2.42$, $p < .06$, although it was in the hypothesized direction; pre-recess inattention ($M = 6.39$) was higher than post-recess inattention ($M = 5.5$).

SOME THINGS TO THINK ABOUT

If you are a parent or a caregiver of children, schedule two sets of time for them to complete a puzzle. In one case have them work for 20-minute intervals and then give them a break. In another case have them work 30 minutes and then give them breaks.

Observe them and enter behaviors in each category.

	Fidgets/Looks Away	Talks to You	Gets up
20-Min Recess			
30-Min Recess			

Now let's try changing the actual break time and see how that effects kids' behavior on their break.

If you are a parent or a caregiver of children, schedule two sets of time for them to complete a puzzle. In one case have them work for 20 minute intervals and then give them a break. In another case have them work 30 minutes and then give them breaks.

Observe them and enter behaviors in each category.

	Runs	Walks	Peer Interaction	Bored	Talks to Adult
20-Min Recess					
30-Min Recess					

Chapter 9

Summing Up:
What Are the Implications of Recess
for Children in School?

In this chapter, I integrate some of the theory and research discussed throughout the book with a specific eye on implications for educational policy. A common mantra in this book has been that policy and educational practice should follow the best theory and empirical evidence available to us. To this end, I have presented my arguments for the role of recess in schools in the context of theory and research findings. Here, I touch upon what I see as some of the central issues to be addressed.

First, I discuss the role of recess in relation to a very current and visible classroom issue: The current debate surrounding Attention Deficit/Hyperactive Disorder (ADHD). I chose the case of ADHD because I think its overdiagnosis may represent children being subjected to too many sustained hours of concentrated work. I argue that providing children with more breaks in the course of their school days may reduce ADHD symptoms among children, especially among boys.

Second, and very briefly, I discuss the role of recess in helping to address what has been recently labeled a national obesity epidemic. Obesity is particularly problematic in childhood, and providing opportunities for self-initiated exercise at recess may help.

And finally, I make some suggestions for ways in which parents, teachers, students, and other stakeholders in the educational enterprise can document the effectiveness (or ineffectiveness) of recess. These data should guide school policy and how resources are allocated.

CAN RECESS PERIODS MODERATE BEHAVIORS ASSOCIATED WITH ADHD DIAGNOSES?

Childhood ADHD is a significant educational and public health problem because of its prevalence—about 4% of the primary school population are believed to suffer from some form of ADHD. Of these, more than 80% are boys (Barkley, Dupaul, & McMurray, 1990; Nigg, 1993). Additionally, ADHD has a sustained effect on children's school and more general societal functioning (Klein & Mannuzza, 1991). Children classified as ADHD seem to have social and academic difficulties very soon after they enter the primary grades. They are impulsive and have difficulty sitting still, attending to sedentary tasks, and working cooperatively with peers (Cunningham & Siegal, 1987). Thus, it is imperative for both individual and societal reasons to explicate the limitations and strengths of the ADHD construct and to examine the degree to which some school conditions may actually exacerbate the problem. In keeping with our earlier discussions of the role of recess in maximizing children's attention to demanding classroom tasks, I suggest that providing frequent breaks during periods of prolonged and intense work will maximize attention and reduce behavioral symptoms associated with ADHD.

WHAT IS ADHD AND HOW IS IT PRESENTED IN THE CLASSROOM?

At face level, ADHD is comprised of two seemingly related factors: high levels of physical activity and low levels of attention. By physical activity, I mean the intensity level, frequency, and duration of small motor behavior, such as fidgeting, ticks, tapping of feet and hands, and locomotion. In other words: Not being able to sit still. Younger, compared with older, primary school children more frequently exhibit high activity symptoms.

Attention is often defined as engagement on specific tasks and can be measured by the degree to which children maintain their gaze on the immediate task at hand. These two dimensions of children's classroom behavior, activity and attention, are reliable indicators of school achievement and social competence (Whalen, 1983): children with high, compared with low, physical activity levels typically are low achievers and more frequently experience social problems, such as peer rejection. Inattention to academic tasks has an obvious, negative impact on learning.

While exhibition of either high physical activity or low attention is problematic in terms of adaptation to school, they are particularly problematical when children exhibit a combination of the two; indeed they form the core of the *Diagnostic and Statistical Manual of Mental Disorders* (DSM) definition of ADHD. ADHD, though controversial in terms of definition (Lerner & Lowenthal, 1994), is currently conceptualized as two empirically distinct constructs, composed of inattention and hyperactivity-impulsivity (Bauermeister, Alegria, Bird, Rubio-Stipec, & Canino, 1992).

The incidence of ADHD-related behavior and diagnosis are relatively low in preschool and kindergarten, increasing significantly in first grade and remain relatively stable thereafter. In order to be diagnosed as ADHD, symptoms must be observed in different situations (usually home and school) and must appear early in children's primary school careers (by age 7). Even though many ADHD children (40%) are within the normal IQ range, most children who exhibit ADHD-related behaviors are at-risk for school failure, because dysfunctions are occurring at a crucial time in their development and school careers. Further, ADHD often results in children having difficulty in peer relations, resulting in them associating with other children disaffected from school, eventually leading to school dropout (Coie & Dodge, 1998). It is not surprising that these children have difficulty with peer relations, as they are probably not fun to be with. They can't sustain attention and interaction around social tasks, such as games, that kids enjoy and they often pester their peers by poking, interrupting, and talking nonstop.

Importantly, negative early school experiences have a negative *cumulative* effect on subsequent functioning (Walberg & Tsai, 1983). A significant number of ADHD-diagnosed children experience numerous problems in school, from low achievement in reading and other academic areas, to learning disabilities (e.g., Stanford & Hynd, 1994), to conduct-related problems, such as juvenile delinquency (Loeber, 1990; Rutter & Garmezy, 1983, p. 817; Whalen, 1983). The diversity in school-related problems (and by implication, diversity in definitions for ADHD) associated with ADHD resulted in the U.S. Department of Education issuing a 1991 policy memorandum stating that ADHD children could be served under one of the following disability categories: learning disability, emotional disturbance, or other health impaired.

The history of the definition of the syndrome is helpful in gaining insight into its etiology. The definition of ADHD has been in a state of flux almost since its inception. ADHD has its roots in Attention Deficit Disorder (ADD), which was first recognized in the 1960s as an extension of Minimal Brain Disfunction (MBD). Then, as now, inattention and impulsivity are thought to be the result of biology, more specifically, "gene inheritance" (Dykman, Ackerman, & Raney, 1993, p. 7). This complex set of behaviors is conceptualized in an "executive summary of research syntheses" for the U.S. Department of Education as a genetic expression, with minimal environmental mediation. Thus, the definition of ADHD is a unidirectional model of adaptation where ADHD is organic and resides primarily within the child. From this view, children's failure to adapt to school is a direct result of their biological condition. I have argued earlier in this book against the simplistic dichotomizing of biology and experience, and this is equally true for understanding a "medical problem" such as ADHD as it is for understanding patterns of children's play.

It should also be noted that diagnostic rates of ADHD in the USA are considerably higher than in other similar countries, such as the UK (British Psychological Society, 2000). This finding presents an interesting comparative case where two relatively similar societies (similar in terms of demographics) have very different rates of diagnosed ADHD. One interpretation of this comparison is that US children are overdiagnosed. Correspondingly, it also provides some insight into the organic bases of ADHD. If the syndrome was primarily due to inheritance or individual constitutional differences, we would expect (other things being equal— such as levels of diagnosis) similar rates of ADHD in both countries. That this is not the case suggests that cultural differences are due to the differences in the way schooling is organized.

The view that I have advanced and discussed earlier and in more depth, has its roots in evolutionary biology and ethology (e.g., Gottlieb, 1983, 1998; Hinde, 1982), and has more recently been extended to programmatic examinations of children and adolescents in family and school contexts (Bjorklund & Pellegrini, 2002; Lerner, 1978, 1984, 1989; Pellegrini & Long, 2003). This view posits a transactional, not unidirectional, relation between individual organisms and their environments. Unidirectional relations are characterized by an individual affecting its environment (e.g., a "problem" child eliciting specific expectations and instructional strategies from a teacher) or by an environment "coercing" (Barker, 1968) an individual (e.g., "special" classes teaching some "marginally" ADHD children to act like "special" children). The current view of ADHD as biologically determined is consistent with a unidirectional model.

In contrast, a transactional model posits that children and their environments influence each other (e.g., special children elicit different reactions from different teachers; the reactions/expectations of these different teachers "feedback" to affect individual children's behavior). Although most children may be sensitive to such change, those who display extreme symptoms of ADHD may be relatively insensitive to environmental change. These propositions certainly should be tested empirically.

Timing of these transactions is also crucial in this view. By timing, I mean that specific behaviors have different meaning depending upon the specific phase of development in which they occur in specific contexts (Lerner, 1989). Thus, development is expressed in terms of probability, not in deterministic terms. The likelihood of a specific outcome, such as ADHD classification, depends upon a child exhibiting a specific set of behaviors in a certain place at a certain time. As noted above, a child's developmental trajectory will vary if those same behaviors are expressed in a different place (such as with a different teacher) or at a different time (such as during preschool rather than during first grade).

Another example of the importance of timing is illustrated in studies examining the impact of age of school entry on grade retention and adjustment to school problems (DePasquale, Moule, & Flewelling, 1980; Langer, Kalk, & Searls, 1984). For example, younger children (i.e., those born right before the cut-off date for school entry) compared with older children (children whose birthday fell just after the cut-off and had to delay school entry until the following year), were more likely to be retained during the elementary school years. Further, boys, whose physical maturation lags behind girls (Tanner, 1978), were twice as likely as girls to be retained. Indeed, girls' rapid maturity, relative to boys, may partially explain these as well as other school-achievement issues.

The educational implications of my view are clear. Children's functioning in school is the result of within-individual factors (such as being active) being embedded within specific school systems. Responsibility (or blame) lies in the transaction between the two systems. As Lerner (1984) notes, the consequence of this theory is recognition of developmental plasticity, where childhood functioning is facilitated or inhibited by the placement of specific children in specific environments at specific times. It is not predetermined by biological or environmental imperatives.

Simply put, direct causal statements about the effect of individuals' biology on behaviors related to most cases of ADHD should not be made. It is too simplistic to dichotomize individual/biological and environmental effects on a complex constellation of behaviors, such as those comprising ADHD. Similar warnings have been voiced about learning disabilities (e.g., Spear-Swerling & Sternberg, 1994).

The point of this discussion is to re-state the notion that biology and environment are interactive. The interactive role of biology and the environment ought to be included in any such model of ADHD. Part of an organism's biological endowment is the selection of a specific environment. The environment, in turn, affects the expression of one's biology. To separate them is to misunderstand the way in which organisms develop. Biological expression of behavior is realized in specific environments. Of course, in a few cases, children may have experienced extreme biological events which predisposed them to high levels of activity and inattention. These extreme cases probably also show up earlier, rather than later. Yet even rather stable and heritable traits, such as probable height, are affected by perinatal environmental factors, such as mothers' nutrition during pregnancy (Hinde, 1982).

What Factors Influence the Expression of ADHD Symptoms?

Classroom structure is an aspect of the school environment that affects the ways in which ADHD may be expressed. I have already documented (in the discussion of gender segregation on the playground) differences between boys' and girls' levels of physical activity when they are confronted with the same behavioral requirements and task demands. Differences are maximized in low-structure contexts, such as free-play time, compared with more structured situations, such as silent-reading time (Eaton & Enns, 1986). To complicate the picture, researchers studying children's ADHD-related behaviors, such as physical activity and attention, often confound gender-role stereotype of classroom tasks (e.g., blocks are male-preferred props) with task structure (e.g., math usually requires a convergent solution). Consequently, we do not know if the ADHD behaviors are due to a trans-situational difference between boys and girls, the structure of the task, gender preference, or an interaction between task and gender. So it could be the case that boys are less attentive than girls simply because they are observed while working on a female-preferred task. If they were observed while working on a male-preferred task, they may be more attentive. One should never underestimate the role of motivation on children's classroom behavior.

Illustrative of this point, one group of researchers unknowingly included both male- and female-preferred activities in their unstructured setting (respectively, math/spatial and word games activities) and only male-preferred activities in the structured settings (i.e., math activities; Jacob et al., 1978). That male and female stereotyped subject matter, such as mathematics and reading/spelling, respectively, are implicated in ADHD status is indirectly supported by other researchers (O'Brien et al., 1992), who found that ADHD children were more attentive on mathematics tasks than on reading/spelling tasks. This may be because ADHD children are predominantly boys and mathematics is a male-preferred subject; thus, boys may have been more attentive to this task than to the female-preferred reading tasks. These hypotheses are consistent with the literature on gender preference (Huston, 1983) and with the classroom attention literature (Pellegrini et al., 1995). In this latter study, boys were more attentive to male-preferred tasks than to female-preferred tasks.

Scheduling of lessons is another important, yet understudied, aspect of the classroom context that affects ADHD-related behavior. This is the place where the role of recess is most clear, I think.

As I noted in Chapters 1 and 8, explanations for the role of recess scheduling on attention and activity can be derived from mass versus distributed practice. Concentration is high and physical activity low when tasks are presented in short but frequent formats, compared with longer, less frequent formats. Applying this construct to children in classrooms, we would expect that longer, compared with shorter, periods of work with infrequent breaks, or recesses, to have negative effects on classroom attention (Pellegrini & Davis, 1993; Pellegrini et al., 1995). All children, but especially ADHD children, should become less attentive to seat work as the time assigned to seat work increases. In short, children, like the rest of us, need a break after sitting at a task for a period of time.

The data support the theory to the extent that children's attention to tasks wanes as a function of time (Pellegrini & Smith, 1993). The cross-national record also supports the theory. Harold Stevenson and colleagues (Stevenson & Lee, 1990; Stevenson et al., 1987) observed that Taiwanese and Japanese elementary school children have, across the school day, play breaks of 10–15 minutes after 40–45 minutes of lessons. Stevenson and colleagues posit that the "rapt attention and intense concentration" (Stevenson & Lee, 1990, p. 31) to class work may be because of the periods of vigorous play surrounding the lessons.

This explanation has been supported empirically and documented extensively in this volume (in the previous chapter, on cognitive performance). Here, I only highlight some of the findings. Experimental data involving adults show a positive effect of physical exercise on attention (Tomporowski & Ellis, 1988) and, in one study presented in Chapter 8 of this volume, where the gender preference of the seat work was manipulated, boys were more attentive to the male-preferred task than to the female preferred task. Further, children, but especially boys, were more attentive to these standardized tasks after recess than before.

Regarding age and achievement, the effects of age of entry into school is relevant. Take the example of two children of equal age and familial circumstances entering school one year apart. They will probably have very different school experiences. As noted above, younger children, compared with older ones, are more likely to experience difficulty (DePasquale et al., 1980; Langer et al., 1984). Of course, individual teachers and the classroom environments they create also influence these differential experiences.

There are robust gender differences in ADHD, as noted at the beginning of this chapter. Boys are diagnosed more than girls. An implication of this practice is that boys have been studied, almost exclusively; consequently, we really do not understand much about girls who show ADHD-related symptoms. The exclusion of girls from the ADHD literature is a limitation of the extant research because they represent a sizable minority (e.g., one girl for every five boys in primary school children). ADHD in girls must be considered because it is both an important equity issue and, from scientific and pedagogical perspectives, it is important to know the ways in which boys and girls negotiate their ADHD experiences. Are girls' developmental trajectories, both leading to and following diagnosis, similar to those of boys? Do differences relate to the fact that most primary teachers are female rather than male? These are important issues for understanding potential differences between boys and girls in primary school classrooms.

Studying boys and girls with and without ADHD would also be an interesting venue to explore the ways in which biology and context interact to affect children's development. It would probably be fruitful to examine the "goodness of fit" (Thomas & Chess, 1977) between environmental demands or expectations (such as classroom organization) and children's capacities (aspects of temperament such as "activity"). Part of this process involves describing the environments in which these children function, in terms of demands for specific behaviors, such as physical activity and sociability.

To speculate a bit, it may be the case that physically active girls may be viewed as "problems" in some families and classrooms, but not in others. Children considered problems, consequently, may experience coercive socialization and educational practices. The family socialization literature indicates clearly that coercive parenting is a reliable predictor of maladaptation to school and antisocial behavior (Maccoby & Martin, 1983).

Currently in much of the ADHD literature, maturation, or age-related change, is divorced from the social context in which it occurs. A maturational, or biological-determinism, perspective assumes, as noted above, that development unfolds according to a biological clock, with minimal transaction with context. My position, in contrast, assumes that developmental processes, per se, and the function of behaviors characterizing these processes, are differentially significant according to contextual and timing variables. Specifically, behaviors for children of different ages are adaptive, or maladaptive, depending on the situation in which they are embedded. For example, kindergartners' high level of physical activity may be viewed positively by a teacher who thinks that children learn best by moving around their environments, by manual activities, and short but intense academic periods; these same behaviors would be viewed negatively in a more sedentary kindergarten classroom and in later grades. Feedback provided by each teacher would, in turn, shape the child's subsequent behavior.

Also related to age/maturation is the fact that the incidences of ADHD diagnoses tend to increase as children mature and move into formal primary schooling (Whalen, 1983). Indeed, this age issue is embodied in the DSM criteria for ADHD to such an extent that ADHD must be diagnosed before children are 7 years of age. It is not known whether this dramatic shift in children's status is related primarily to an endogenous process in children, such as maturation, or an exogenous process, such as the structure of primary schooling. My perspective suggests that it is an interaction between individual and external factors.

By ways of illustration, consider a comparison between children in preschool/kindergarten and those in primary schools. It is well known that preschools and kindergartens tend to be less structured than primary schools (Minuchin & Shapiro, 1983). By this I mean that children in preschool and kindergarten, compared with children in primary school, are often given free choice of activities, interact with activities in varied (often divergent) ways, and are allowed to move around the classroom and talk with peers. Thus, many of the behaviors that are often characteristic of ADHD children in primary school are modal, and typically encouraged, in preschools. Consequently, the finding that ADHD-related behavior is minimized in "open," compared with traditional, classrooms is not surprising (Jacob et al., 1978). For some children, then, it may be the case that ADHD is observed during the primary grades, rather than in preschool and kindergarten, not because of maturation but because of the differing demand characteristics of the classrooms.

The construct of a goodness of fit between individual children and specific classrooms is a useful explanatory concept (Thomas & Chess, 1977). A basic premise of this research is that children's individual difference characteristics alone (e.g., temperament) do not determine their success or failure in school; adaptation is the result of a match/mismatch between the child and the environment. To test this proposition, researchers have studied the ways in which children with different temperaments (e.g., active/energetic, compliant/passive) fit into different classroom regimens. Results support the idea that adjustment to primary school is determined by the match between child-level variables and classroom-level variables. For example, children with self-control problems did poorly in open classrooms, while sociable children did well in those same classrooms (Barclay, 1983). In short, the probability of school success is maximized when there is a match between children and their classroom.

I suggest that the high rates of ADHD diagnosis in American schools is, in part, because of the interaction between children's characteristics and the demands of formal schooling. If ADHD is primarily an organic problem we would expect high levels of activity (especially in boys) and low levels of attention to appear relatively early in children's lives and to manifest themselves in various contexts. Only in more marginal cases would we expect ADHD-related behaviors to surface during the primary school, rather than preschool years. Correspondingly, these behaviors should vary considerably, depending upon the nature of the tasks in which children are engaged and the duration which they are expected to sit. In short, classifying children as ADHD is an incredibly high-stakes decision. We should base our decisions on systematic study of individual children across various contexts. If our hunches are correct, we should then try to have classrooms that accommodate different children.

As children move into primary grades there is increased demand for children to engage in more sedentary activities. Correspondingly, during this time children's ability to attend to sedentary, cognitive tasks increases substantially (Bjorklund & Green, 1992). Consequently, children need frequent breaks between cognitively demanding tasks; younger children probably need breaks more frequently than do older children.

The task remains for us to determine what might be optimal durations for classroom seat work and recess/break periods. Children's levels of attention, physical activity, and social interaction should be measured across periods of varying durations, and curve-fitting techniques should be used to determine what may be the optimal duration for maximizing the exhibition of desired behaviors. The manipulation of prerecess and recess periods in field experimental studies is crucial in this work.

Another corresponding issue relates to the length of the school day. As we have all heard, American children do not fare particularly well in terms of academic achievement when they are compared with children from other countries (e.g., Stevenson & Lee, 1990). Part of the reason for this seems to be due to the length of the school day and to the length of the school year. American children attend school fewer hours per year, relative to children in most other industrialized countries. It makes intuitive sense that the longer kids are in school, the more they will learn. A major qualifier here, of course, is that children need breaks during these long school days, as is the case in Japan and Taiwan.

Extended school days would also benefit parents. Most American children live in families where either both parents work or in single-parent families where that parent works. Unless parents provide very expensive afterschool care, children will be unsupervised for long periods of time until parents get home (Steinberg, 1986). The danger, here, of course, is that when children are unsupervised they tend to get in trouble (Patterson, 1986). So, an extended school day, with frequent breaks, would maximize children's learning and provide parents and children with a safe and productive place for children to spend time while parents are working.

In the long run this practice may also save communities money. Kids who get into trouble are expensive to deal with. Time missed in school, therapy, or residential treatment/confinement, and low achievement, are all very expensive. To borrow from a TV ad of a few years ago advocating preventative maintenance for cars—you can pay me now, or you can pay me later. Paying earlier is probably cheaper, and more humane, than paying later.

SUPER-SIZED!

Americans, children included, are overweight (DeAngelis, 2004; Rich, 2004). Indeed, the problem of childhood obesity has been called an epidemic. This current state of affairs is due to a combination of factors, including large, or jumbo, portions (especially if one eats out) of high fat and high carbohydrate foods (especially if one eats fast foods) and easily accessible and ever-present snack foods.

Add to this poor diet children's lack of exercise. Children are especially sedentary during the typical school day (Simons-Morton, O'Hara, Parcel, Huang, Baranowski, & Wilson, 1990). Opportunities for recess in spacious settings equipped with apparatus to encourage exercise (basketball hoops, four-square grids, balls, etc.) would help moderate children's weight problems, especially if it were paired with physical education and participation-oriented sports (in contrast to sports where only the "best" make the team). It may be the case that by merely providing opportunities for children to engage in free play may be enough to boost their sedentary life in school. For example, some research has shown that when children are out of school (before and after school), relative to being in school, they engage in close to double the amount of vigorous exercise (Simons-Morton et al., 1990).

However, in more systematic studies of the physical activity of both preschool (McKenzie et al., 1997) and primary school children (Hovell et al., 1978), it was found that most children did not engage in adequate levels of physical activity during the recess period. For example, primary school children spent only 60% of the recess period engaged in physical activity (Hovell et al., 1978), and the rest of the time was spent standing around, often waiting in line. Further, most of children's physical activity was observed at the start of the recess period and declined as the recess period progressed (McKenzie at al., 1998; Smith & Hagen, 1980).

If teachers or playground supervisors encouraged physical activity on the playground, however, children's physical activity was maintained across a longer period of time. In short, just providing opportunity to exercise does not seem to be enough. After a short period of time, children seem to just hang around—they do not engage in active behavior. Kids need to be encouraged to do so. Indeed, even during physical education periods children do not engage spontaneously and voluntarily in vigorous activity (Cuming et al., 1969; Simons-Morton et al., 1987).

It may be the case that both at recess and in physical education classes, children are spending substantial periods of time waiting around. They could be waiting for instruction or a turn in their PE classes or waiting in line to go in or out for recess. Time might be better spent with less waiting around and more exercise. If encouragement is needed, and it appears that it may be, playground supervisors should spend more of their time doing that than having kids wait around.

WHAT IS TO BE DONE? IMPACTING POLICY

I believe that instructional decisions should be based upon the hallmarks of specific periods during children's development. Thus, the "what" and "how" of classroom instruction for preschool and kindergarten children would be different from those of primary school children. In keeping with this idea, the educational goals should be developmentally specific. Preschool and kindergarten educators should be concerned primarily with children's peer relations (Waters & Sroufe, 1983). Thus, classrooms should be places where children walk around and talk with each other. Introduction of basic skills, such as reading, to this group can be accomplished in developmentally appropriate ways by encouraging children's pretend play with their peers; preschool children's social pretense and accompanying forms of oral language reliably predict early literacy (Pellegrini & Galda, 1993).

Following this logic and using the research presented in this book as a base, educational practice and policy should implement recess across the curriculum. With this said, this final section is a call to action. Stakeholders in the educational process (and who isn't?) can and should let politicians and educators know what they think about these issues. After all, our children are the individuals being educated and our tax and tuition dollars are supporting the schools. As I advocated throughout this book, research should guide practice and policy, and most of this book has been dedicated to providing that evidence.

There may be cases, however, when a specific question is not readily answered in the research literature, or when a person wants to determine if their specific school or school system is similar to or different from what has already been reported in the literature. In these cases, an action research approach can be applied. Action research is different from traditional academic research to the extent that the latter is theory and hypothesis driven, trying to establish general principles, whereas action research is oriented toward a very specific problem or question.

Action research has its origins in social-action movements. Specifically, one very early example (before World War I) of action research involved R. H. Tawney, an eminent English economic historian at London University. Tawney spent much of his free time in the coal fields of Midlands, England, teaching miners about economics so that they could improve their lot (Terrill, 1973). More currently, action research has been used by parents and teachers to improve conditions in their schools.

Like more traditional research, action researchers begin with identifying a problem, very clearly. Next they plan a way in which to study the problem. This process often involves a variety of different stake holders, such as parents, children, teachers, and administrators. In short, you should try to involve all the folks who have a stake in this problem. Once the plan is implemented, it is imperative that the researchers monitor the process. They must make sure that they are actually implementing the plan that they said they were implementing.

Once all the data are collected, the findings should be objectively assessed. Were your questions answered? Did you learn anything that could help you study this better in the future?

With results in hand you should then write up a formal report, outlining your questions, methods, data analyses, and results. In terms of format for presenting your results, it may be best if you used an abbreviated, poster-like format. You could use Power Point to construct a presentation that could be given to different groups as well as printed out and distributed.

As I have stressed throughout this book, research and theory should guide school policy. In cases where policy is not being so guided, it is up to you, the parents, tax and tuition payers, and interested citizens, to make the larger public aware of the inconsistencies in policy and our current state of knowledge. After all, most of us have a vested interest in schools doing the right thing and being reminded when they are not. In open societies, information is a very powerful stimulus for change. If we make strong arguments loud enough and often enough, things will change.

If schools are reluctant to implement these practices, it is necessary to contact other like-minded parents, educators, and citizens to demand "accountability." Accountability here means that educational practice should follow data. Ask educators who refuse to implement recess how they know—empirically—that eliminating or reducing recess improves instruction. Do this at PTA meetings, school board meetings, and when superintendents of school are interviewing for jobs in your district. These are your children and your tax dollars, so demand accountability.

It's now time to take it to the streets and the playgrounds!

References

Alexander, G. M., & Hines, M. (1994). Gender labels and play styles: Their relative contributions to children's selection of playmates. *Child Development, 65,* 869–879.

Alexander, R. D. (1989). Evolution of the human psyche. In P. Mellers & C. Stringer (Eds.), *The human revolution: Behavioural and biological perspectives on the origins of modern humans* (455–513). Princeton, NJ: Princeton University Press.

Alexander, R. D., Hoogland, J. L., Howard, R. D., Noonan, K. M., & Sherman, P. W. (1979). Sexual dimorphisms and breeding systems in pinnipeds, ungulates, primates, and humans. In N. A. Chagnon & W. Irons (Eds.), *Evolutionary biology and human social behavior* (pp. 402–435). N. Scituate, MA: Duxbury Press.

Allport, G. M. (1954). *The nature of prejudice.* Cambridge, MA: Addison-Wesley.

Archer, J. (1992). *Ethology and human development.* Hemel Hemstead, UK: Harvester Wheatsheaf.

Archer, J., & Lloyd, B. (2002). *Sex and gender* (2nd ed.). London: Cambridge University Press.

Aronowitz, S. (1973). Together and equal: The egalitarian promise of children's games. *Social Policy* (November/December), 78–84.

Bakeman, R., & Brownlee, J. (1980). The strategic use of parallel play: A sequential analysis. *Child Development, 51,* 873–878.

Barclay, J. (1983). A meta-analysis of temperament-treatment interactions with alternative learning and counseling treatments. *Developmental Review, 3,* 410–443.

Barker, R. (1968). *Ecological psychology.* Stanford, CA: Stanford University Press.

Barkley, R., Dupaul, G., & McMurray, M. (1990). Comprehensive evaluation of attention deficit disorder with and without hyperactivity as defined by research criteria. *Journal of Clinical and Counseling Psychology, 58,* 775–789.

Bateson, P. P. G. (1976). Rules and reciprocity in behavioral development. In P. P. G. Bateson & R. A. Hinde (Eds.), *Growing points in ethology* (pp. 401–421). London: Cambridge University Press.

Bateson, P. P. G. (1981). Discontinuities in development and changes in organization of play in cats. In K. Immelmann, G. Barlow, L. Petrinovich, & M. Main (Eds.), *Behavioural development* (pp. 281–295). Cambridge, UK: Cambridge University Press.

Bateson, P. P. G. (2005). Play and its role in the development of great apes and humans. In A. D. Pellegrini & P. K. Smith (Eds.) *The nature of play: Great apes and humans.* New York: Guilford.

Bateson, P. P. G., & Martin, P. (1999). *Design for a life: How behaviour develops.* London: Jonathan Cape.

Bauermeister, J., Alegria, M., Bird, H., Rubio-Stipec, & Canino, G. (1992). Are attentional-hyperactivity deficits unidimensional or multidimensional? Empirical findings from a community survey. *Journal of the Academy of Child and Adolescent Psychiatry, 31,* 423–431.

Bekoff, M., & Byers, J. A. (1981). A Critical re-analysis of the ontogeny and phylogeny of mammalian social and locomotor play. In K. Immelmann, G. Barlow, L. Petronovich, & M. Main (Eds.), *Behavioural Devleopment* (pp. 296–337). Cambridge, UK: Cambridge University Press.

Belsky, J., & Most, R. (1981). From exploration to play: A cross-sectional study of infant free-play behavior. *Developmental Psychology, 17,* 630–639.

Bjorklund, D. F. (1978). Negative transfer in children's recall of categorized material. *Journal of Experimental Child Psychology, 26,* 299–307.

Bjorklund, D. F. (1997). The role of immaturity in human development. *Psychological Bulletin, 122,* 153–169.

Bjorklund, D. F. (2004). *Children's thinking: Cognitive development and individual differences* (4th ed.). Pacific Grove, CA: Brooks/Cole.

Bjorklund, D. F., & Green, B. L. (1992). The adaptive nature of cognitive immaturity. *American Psychologist, 47,* 46–54.

Bjorklund, D. F., & Harnishfeger, K. K. (1990). The resources construct in cognitive development: Diverse sources of evidence and a theory of inefficient inhibition. *Developmental Review, 10,* 48–71.

Bjorklund, D. F., & Pellegrini, A. D. (2000). Child development and evolutionary psychology. *Child Development, 71,* 1687–1708.

Bjorklund, D. F., & Pellegrini, A. D. (2002). *Evolutionary developmental psychology.* Washington, DC: American Psychological Association.

Blatchford, P. (1989). *Playtime in the Primary School: Problems and Improvements.* Windsor, Berkshire, UK: NFER-Nelson.

Blatchford, P. (1996). We did more then: Changes in pupils' perceptions of breaktime from 7 to 16 years. *Journal of Research in Childhood Education, 11,* 14–24.

Blatchford, P. (1998). *Social life in school.* London: Falmer.

Blatchford, P., & Sumpner, C. (1998). What do we know about break time? Results from a national survey of breaktime and lunch time in primary and secondary schools. *British Educational Research Journal, 24,* 79–94.

Bloch, M. N. (1989). Young boys' and girls' play at home and in the community: A cultural ecological framework. In M. Bloch & A. Pellegrini (Eds.), *The ecological context of children's play* (pp. 120–154). Norwood, NJ: Ablex.

Blurton Jones, N. (1972). Categories of child interaction. In N. Blurton Jones (Ed.), *Ethhological studies of child behaviour* (pp. 97–129). London: Cambridge University Press.

Blurton Jones, N. (1976). Rough-and tumble play among nursery school children. In J. Bruner, A. Jolly, & K. Sylva (Eds.), *Play—Its role in development and evolution* (pp. 352–363). New York: Basic Books.

Borman, K. M., & Kurdek, L. A. (1987). Grade and gender differences in the stability and correlates of the structural complexity of children's playground games. *International Journal of Behavioral Development, 10,* 241–251.

Bornstein, M., Haynes, O. M., Pascual, L., Painter, K. M., & Galperin, C (1999). Play in two societies. *Child Development, 70,* 317–331.

Boulton, M. J. (1992). Participation in playground activities at middle school. *Educational Research, 34,* 167–182.

Boulton, M., Smith, P. K. (1993). Ethnic, gender partner, and activity preferences in mixed-race children's social competence develops in the context of interacting with their peers schools in the UK: Playground observations. In C. Hart (Ed.), *Children on playgrounds* (pp. 210–238). Albany: SUNY Press.

Brainerd, C. J., & Reyna, V. F. (1990). Gist is the Grist: Fuzzy-trace theory and the new intuitionism. *Development Review, 10,* 3–47.

Brainerd, C. J., & Reyna, V. F. (1993). Domains of fuzzy trace theory. In M. L. Howe & R. Pasnak (Eds.), *Emerging themes in cognitive development, Vol 1. Foundations* (pp. 50–93). New York: Springer-Verlag.

Bretherton, I. (1984). Representing the social world in symbolic play. Reality and fantasy. In I. Bretherton (Ed.) *Symbolic play* (pp. 3–41). New York: Academic.

British Psychological Society Working Party. (2000). *Attention Deficit/Hyperactivity Disorder: Guidelines and principles for successful multi-agency working.* Leicester, UK: Author.

Brody, G. H., Graziano, W. G., & Musser, L. M. (1983). Familiarity and children's behavior in same-sex and mixed sex peer groups. *Developmental Psychology, 19,* 568–576.

Bronfenbrenner, U. (1973). *Two worlds of childhood: US and USSR.* New York: Pocket Books.

Bronfenbrenner, U. (1979). *The ecology of human development.* Cambridge, MA: Harvard University Press.

Bronfenbrenner, U., & Ceci, S. J. (1994). Nature-nurture reconceptualized in developmental perspective: A bioecological model. *Psychological Review, 101,* 568–586.

Brophy, J., & Good, T. (1974). *Teacher–student relationships.* New York: Holt, Rinehart & Winston.

Brown, B. B. (1990). Peer groups and peer cultures. In S. Feldman & G. Elliot (Eds.), *At the threshold* (pp. 171–196). Cambridge, MA: Harvard University Press.

Bruner, J. (1972). The nature and uses of immaturity. *American Psychologist, 27,* 687–708.

Burghardt, G. M. (1998). Play. In G. Greenberg & M. M. Haraway (Eds.), *Comparative psychology: A handbook* (pp. 725–733). New York: Garland.

Butterfield, H. (1931/1965). *The Whig interpretation of history.* New York: Norton.

Byers, J. A., & Walker, C. (1995). Refining the motor training hypothesis for the evolution of play. *American Naturalist, 146,* 25–40.

Cairns, R. (1983). The emergence of developmental psychology. In W. Kessen (Ed.), *Handbook of child psychology* (Vol. 1, pp. 41–102). New York: Wiley.

Cairns, R., & Cairns, B. (1988). The developmental-interactional view of social behavior. Four issues of adolescent aggression. In D. Olweus, J. Block, M. Radkye-Yarrow (Eds), *Developmental of antisocial and prosocial behavior: Research, theory, and issues* (pp. 315–342). New York: Academic.

Campbell, A., Shirley, L., Heywood, C., & Crook, C. (2000). Infants' visual preference for sex-congruent babies, children, toys, and activities: A longitudinal study. *British Journal of Developmental Psychology, 18,* 479–498.

Carmichael, L. (Ed.). (1946). *Manual of child psychology* (1st ed.). New York: Wiley.

Carmichael, L. (Ed.). (1954). *Manual of child psychology* (2nd ed.). New York: Wiley.

Caro, T. M. (1995). Short-term costs and correlates of play in cheetahs. *Animal Behaviour, 49,* 333–345.

Caro, T. M., & Bateson, P. (1986). Ontogeny and organization of alternative tactics. *Animal Behaviour, 34,* 1483–1499.

Carpenter, C. J., Huston, A. C, & Spera, L. (1989). Children's use of time in their everyday activities during middle childhood. In M. N. Bloch & A. D. Pellegrini (Eds.), *The ecological context of children's play* (pp. 165–190). Norwood, NJ: Ablex.

Carson, J., Burks, V. & Parke, R. (1993). Parent-child physical play: Determination and consequences. In K. MacDonald (Ed.), *Parent-child play* (pp. 197–220). Albany: State University of New York Press.

Case, R. (1985). *Intellectual development: Birth to adulthood.* New York: Academic Press.

Cavallo, D. (1979). The politics of latency: Kindergarten pedagogy, 1860–1930. In B. Finkelstein (Ed.), *Regulated children/liberated children* (pp. 158–183). New York: Psychohistory Press.

Cavallo, D. (1981). *Muscles and morals: Organized playgrounds and urban reform, 1880–1920.* Philadelphia: University of Pennsylvania Press.

Chance, M. R. A. (1967). Attention structure as the basis for primate rank orders. *Man, 2,* 503–518.

Charlesworth, W. R., & Dzur, C. (1987). Gender comparisons of preschoolers' behavior and resource utilization in group problem solving. *Child Development, 58,* 191–200.

Chepko, B. (1971). A preliminary study of the effects of play deprivation on young goats. *Zeitschrift für Tierpsychologie, 28,* 517–526.

Clark, R. W. (1971). *Einstein. The life and times.* New York: Avon Books.

Coie, J., & Dodge, K. (1983). Continuities and changes in children's social status: A five-year longitudinal study. *Merrill-Palmer Quarterly, 29,* 261–287.

Coie, J. D., & Dodge, K. A. (1998). Aggression and antisocial behaviour. In N. Eisenberg (Ed.), *Handbook of child psychology* (Vol. 3, pp. 779–862). New York: Wiley.

Conradt, L. (1998). Measuring the degree of sexual segregation in group-living animals. *Journal of Animal Ecology, 67,* 217–226.

Costabile, A., Smith, P., Matheson, L., Aston, J., Hunter, T., & Boulton, M. (1991). Cross-national comparison of how children distinguish serious and playful fighting. *Developmental Psychology, 27,* 881–887.

Council on Physical Education for Children. (2001). Recess in elementary schools: A position paper from the National Association for Sport and Physical Education. http://eric.ed.uiuc.edu/naecs/position/recessplay.html

Cronbach. L. J. (1971). Test validation. In R. L. Thorndike (Ed.), *Educational measurement.* Washington, DC: American Council on Education.

Cuming, G. R., Goulding, D., & Bagely, G. (1969). Failure of school physical education to improve cardiovascular fitness. *Canadian Medical Association Journal, 101,* 69–73.

Cunningham, C., & Siegal, L. (1987). Peer interactions of normal and attention-deficit-disordered boys during free play, cooperative task and simulated classroom situations. *Journal of Abnormal Child Psychology, 15,* 247–268.

Dansky, J., & Silverman, I. W. (1973). Effects of play on associative fluency in preschool-age children. *Developmental Psychology, 9,* 38–43.

Dansky, J., & Silverman, I. W. (1975). Play: A general facilitator of associative fluency. *Developmental Psychology, 11,* 104.

DeAngelis, T. (2004). What's to blame for the surge in super-sized Americans? *Monitor on Psychology, 35*(1), 44–49.

Dempster, F. N. (1988). The spacing effect. *American Psychologist, 43,* 627–634.

Dempster, F. N. (1992). The raise and fall of inhibitory mechanisms: Toward a unified theory of cognitive development and aging. *Developmental Review, 12,* 45–75.

Dempster, F. N. (1993). Resistance to interference: Developmental changes in a basic processing mechanism. In M. L. Howe & R. Pasnak (Eds.), *Emerging themes in cognitive development. Vol. 1: Foundations* (pp. 3–27). New York: Springer-Verlag.

de Waal, F. B. M. (1982). *Chimpanzee politics.* London: Jonathan Cape.

deWaal, F. B. M. (1986). The integration of dominance and social bonding in primates. *Quarterly Review of Biology, 61,* 459–479.

deWaal, F., & Lanting, F. (1997). *Bonobo: The forgotten ape.* Berkeley: University of California Press.

DePasquale, G., Moule, A., & Fleweling, A. (1980). The birthdate effect. *Journal of Learning Disabilities, 13,* 234–238.

Dodge, K. A., & Coie, J. D. (1987). Social information processing factors in reactive and proactive aggression in children's peer groups. *Journal of Personality and Social Psychology, 53,* 1146–1158.

Dodge, K., Pettit, G., McClaskey, & Brown, M. (1986). Social competence in children. *Monographs of the Society for Research in Child Development, 5*(2).

Douglas, J. D., & Corsale, K. (1977). The effects of mode and rate of presentation on evaluative encoding in children's memory. *Child Development, 48,* 46–50.

Dunbar, R. I. M. (1988). *Primate social systems.* Ithaca, NY: Cornell.

Dykman, R., Ackerman, P., & Raney, T. (1993). Research syntheses on assessment and characteristics of children with attention deficit disorder. In Chesapeake Institute (Ed.), *Executive summaries of research syntheses and promising practices on the education of children with attention deficit disorder* (pp. 4–21). Washington, DC: Chesapeake Institute.

Eaton, W. O., & Enns, L. (1986). Sex differences in human motor activity level. *Psychological Bulletin, 100,* 19–28.

Eaton, W. O., Enns, L., & Presse, M. (1987). Scheme for observing activity. *Journal of Psychoeductional Assessment, 3,* 273–280.

Eaton, W., & Yu, A. (1989). Are sex differences in child motor activity level a function of sex differences in maturational status? *Child Development, 60,* 1005–1011.

Ebinghaus, H. (1964). *Memory.* New York: Teachers College Press. (Original work published 1885)

Eder, D., & Felmlee, D. (1984). The development of attention norms in ability groups. In P. Peterson, L. C. Wilkinson, & M. Hallinan (Eds.), *The social context of instruction* (pp. 189–208). New York: Academic.

Ehrhardt, A. (1984). Gender differences: A biosocial perspective. In Sondergegger (Ed.), *Nebraska Symposium on motivation* (pp. 37–57). Lincoln: University of Nebraska Press.

Eisenberg, N. (Ed.). (1998). *Manual of child psychology: Vol. 3. Social, emotional, and personality development.* New York: Wiley.

Entwsile, D., Alexander, K., Cadigan, D., & Pallas, A. (1987). Kindergarten experience: Cognitive effects or socialization. *American Educational Research Journal, 24.*

Evans, J., & Pellegrini, A. D. (1997). Surplus energy theory: An enduring but inadequate justification for break time. *Educational Review, 49,* 229–236.

Fabes, R. A., Martin, C. L., Hanish, L. D., Anders, M. C., & Madden-Derdich, D. A. (2003). Early school competence: The roles of sex-segregated play and effort control. *Developmental Psychology, 39,* 848–858.

Fagen, R. (1981). *Animal play behavior.* New York: Oxford University Press.

Fagen, R. (1993). Primate juveniles and primate play. In M. Perieria & L. Fernbanks (Eds.), *Juvenile primates* (pp. 182–196). New York: Oxford University Press.

Fagot, B. I. (1974). Sex differences in toddlers' behavior and parental reaction. *Developmental Psychology, 10,* 554–558.

Fein, G. (1981a). The physical environment: Stimulation or evocation. In R. Lerner & N. Busch-Rossnagel (Eds.), *Individuals as producers of their environment* (pp. 257–279) New York: Wiley.

Fein, G. (1981b). Pretend play in childhood: An integrative review. *Child Development, 52,* 1095–1118.

Field, T. (1994). Infant day care facilitates later social behavior and school performance. In E. Jacobs & H. Goelman (Eds.), *Children's play in day care centers.* Albany: SUNY Press.

Fine, G., Mortimer, J., & Roberts, D. (1990). Leisure, work, and the mass media. In S. Feldman & G. Elliot (Eds.), *At the threshold* (pp. 225–252). Cambridge, MA: Harvard University Press.

Finkelstein, B. (Ed.). (1979). *Regulated children/liberated children.* New York: Psychohistory Press.

Finkelstein, B. (1987). Historical perspectives on children's play in schools. In J. Block & N. King (Eds.), *School play* (pp. 17–37). New York: Garland.

Flavell, J. H., Miller, P. A., & Miller, S. A. (1993). *Cognitive development* (3rd ed.). Englewood Cliffs, NJ: Prentice Hall.

Frost, J. (1986). Children's playgrounds: Research and practice. In G. Fein and M. Rivkin (Eds.), *The young child at play: Reviews of research,* Vol. 4 (pp. 195–212). Washington, DC: National Association for the Education of Young Children.

Frost, J., & Sunderlin, S. (Eds.) (1985). *When children play.* Wheaton, MD: Association for Childhood Education International.

Fry, D. P. (1987). Difference between play fighting and serious fighting among Zapotec children. *Ethology and Sociolbiology, 8,* 285–306.

Garton, A., & Pratt, C. (1987). Participation and interest in leisure activities by adolescent school children. *Journal of Adolescence, 10,* 341–351.

Garvey, C. (1977). *Play.* Cambridge, MA: Harvard University Press.

Garvey, C. (1990). *Play* (2nd ed.). Cambridge, MA: Harvard University Press.

Goodwin, M. (1990). *He-said-she-said: Talk as social organization among black children.* Bloomington: Indiana University Press.

Gottlieb, G. (1983). The psychobiological approach to developmental issues. In M. tHaith & J. Campos (Eds.), *Handbook of child psychology* (Vol. 2, pp. 1–26). New York: Wiley.

Gottlieb, G. (1998). Normally occurring environmental and behavioral influences on gene activity: From central dogma to probabilistic epigenesis. *Psychological Review, 105,* 792–802.

Gottman, J. M. (1983). How children become friends. *Monographs of the Society for Research in Child Development, 48*(3)Serial No. 201).

Greeno, J. (1991). Number sense as situated knowing in a conceptual domain. *Journal of Research in Mathematics Education, 22,* 170–218.

Grice, H. P. (1975). Logic and conversation. In P. Cole & J. Morgan (Eds.), *Syntax and semantics* (Vol. 3, pp. 41–58). New York: Academic.

Groos, K. (1898). *The play of animals.* New York: Appleton.

Groos, K. (1901). *The play of man.* New York: Appleton.

Guerra, N. G., Husemann, L. R., & Spindler, A. (2003). Community violence exposure, social cognition, and aggression among urban elementary school children. *Child Development, 74,* 1561–1576.

Gump, P. V., & Sutton-Smith, B. (1953). The "It" role in children's games. *The Group, 17,* 3–8.

Haight, W. L., & Miller, P. J. (1993). *Pretending at home.* Albany, NY: State University of New York Press.

Hall, G. S. (1904). *Adolescence: Its psychology and its relation to physiology, anthropology, sociology, sex, crime, religion, and education* (Vols. 1–2). New York: Appleton.

Hall, G. S. (1916). *Adolescence.* New York: Appleton.

Harlow, H. (1962). The heterosexual affection system in monkeys. *American Psychologist, 17,* 1–9.

Harnishfeger, K. K., & Bjorklund, D. F. (1993). The ontogeny of inhibition mechanisms: A renewed approach to cognitive development. In M. L. Howe & R. Pasnak (Eds.), *Emerging themes in cognitive development: Vol 1. Foundations.* New York: Springer Verlag.

Harnishfeger, K. K., & Bjorklund, D. F. (1994). Individual differences in inhibition: Implications for children's cognitive development. *Learning and Individual Differences, 6,* 331–355.

Harper, L., & Huie, K. (1985). The effects of prior group experience, age, and familiarity on the quality and organizational of preschoolers' social relations. *Child Development, 56,* 704–717.

Harper, L., & Sanders, K. (1975). Preschool children's use of space: Sex differences in outdoor play. *Developmental Psychology, 11,* 119.

Hart, C. H. (Ed.). (1993). *Children on playgrounds: Research perspectives and applications.* Albany, NY: State University of New York Press.

Hart, C. (1993). Children on playgrounds: Applying current knowledge to future practice and inquiry. In C. Hart (Ed.), *Children on playgrounds* (pp. 418–432). Albany: State University of New York Press.

Hart, C., & Sheehan, R. (1986). Preschoolers' play behavior in outdoor environments: Effects of traditional and contemporary playgrounds. *American Educational Research Journal, 23,* 669–679.

Hartup, W. (1983). Peer relations. In E. M. Hetherington (Ed.), *Handbook of child psychology* (Vol. IV, pp. 103–196). New York: Wiley.

Hartup, W. W. (1996). The company they keep: Friendships and their developmental significance. *Child Development, 67,* 1–13.

Hayward, G., Rothenberg, M., & Beasley, R. (1974). Children's play and urban playground environments: A comparison of traditional contemporary, and adventure types. *Environment and Behavior, 6,* 131–168.

Hawley, P. H. (1999). The ontogenesis of social dominance: A strategy-based evolutionary perspective. *Developmental Review, 19,* 97–132.

Hawley, P. H. (2002). Social dominance and prosocial and coercive strategies of resource control in preschoolers. *International Journal of Behavioral Development, 26,* 167–176.

Heath, S. (1983). *Ways with words.* New York: Cambridge University Press.

Hetherington, E. M. (Ed.). (1983). *Handbook of child psychology: Vol. IV. Socialization, personality and social development* (pp. 693–774). New York: Wiley.

Hillman, M. (1993). One false move. In M. Hillman (Ed.), *Children, transport and the quality of life.* London: Policy Studies Institute.

Hinde, R. (1982). *Ethology.* London: Fontana.

Hinde, R. (1983). Ethology and child development. In J. J. Campos and M. H. Haith (Eds.), *Handbook of child psychology: Infancy and developmental psychobiology, Vol. II.* New York: Wiley.

Hines, M., & Kaufman, F. R. (1994). Androgen and the development of human sex-typical behaviour: Rough and tumble play and sex preferred play mates in children with Congenital Adrenal Hyperplasia (CAH). *Child Development, 65,* 1042–1053.

Hodges, E. V., & Perry, D. G. (1999). Personal and interpersonal antecedents of victimization by peers. *Journal of Personality and Social Psychology, 76,* 677–685.

Hovell, M. F., Bursick, J. H., Sharkey, R., & McClure, J. (1978). An evaluation of elementary students' voluntary physical activity during recess. *Research Quarterly for Exercise and Sport, 49,* 460–474.

Howes, C. (1993). *The collaborative construction of pretense.* Albany: State University of New York Press.

Hrdy, S. B. (1976). Care and exploitation of nonhuman primate infants by conspecifics other than the mother. In J. S. Rosenblatt, R. A. Hinde, E. Shaw, & C. Beer (Eds.), *Advances in the study of behavior, Volume 6* (pp. 101–158). New York: Academic Press.

Hughes, T. (1895). *Tom Brown's school days.* Cambridge, UK: The Riverside Press.

Huizinga, J. (1939/1955). *Homo ludens: A study of the play element in culture.* Boston: The Beacon Press.

Humphreys, A., & Smith, P. K. (1984). Rough-and-tumble in preschool and playground. In P. K. Smith (Ed.), *Play in animals and humans* (pp. 241–270). London: Blackwell.

Humphreys, A., & Smith, P. K. (1987). Rough-and-tumble play, friendship and dominance in school children: Evidence for continuity and change with age. *Child Development, 58,* 201–212.

Humphrey, N. (1976). The social function of intellect. In P. Bateson and R. Hinde (Eds.), *Growing points in ethology* (pp. 303–317). Cambridge: Cambridge University Press.

Hunter, W. (1929). Learning III: Experimental studies of learning. In C. Murchison (Ed.), *The foundations of experimental psychology* (pp. 564–627). Worcester, MA: Clark University Press.

Huston, A. (1983). Sex typing. In E. Hetherington (Ed.), *Manual of child psychology, Vol 4* (pp. 387–468). New York: Wiley.

Hutt, C. (1966). Exploration and play in children. *Symposia of the Zoological Society of London, 18,* 61–81.

Jacob, R., O'Leary, K., & Rosenblad, C. (1978). Formal and informal classroom settings: Effects on hyperactivity. *Journal of Abnormal Child Psychology, 6,* 47–59.

James, W. (1901). *Talks to teachers on psychology: And to students on some of life's ideals.* New York: Holt.

Janikas, K. (1993). Hand clapping games: Rhythmic recordings of girlhood socialization. *Newsletter of the Laboratory of Comparative Human Cognition, 15,* 97–102.

Kagan, J. (1971). *Continuity and change in infancy.* New York: Wiley.

Kamii, C., & DeVries, R. (1978). *Physical knowledge in preschool education.* Engelwood Cliffs, NJ: Prentice-Hall.

Keogh, B. (1982). Children's temperament and teacher decisions. In R. Porter & G. Collins (Eds.), *Temperamental differences in infants and young children* (pp. 267–278). London: Pitman.

Kessen, W. (1965). *The child.* New York: Wiley.

Kessen, W. (Ed.). (1975). *Childhood in China.* New Haven, CT: Yale University Press.

Kleiber, D., Larson, R., & Csikszentmihalyi, M. (1986). The experience of leisure in adolescence. *Journal of Leisure Studies, 18,* 169–176.

Klein, R., & Mannuzza, S. (1991). Longterm outcome of hyperactive children. *Journal of the American Academy of Child and Adolescent Psychiatry, 30,* 383–387.

Konner, M. J. (1972). Aspects of the developmental ethology of a foraging people. In N. Blurton Jones (Ed.), *Ethological studies of child behaviour* (pp. 285–304). London: Cambridge University Press.

Ladd, G. W., Kochenderfer, B. J., & Coleman, C. C. (1996). Friendship quality as a predictor of young children's early school adjustment, *Child Development, 67,* 1103–1118.

Ladd, G. W., & Price, J. M. (1987). Predicting children's social and school adjustment following the transition from preschool to kindergarten. *Child Development, 58,* 1168–1189.

Ladd, G. W., & Profilet, S. M. (1996). The Child Behavior Scale: A teacher-report measure of young children's aggressive, withdrawn, and prosocial behavior. *Developmental Psychology, 32,* 1008–1024.

Langer, P., Kalk, J., & Searls, D. (1984). Age of achievement and trends in achievement. *American Educational Research Journal, 21,* 61–78.

Lerner, R. (1978). Nature, nurture, and dynamic interactionism. *Human Development, 21,* 1–20.

Lerner, R. (1984). *On the nature of human plasticity.* New York: Cambridge University Press.

Lerner, R. (1989). Developmental contextualism and the life-span view of person-context interaction. In M. Bornstein & J. Bruner (Eds.), *Interaction in human development* (pp. 217–239). Hillsdale, NJ: Lawrence Erlbaum Associates.

Lever, J. (1975/1976). Sex differences in the games children play. *Social Problems, 23,* 479–487.

Lockheed, M. S., Harris, A. M., & Nemceff, W. P. (1983). Sex and social influence: Does sex function as a status characteristic in mixed-sex groups? *Journal of Educational Psychology, 75,* 877–888.

Loeber, R. (1990). Development and risk factors of juvenile antisocial behavior and delinquency. *Clinical Psychology Review, 10,* 1–42.

Lykken, D. (1968). Statistical significance in psychological research. *Psychological Bulletin, 70,* 151–159.

Maccoby, E. E. (1998). *The two sexes: Growing up apart, coming together.* Cambridge, MA: Harvard University Press.

Maccoby, E., & Jacklin, C. (1974). *The psychology of sex differences.* Stanford, CA: Stanford University Press.

Maccoby, E., & Martin, J. (1983). Socialization in the context of the family. *Handbook of child psychology, Vol 4,* (pp. 1–102). New York: Wiley.

MacDonald, K., & Parke, R. D. (1984). Bridging the gap: Parent-child play interactions and peer interactive competence. *Child Development, 55,* 1265–1277.

MacDonald, K., & Parke, R. (1986). Parent-child physical play. *Sex Roles, 15,* 367–378.

Martin, P., & Bateson, P. P. G. (1993). *Measuring behaviour.* Cambridge, UK: Cambridge University Press.

Martin, P., & Caro, T. (1985). On the function of play and its role in behavioral development. In J. Rosenblatt, C. Beer, M-C. Bushnel, & P. Slater (Eds.), *Advances in the study of behavior* (Vol. 15, pp. 59–103). New York: Academic Press.

Marx, K. (1906). *Capital, Volume 1.* Chicago: Charles Kerr & Co.

Masten, A. S., & Coatsworth, J. D. (1998). The development of competence in favorable and unfavorable environments. *American Psychologist, 53,* 205–220.

McGrew, W. (1972a). *An ethological study of children's behaviour.* London: Methuen.

McGrew, W. (1972b). Aspects of social development in nursery school children, with emphasis on introduction to the group. In N. Blurton Jones (Ed.), *Ethological studies in child behaviour* (pp. 129–156). London: Cambridge University Press.

McKenzie, T. L., Sallis, J. F., Elder, J. P., Berry, C. B., Hoy, P. L., Nader, P. R., Zive, M. M., & Broyles, S. L. (1997). Physical activity levels and prompts in young children at recess: A two-year study of a bi-ethnic sample. *Research Quarterly for Exercise and Sport, 68,* 195–202.

McLoyd, V. (1980). Verbally expressed modes of transformation in the fantasy and play of black preschool children. *Child Development, 51,* 1133–1139.

McLoyd, V. (1982). Social class differences in sociodiamatic play. A critical review. *Developmental Review, 2,* 1–30.

Mergen, B. (1995). Past play: Relics, memory, and history. In A. D. Pellegrini (Ed.), *The future of play theory* (pp. 257–274). Albany, NY: SUNY Press.

Messick, S. (1983). Assessment of children. In W. Kessen (Ed.), *Handbook of Child Psychology: Vol. 1, History, Theory, and Methods* (pp. 477–526). New York: Wiley.

Minuchin, P., & Shapiro, E. (1983). The school as a context for social development. In E. Hetherington (Ed.), *Manual of child psychology: Vol 4* (pp. 197–274). New York: Wiley.

Money, J., & Ehrhardt, A. (1972). *Man & woman, boy & girl.* Baltimore: Johns Hopkins.

Monson, D., & Sebesta, S. (1991). Reading preferences. In J. Flood, J. Jensen, D. Lapp, and J. Squire (Eds.), *Handbook of research on teaching the English language arts* (pp. 664–673). New York: Macmillan.

Moore, R. (1988). Before and after asphalt: Diversity as an ecological measure of quality of children's outdoor environments. In M. Bloch and A. Pellegrini (Eds.), *The Ecological context of children's play* (pp. 191–213). Norwood, NJ: Ablex.

Müller-Schwarze, D. (1984). Analysis of play behaviour. In P. K. Smith (Ed.), *Play in animals and humans* (pp. 147–158). Oxford: Blackwell.

Müller-Schwarze, D., & Müller-Schwarze, C. (1982). Play behavior in mammals: Persistence, decrease and energetic compensation after play deprivation in deer fawns. *Science, 215,* 85–87.

Mussen, P. H. (1970). *Handbook of child psychology, Volumes 1 and 2* (3rd ed.). New York: Wiley

Mussen, P. H. (1983). *Handbook of child psychology, Volumes 1–3* (4th ed.). New York: Wiley.

National Association for the Education of Young Children. (1992). *Developmentally appropriate practice in early childhood programs serving infancts, toddlers, younger preschoolers.* Washington, DC: Author.

National Association of Elementary School Principals. (1989). *National Recess Survey.* Unpublished.

Naylor, H. (1985). Outdoor play and play equipment. *Early Child Development and Care. 19*(1,2), 109–130.

Neill, S. (1976). Aggressive and non-aggressive fighting in twelve-to-thirteen year old pre-adolescent boys. *Journal of Child Psychology and Psychiatry, 17,* 213–220.

Nigg, J. (1993, March). *Personality traits and psychopathology in the parents of ADHD boys.* Poster at the biennial meetings of the Society for Research in Child Development, New Orleans.

Nurss, J., & McGauvran, M. (1976). *The Metropolitan Readiness Test.* New York: Harcourt, Brace, & Jovanovich.

O'Brien, J., Halperin, J., Newman, J., Vanshdeep, S., Wolf, L., & Morganstein, A. (1992). Psychometric differentiation of conduct disorders and attention deficit disorder with hyperactivity. *Developmental and Behavioral Pediatrics, 13,* 274–277.

Opie, I., & Opie, P. (1969). *The lore and language of school children.* New York: Oxford.

Parke, R. D., & Suomi, S. J. (1981). Adult male infant relationships: Human and nonhuman primate evidence. In K. Immelman, G. W. Barlow, L. Petronovitch, & M. Main (Eds.), *Behavioral development* (pp. 700–725). New York: Cambridge University Press.

Parker, J., & Asher, S. (1987). Peer relations and later personal adjustment: Are low accepted children at-risk? *Psychological Bulletin, 102,* 357–389.

Parten, M. (1932). Social participation among preschool children. *Journal of Abnormal and Social Psychology, 27,* 243–269.

Patterson, G. (1986). Performance models for anti-social boys. *American Psychologist, 41,* 432–444.

Pellegrini, A. (1982). Explorations in preschooler's construction of cohesive test in two play contexts. *Discourse Processes, 5,* 101–108.

Pellegrini, A. D. (1984). The social cognitive ecology of preschool classrooms. *International Journal of Behavioral Development, 7,* 321–332.

Pellegrini, A. D. (1988). Elementary school children's rough-and-rumble play and social-competence. *Developmental Psychology, 24,* 802–806.

Pellegrini, A. D. (1991). Outdoor recess: Is it really necessary? *Principal, 70*(5), 40.

Pellegrini, A. D. (1992). Preference for outdoor play during early adolescence. *Journal of Adolescence, 15,* 241–254.

Pellegrini, A. D. (1993). Boy's rough-and-tumble play, social competence, and group composition. *British Journal of Developmental Psychology, 11,* 237–248.

Pellegrini, A. D. (1995). *School recess and playground behavior.* Albany: State University of New York Press.

Pellegrini, A. D. (1995). A longitudinal study of boys' rough and tumble play and dominance during early adolescence. *Journal of Applied Developmental Psychology, 16,* 77–93.

Pellegrini, A. D. (2001). A longitudinal study of heterosexual relationships, aggression, and sexual harassment during the transition from primary school through middle school. *Journal of Applied Developmental Psychology, 22,* 1–15.

Pellegrini, A. D. (2002a). Bullying, victimization, and sexual harassment during the transition to middle school. *Educational Psychologist, 37,* 151–163.

Pellegrini, A. D. (2002b). Rough-and-tumble play from childhood through adolescence: Development and possible functions. In C. H. Hart and P. K. Smith (Eds.), *Handbook of childhood social development* (pp. 438–454). Oxford, UK: Blackwell.

Pellegrini, A. D. (2003). Perceptions and possible functions of play and real fighting in early adolescence. *Child Development, 74,* 1459–1470.

Pellegrini, A. D. (2004a). *Observing children in their natural worlds: A primer in observational methods* (2nd ed.). Mahwah, NJ: Lawrence Erlbaum Associates.

Pellegrini, A. D. (2004b). Sexual segregation in children: A review of evidence for two hypotheses. *Animal Behaviour, 68,* 435–443.

Pellegrini, A. D. (in press). Sexual segregation in human juveniles. In K. Ruckstuhl & P. Neuhas (Eds.), *Sexual segregation in vertebrates.* Cambridge, UK: Cambridge University Press.

Pellegrini, A. D., & Archer, J. (2005). Sex differences in competitive and aggressive behaviour: A view from sexual selection theory. In B. J. Ellis & D. J. Bjorklund (Eds.), *Origins of the social mind: Evolutionary psychology and child development.* New York: Guilford.

Pellegrini, A. D., Bartini, M. (2000). An empirical comparison of methods of sampling aggression and victimization in school settings. *Journal of Educational Psychology, 92,* 360–366.

Pellegrini, A. D., & Bartini, M. (2001). Dominance in early adolescent boys: Affiliative and aggressive dimensions and possible functions. *Merrill-Palmer Quarterly, 47,* 142–163.

Pellegrini, A. D., & Bjorklund, D. F. (1996). The place of recess in school: Issues in the role of recess in children's education and development: An introduction to the theme of the Special Issue. *Journal of Research in Childhood Education, 11,* 5–13.

Pellegrini, A. D., & Bjorklund, D. F. (1997). The role of recess in children's cognitive performance. *Educational Psychologist, 32,* 35–40.

Pellegrini, A. D., & Blatchford, P. (2000). *The child at school: Interactions with peers and teachers.* London: Arnold.

Pellegrini, A. D., & Davis, P. (1993). Confinement effects on playground and classroom behavior. *British Journal of Educational Psychology, 63,* 88–95.

Pellegrini, A. D., & Galda, L. (1982). The effects of thematic fantasy play training on the development of children's story comprehension. *American Educational Research Journal, 19,* 443–452.

Pellegrini, A. D., & Galda, L. (1993). Ten years after: A reexamination of symbolic play and literacy research. *Reading Research Quarterly, 28,* 162–175.

Pellegrini, A., & Galda, L. (1998). *The development of school-based literacy: A social ecological approach.* London: Routledge.

Pellegrini, A. D., & Horvat, M. (1995). A developmental contextual critique of Attention Deficit Hyperactivity Disorder (ADHD). *Educational Researcher, 24,* 13–20.

Pellegrini, A. D., Horvat, M., & Huberty, P. D. (1998). The relative cost of children's physical activity play. *Animal Behaviour, 55,* 1053–1106.

Pellegrini, A. D., Huberty, P. D., & Jones, I. (1995). The effects of play deprivation on children's recess and classroom behaviors. *American Educational Research Journal, 32,* 845–864.

Pellegrini, A. D., Kato, K., Blatchford, P., & Baines, E. (2002). A short-term longitudinal study of children's playground games across the first year of school: Implications for social competence and adjustment to school. *American Educational Research Journal, 39,* 991–1015.

Pellegrini, A. D., & Long, J. D. (2003). A sexual selection theory longitudinal analysis of sexual segregation and integration in early adolescence. *Journal of Experimental Child Psychology, 85,* 257–278.

Pellegrini, A. D., & Perlmutter, J. C. (1987). A re-examination of the Smilansky-Parten matrix of play behavior. *Journal of Research in Childhood Education, 2,* 89–96.

Pellegrini, A. D., & Perlmutter, J. (1989). Classroom contextual effects on children's play. *Developmental Psychology, 25,* 289–296.

Pellegrini, A. D., & Smith, P. K. (1998). Physical activity play: The nature and function of a neglected aspect of play. *Child Development, 69,* 577–598.

Piaget, J. (1952). *The origins of intelligence in children.* New York: Norton.

Piaget, J. (1962). *Play, dreams, and imitation in childhood.* C. Gattengno & F. M. Hodgson (Trans.). New York: Norton. (Original work published 1951).

Piaget, J. (1932/1965) *The moral judgment of the child.* London: Routledge & Kegan Paul.

Piaget, J. (1983). Piaget's theory. In W. Kessen (Ed.), *Handbook of child psychology: History, theory, and methods* (pp. 103–128). New York: Wiley.

Power, T. G. (2000). *Play and exploration in children and animals.* Mahwah, NJ: Lawrence Erlbaum Associates.

Pusey, A. E. (1990). Behavioural changes at adolescence in chimpanzees. *Behaviour, 115,* 203–246.

Rahmani, L. (1973). *Soviet psychology. Philosophical, theoretical, and experimental issues.* New York: International Universities Press.

Ramey, C. T., & Campbell, F. A. (1987). The Carolina Abecedarian Project: An educational experiment concerning human malleability. In J. J. Gallagher & C. T. Ramey (Eds.), *The malleability of children* (pp. 127–140). Baltimore: Brookes.

Repina, T. A. (1971). Development of imagination. In A. V. Zaporozhets & D. B. Elknonin (Eds.), *The psychology of preschool children* (pp. 255–277). Cambridge, MA: MIT Press.

Rich, L. E. (2004). Bringing more effective tools to the weight-loss table. *Monitor on Psychology, 4*(1), 52–55.

Roggman, L., and Langlois, J. (1987). Mothers, infants, and toys: Social play correlates of attachment. *Infant Behavior and Development, 10,* 233–237.

Roopnarine, J. L., Hooper, F., Ahmeduzzaman, M., & Polack, B. (1993). Gentle play partners: Mother-child and father-child play in New Delhi, India. In K. MacDonald (Ed.), *Parent-child play* (pp. 287–304). Albany: SUNY Press.

Rosenthal, M. K. (1994). Social and nonsocial play of infants and toddlers in family day care. In H. Goelman and E. Jacobs (Eds.), *Children's play in day care settings* (pp. 163–192). Albany, NY: SUNY Press.

Rubin, K., Fein, G., & Vandenberg, B. (1983). Play. In E.M. Hetherington (Ed.), *Handbook of child psychology, socialization, personality and social development, Vol IV* (pp. 693–774). New York: Wiley.

Rubin, K., Watson, R., & Jambor, T. (1978). Free-play behaviors in preschool and kindergarten children. *Child Development, 49,* 534–546.

Ruckstuhl, K. E. (1998). Foraging behaviour and sexual segregation in bighorn sheep. *Animal Behaviour, 56*, 99–106.

Ruckstuhl, K. E., & Neuhaus, P. (2002). Sexual segregation in ungulates: A comparative test of three hypotheses. *Biological Review, 77*, 77–96.

Ruckstuhl, K., & Neuhaus, P. (Eds.). (in press). *Sexual segregation in vertebrates*. Cambridge, UK: Cambridge University Press.

Russell, B. (1931/1959). *The scientific outlook*. New York: Norton.

Russell, B. (1932/1972). *In praise of idleness and other essays*. New York: Simon and Schuster.

Rutter, M. (1967). A children's behaviour questionnaire for completion by teachers: Preliminary findings. *Journal of Child Psychology and Psychiatry, 8*, 1–11.

Rutter, M., & Garmezy, N. (1983). Developmental psychopathology. In E. Hetherington (Ed.), *Manual of child psychology, Vol 4* (pp. 775–912). New York: Wiley.

Saltz, E., Dixon, D., & Johnson, J. (1967). Training disadvantaged preschoolers on various fantasy activities: Effects on cognitive functioning and impulse control. *Child Development, 48*, 367–380.

Schofield, J. W. (1981). Complementary and conflicting identities: Images and interactions in an inter-racial school. In S. R. Asher & J. M. Gottman (Eds.), *The development of children's friendships* (pp. 53–90). New York: Cambridge University Press.

Schwartzmann, H. (1978). *Transformations: The anthropology of children's play*. New York: Plenum Press.

Serbin, L., Connor, J., Burchardt, C., & Citron, C. (1979). Effects of peer presence on sex-typing of children's play behavior. *Journal of Experimental Child Psychology, 27*, 303–309.

Serbin, L. A., Tonick, I. J., & Sternglanz, S. H. (1977). Shaping cooperative cross-sex play. *Child Development, 48*, 924–929.

Siegler, R. S. (1996). *Emerging minds: the process of change in children's thinking*. New York: Oxford University Press.

Simons-Morton, B. G., O'Hara, N. M., Parcel, G. S., Huang, I. W., Baranowski, T., & Wilson, B. (1990). Children's frequency of participation in moderate to vigorous physical activities. *Research quarterly for Exercise and Sport, 61*, 307–314.

Simons-Morton, B. G., O'Hara, N. M., Simons-Morton, D. G., & Parcel, G. S. (1987). Children and fitness: A public health perspective. *Research Quarterly for Exercise and Sport, 58*, 293–302.

Slaughter, D. T., & Dombrowski, J. (1989). Cultural continuities and discontinuities: Impact on social and pretend play. In M. N. Bloch and A. D. Pellegrini (Eds.), *The ecological context of children's play* (pp. 282–310). Norwood, NJ: Ablex.

Sluckin, A. (1981). *Growing up on the playground*. London: Routledge and Kegan Paul.

Smilansky, S. (1968). *The effects of sociodramatic play on disadvantaged preschool children*. New York: Wiley.

Smith, P. K. (1974). Social and fantasy play in young children. In B. Tizard & D. Harvey (Eds.), *Biology of play* (pp. 123–145). London: SIMP/Heinemann.

Smith, P. K. (1982). Does play matter? Functional and evolutionary aspects of animal and human play. *The Behavioral and Brain Sciences, 5*, 139–184.

Smith, P. K., & Boulton, M. (1990). Rough-and-tumble play, aggression, and dominance: Perception and behavior in children's encounters. *Human Development, 33*, 271–282.

Smith, P. K., & Connolly, K. (1980). *The ecology of preschool behaviour.* London: Cambridge University Press.

Smith, P. K., & Dodsworth, C. (1978). Social class differences in the fantasy play of preschool children. *Journal of Genetic Psychology, 133,* 183–190.

Smith, P. K., & Hagen, T. (1980). Effects of play deprivation on exercise play of nursery school children. *Animal Behaviour, 28,* 922–928.

Smith, P. K., Hunter, T., Carvalho, A. M. A., & Costabile, A. (1992). Children's perceptions of playfighting, playchasing and real fighting: A cross-national interview. *Social Development, 1,* 1992.

Smith, P. K., & Lewis, K. (1985). Rough-and-tumble play, fighting, and chasing in nursery school children. *Ethology and Sociobiology, 6,* 175–181.

Smith, P. K., Smees, R., & Pellegrini, A. D. (2004). Play fighting and real fighting: Using video playback methodology with young children. *Aggressive Behavior, 30,* 164–173.

Smith, P. K., & Vollstedt, R. (1985). On defining play: An empirical study of the relationship between play and various play criteria. *Child Development, 56,* 1042–1050.

Snow, C. E. (1989). Understanding social interaction and language acquisition: Sentences are not enough. In M. Bornstein and J. S. Bruner (Eds.), *Interaction in human development* (pp. 83–103). Hillsdale, NJ: Lawrence Erlbaum Associates.

Spear-Swerling, L., & Sternberg, R. (1994). The road not taken: An integrated theoretical model of reading disability. *Journal of Learning Disabilities, 27,* 91–103.

Sroufe, L. (1979). The coherence of individual development: Early care attachment, and subsequent development issues. *American Psychologist, 34,* 834–841.

Sroufe, L. A., Egelund, B., & Carlson, E. A. (1999). One social world: The integrated development of parent-child and peer relationships. In W. A. Collins & B. Laursen, *Relationships as developmental contexts. The Minnesota symposia on child psychology, Vol. 30* (pp. 241–261). Mahwah, NJ: Erlbaum.

Stamps, J. (2003). Behavioural processes affecting development: Tinbergen's fourth question comes to age. *Animal Behaviour, 66,* 1–13.

Stanford, L., & Hynd, G. (1994). Congruence of behavioral sympotomology in children with ADD/H, ADD/WO, and Learning Disabilities. *Journal of Learning Disabilities, 27,* 243–253.

Steinberg, L. (1986). Latchkey children and susceptibility to peer pressure. *Developmental Psychology, 22,* 433–439.

Stevenson, H., & Lee, S. (1990). Contexts of achievement. *Monographs of the Society for Research in Child Development* (Serial No. 221), *55*(1–2).

Stevenson, H., Stigler, J., Lucker, G., Lee, S., Hsu, C., & Kitamura, S. (1987). Classroom behavior and achievement of Japanese, Chinese, and American children. In R. Glaser (Ed.), *Advances in instructional psychology* (Vol. 3, pp. 153–204). Hillsdale, NJ: Lawrence Erlbaum Associates.

Strayer, F. F. (1980). Social ecology of the preschool peer group. In W. A. Collins (Ed.), *Minnesota symposium on child development, Vol 13* (pp. 165–196). Hillsdale, NJ: Lawrence Erlbaum Associates.

Strayer, F. F., & Noel, J. M. (1986). The prosocial and antisocial functions of aggression. In C. Zahn-Waxler, E. M. Cummings, & R. Iannoti (Eds.), *Altruism and aggression* (pp. 107-131). New York: Cambridge University Press.

Suomi, S., & Harlow, H. (1972). Social rehabilitation of isolate-reared monkeys. *Developmental Psychology, 6,* 487–496.

Sutton-Smith, B. (1973). *The folk games of children.* Austin: University of Texas Press.

Sutton-Smith, B. (1975). *The study of games: An anthropological approach.* New York: Teachers College Developmental Studies.

Sutton-Smith, B. (1981). *A history of children's play: The New Zealand playground 1840–1950.* Wellington, New Zealand: New Zealand Council for Educational Research.

Sutton-Smith, B. (1990). School playground as festival. *Children's Environment Quarterly, 7,* 3–7.

Sutton-Smith, B. (1995). Conclusion: The persuasive rhetorics of play. In A. D. Pellegrini (Ed.), *The future of play theory* (pp. 275–295). Albany: State University Press of New York.

Sutton-Smith, B. (1997). *The ambiguity of play.* Cambridge, MA: Harvard University Press.

Sutton-Smith, B., Rosenberg, B. G., & Morgan, E. (1963). Development of sex differences in play choices during preadolescence. *Child Development, 34,* 119–126.

Symons, D. (1978). *Play and aggression: A study of rhesus monkeys.* New York: Columbia University Press.

Takhvar, M., & Smith, P. K. (1990). A review and critique of Smilansky's classification scheme and the "nested hierarchy" of play categories. *Journal of Research in Early Childhood, 4,* 112–122.

Tanner, J. (1978). *Fetus in man: Psychical growth from conception to maturity.* Cambridge: Harvard University Press.

Tawney, R. H. (1969/1926). *Religion and the rise of capitalism.* Harmondsworth, UK: Penguin. (Original work published 1926)

Terrill, R (1973). *R. H. Tawney and his times.* Cambridge, MA: Harvard University Press.

Thelen, E. (1979). Rhythmical sterotypies in normal human infants. *Animal Behaviour, 27,* 699–715.

Thelen, E. (1980). Determinants of amounts of sterotyped behavior in normal human infants. *Ethology and Sociobiology, 1,* 141–150.

Thomas, A., & Chess, S. (1977). *Temperament and development.* New York: Brunner/Mazel.

Thompson, G. G. (1944). The social and emotional development of preschool children under two types of education programs. *Psychological Monographs, 56*(5).

Thompson, G. G. (1960). Children's groups. In P. H. Mussen (Ed.), *Handbook of research methods in child development* (pp. 821–853). New York: Wiley.

Thorne, B. (1986). Girls and boys together. But mostly apart: Gender arrangements in elementary school. In W. W. Hartup and Z. Rubin (Eds.), *Relationships and development* (pp. 167–184). Hillsdale, NJ: Lawrence Erlbaum Associates.

Thorne, B. (1993). *Gender play: Boys and girls in school.* Buckingham, UK: Open University Press.

Tinbergen, N. (1963). On the aims and methods of ethology. *Zeitschirift für Tierpsychologie, 20,* 410–413.

Tomporowski, P., & Ellis, N. (1988). Effects of exercise on cognitive processes. *Psychological Bulletin, 99,* 338–346.

Toppino, T., Kasserman, J., & Mrack, W. (1991). The effect of spacing repetitions on the recognition memory of young children and adults. *Journal of Experimental Child Psychology, 51,* 123–138.

Tudge, J., & Rogoff, B. (1989). Peer influences on cognitive development: Piagetian and

Vygotsian perspectives. In M. Bornstein & J. Bruner (Eds.), *Interaction in human development* (pp. 17–40). Hillsdale, NJ: Lawrence Erlbaum Associates.

Vaughn, B. E., & Waters, E. (1981). Attention structure, sociometric status, and dominance: Interrelations, behavioral correlates, and relationships to social competence. *Developmental Psychology, 17,* 275–288.

Vygotsky, L. (1967). Play and its role in the mental development of the child. *Soviet Psychology, 12,* 62–76.

Vygotsky, L. S. (1978). *Mind in society.* Cambridge: Harvard University Press.

Walberg, H., & Tsai, S-L. (1983). Mathews effects in education. *American Educational Research Journal, 20,* 359–373.

Waters, E., & Sroufe, L. A. (1983). Social competence as developmental construct. *Developmental Review, 3,* 79–97.

Weir, R. (1962). *Language in the crib.* The Hague: Mouton.

Werner, H., & Kaplan, E. (1952). The acquisition of word meanings: A developmental study. *Monographs for the Society for Research in Child Development, 18*(1, serial 51).

Whalen, C. (1983). Hyperactivity, learning problems, and attention deficit disorders. In T. Ollenick & M. Hersen (Eds.), *Handbook of child psycholopathology* (pp. 151–199). New York: Plenum.

White, S. (1966). Evidence for a hierarchical arrangement of learning processes. In L. Lipsett & C. Spiker (Eds.), *Advances in child development and behavior, Vol. 2.* New York: Academic.

Wittrock, M. (1986). Students' thought processes. In M. Wittrock (Ed.), *Handbook of research on teaching* (pp. 297–314). New York: Macmillan.

Wohlwill, J. (1973). *The study of behavioral development.* New York: Academic.

Wohlwill, J. (1984). Relationships between exploration and play. In T. Yawkey & A. D. Pellegrini (Eds.), *Child's play* (pp. 143–170). Hillsdale, NJ: Lawrence Erlbaum Associates.

Wood, D., Bruner, J. S., & Ross, G. (1976). The role of tutoring in problem-solving. *Journal of Child Psychology and Psychiatry, 17,* 89–100.

Wright, M. (1980). Measuring the social competence of preschool children. *Canadian Journal of Behavioral Science, 12,* 17–32.

Zakriski, A., & Wright, J. (1991, April). *Perceptions of dominance in children's peer groups: Age differences in the relation between aggression, status, and dominance.* Poster presented at the biennial meeting of the Society for Research in Child Development, Seattle, WA.

Zaporozhets, A. V., & Elknonin, D. B. (Eds.). (1971). *The psychology of preschool children.* Cambridge, MA: MIT Press.

Zigler, E., & Trickett, P. (1978). I.Q., social competence, and evaluation of early childhood intervention programs. *American Psychologist, 33,* 789–798.

Author Index

Subject Index

Printed in the United States
115953LV00002B/147/A

9 780805 853247